Stress
Resets

Stress Resets

How to
Soothe Your
Body and Mind
in Minutes

JENNIFER L. TAITZ
PsyD, ABPP

Workman Publishing • New York

Workman
Workman Publishing
Hachette Book Group, Inc.
1290 Avenue of the Americas
New York, NY 10104
workman.com

Workman is an imprint of Workman Publishing, a division of Hachette Book Group, Inc. The Workman name and logo are registered trademarks of Hachette Book Group, Inc.

Design by Sarah Smith

The publisher is not responsible for websites (or their content) that are not owned by the publisher.

Workman books may be purchased in bulk for business, educational, or promotional use. For information, please contact your local bookseller or the Hachette Book Group Special Markets Department at special.markets@hbgusa.com.

Library of Congress Cataloging-in-Publication Data is available.

ISBN 978-1-5235-2332-0

First Edition January 2024

Printed in the United States of America on responsibly sourced paper.
10 9 8 7 6 5 4 3

Sylvie, Eli, and Asher—I hope you choose courage and kindness in the face of stress.

And to *you*—may resetting enrich your life and the lives of those around you.

Contents

Introduction

WHAT IF IT WERE POSSIBLE to turn down the less helpful aspects of your stress response in just a few minutes, any time you wanted—no ponderous meditations, medications, or martinis required? As a clinical psychologist, I've seen it happen for my clients again and again. I specialize in teaching people evidence-based ways to regulate their emotions and cope with difficult situations. In the fourteen years that I've been a practicing therapist in both New York and Los Angeles, I've taught thousands of people how to consciously stop themselves from obsessing, ruminating, and passively focusing on their challenges so that they can pivot, sit with their emotions, and move forward. I call these strategies *stress resets*, and they're designed to be short: You can do many of them in only five minutes. Just as important, every one is based in research and proven to bring relief (at least temporarily) so you can pause and reset rather than spiral downward.

Most of us need these simple strategies. When life feels overwhelming, human beings often instinctively do things that end up making us—or the situation—feel *worse*. When we're riled up, it's tough to access wisdom. Instead, we react in ways that keep us stuck. Whether we painfully obsess, shoot off aggressive texts, procrastinate, or misuse substances, our instincts can turn against us and exacerbate our suffering. Think of it this way:

stress = stress
stress + overthinking + avoiding = STRESS

But it doesn't have to be that way. Pioneer stress researcher Dr. Hans Selye, an endocrinologist who began studying the topic close to one hundred years ago, saw stress as an adaptive bodily response that pushes us to react when we're feeling overwhelmed. Dr. Selye, who published more than 1,700 articles related to stress, described it like this: *external event → stress response*. Decades later, in the 1980s, Dr. Richard Lazarus, a clinical psychologist who focused on coping and problem solving, broadened the definition of stress to include how we react to it, describing stress as an experience in which a challenge, interpretation, and reaction can all play a role (think *stressful event → stress ← response*). But whatever the equation, the takeaway is: How you choose to respond to what you're facing affects how stressed you ultimately feel.

Let's take an example that unfolded in my house. One morning when my husband, Adam, was tired and rushing (not a good combination), he dropped a full carton of milk on the kitchen floor. Fuming, he cleaned it up rather aggressively, then cut his hand on the kickplate at the bottom of our refrigerator. Unfortunately, we didn't have any bandages in the house, so, feeling even more frustrated, he jumped in the car for a drugstore run.

Agitated and replaying his "horrible" morning on his way home from the store, he then got into a minor car accident. You can't make this stuff up!

Of course, I have plenty of examples of how I've exacerbated an already stressful situation. Years ago, exhausted and newly back to work after the recent birth of my second child, I began gnawing endlessly on my fingernail, to the point where I found myself in the emergency room with an antibiotic-resistant infection that required minor surgery. If I had only paused, observed my stress-fueled urges, taken a few deep breaths, and tried one of the stress resets in this book, I'd have spared myself hours in the emergency room and multiple follow-up visits with an infectious disease specialist.

I'm pretty sure you have examples of your own.

So many of my clients tell me about their own impulsive reactions to stress: feeling stung by rejection, then reaching out to a random stranger or a problematic ex for solace, only to end up feeling more rejected or lonely; feeling overwhelmed by work, then indulging in junk food that makes them feel *more* sluggish. There are countless ways we undermine our ability to live better when we face stress:

> How you choose to respond to what you're facing affects how stressed you ultimately feel.

- *Tight on money → overspending*

- *Big deadline → vacillating between perfecting and procrastinating*

- *Feeling anxious → over-researching or hyperfocusing on the problem to the point of panic*

- *Grieving → relying on substances to try to numb the pain*

- *Feeling exhausted → staying up late scrolling on your phone*

All of these "escapes" take a toll on our *self-efficacy,* or our perceived ability to cope. Metaphorically speaking, I think of it as trying to remove a stain in a way that only spreads the mess. In the pages ahead, I'll encourage you to take a closer look at how you habitually dodge your stressors, which, in itself, can be an empowering way to problem solve. By reflecting on and improving how you cope in tough moments, you'll gain appreciation for your ability to take good care of yourself and, ultimately, harness your emotions to live better and find joy.

It's pretty much impossible to prevent events that elicit our stress. That's why we need to stop waiting to feel less stressed or for life to feel more predictable before taking action. And what better time than now? According to a 2022 survey by the American Psychological Association, 27 percent of adults in the US describe being so stressed by factors such as the country's political divide, the economy, and climate change that they are unable to function. A sizable 76 percent of those surveyed say their stress has taken a toll on their well-being. Left unaddressed, stress can lead to more lasting psychological problems. In 2020, following the onset of the COVID-19 pandemic, the World Health Organization estimated a 25 percent rise in the prevalence of anxiety and depression across the globe, with rates of depression in the US tripling. So many of us continue to face circumstances that would deplete anyone's emotional resources, such as financial adversity, structural racism, and sexism. And it's unbelievably unsettling to worry about issues like gun violence destroying our lives and AI upending our careers. That's all the more reason everyone deserves these doable, quick ways to recalibrate— techniques that allow us to slow down, breathe easier, and problem solve.

First, though, it's important to consider the key underlying habits that may be keeping you stuck. Most people who struggle with their response to stress

STRESS CYCLE

GET MIRED
IN NEGATIVE
THOUGHTS

COPE BY
AVOIDING

JUDGE PHYSICAL
SYMPTOMS OF STRESS

1) get mired in negative thoughts, 2) judge their physical symptoms of stress, and 3) cope by avoiding whatever it is that creates their stress. The trouble is, each of these three components contributes to a stress response in the body that builds on itself, creating even more stress. For example, telling yourself *I can't!* can generate physical symptoms, whether it's trembling, dry mouth, or other sensations. That leads to another common reaction: critiquing your body's natural stress response, which only intensifies catastrophic thinking. And so we focus on avoiding or escaping whatever is stressing us out rather than moving toward what matters to us. You can see what I'm getting at: As the cycle continues, it becomes tougher to gain perspective and actually solve whatever problems are making you stressed in the first place.

Of course, it's human nature to try to escape what worries us. And there is a smorgasbord of distractions readily available to us, including spending hours on social media, smoking weed, or mindlessly drinking and snacking. There's also a popular escape that gives me a lot of anxiety: An increasing number of people are turning to a prescription for a benzodiazepine like Xanax or Klonopin, one of the most common "solutions" for anxiety. To be clear, I fully support pursuing treatment if you're experiencing ongoing psychological problems. I also applaud the courage it takes to seek professional help when you're struggling. My particular concern is with benzos— medications that the US Food and Drug Administration urges physicians to dispense sparingly due to their addiction potential and side effects. Despite this, more than ninety-two million prescriptions for these antianxiety drugs are filled in the US each year. Plus, popping a pill when you're stressed out only perpetuates the idea that you can't manage on your own.

To change our repertoire of destructive behaviors, we need to look inward for solutions, not outward. We need to focus on what we want our lives to stand for. We need to stop prioritizing comfort and distraction at the expense of truly enhancing our lives. We need wiser ways to cope so we can do better in trying moments. One saying that inspires me is commonly attributed to Viktor Frankl, a psychiatrist and Holocaust survivor: "Between stimulus and response there is a space. In that space lies our power to choose our response. In our response lies our growth and freedom."

This book will provide you with concrete instructions to widen that space. In the pages to come, I'll share some of my favorite skills that interweave mindfulness with principles from behavioral therapies to help people cope with intense emotions and circumstances. Here's a bit more detail on these approaches and how they can help you cope with stress.

Dialectical behavior therapy (DBT)[1] is a treatment developed by Dr. Marsha Linehan, a professor emeritus at the University of Washington, that was initially designed and used to help people with borderline personality disorder (BPD), a condition that can include impulsivity and unstable relationships and that experts once considered lifelong and difficult to treat. But countless people with BPD who have pursued DBT end up improving their telltale symptoms, so much so that they no longer meet the criteria for this diagnosis. More recently, DBT has been used to treat post-traumatic stress disorder (PTSD), substance use, binge eating, and bulimia. Many of my clients who are experiencing incredible stress that stems from prolonged loneliness, invalidating relationships, jobs that feel unfulfilling yet all-consuming, or caregiving find DBT skills helpful when dealing with what feels like the emotional equivalent of a triathlon.

One of my passions is teaching a curriculum called *distress tolerance*, a skill set designed for times when you feel overcome by the intensity of your emotions and can't easily solve a problem. Distress tolerance, which is part of DBT, includes increasing your acceptance and willingness; bringing awareness to the pros and cons of your specific urges in response to stress; and brainstorming more uplifting ways to persevere in difficult moments, all of which help us cope more effectively.

I'll also be turning to strategies from acceptance and commitment therapy (ACT), a method pioneered by Dr. Steven Hayes, professor emeritus at the University of Nevada, Reno, that helps people become more flexible,

---

1 If you're wondering what the heck "dialectical" means, the term refers to the concept that ideas that seem in opposition can both be true. A key dialectic in DBT is that you can simultaneously accept what you're facing *and* change your life.

present, and committed to their values. In addition, you'll learn tools from the Unified Protocol, a cognitive behavioral therapy (CBT) program that helps people face whatever they're avoiding. The Unified Protocol was spearheaded by Dr. David Barlow, a professor emeritus at Boston University, and his colleagues and efficiently improves a range of psychological problems.

All of these therapies are evidence-based and designed to improve your ability to disentangle yourself from unhelpful thoughts and practice acceptance so you can fully participate in creating a life that matters to you. If acceptance seems like the total opposite of what you're striving for, know that acceptance doesn't mean staying the same. To the contrary, learning to accept stress and noticing what shows up in your mind and body will allow you to respond more effectively to what's in front of you. And as you will find, supercharging your ability to cope in the face of stress will also help you rise above urges that can make everything harder. DBT, ACT, and CBT therapists, including myself, use these tools in our own lives to cope with everything from daily hassles to chronic pain to grief.

Ideally, all of us could instantly turn to someone for an uplifting pep talk in our worst moments. But that's not always possible. Plus, many of my clients notice that venting to another person during times of peak stress isn't always cathartic. Oversharing your stress can keep you feeling riled up, and experts know that stress can be contagious. And sadly, even our most well-meaning confidants sometimes minimize our stress ("Don't worry, it'll all work out!") or dole out impractical advice ("Can you just get away for a few days?").[2] My hope is that you can turn to this book in those moments, whether you pick it up late at night when you can't sleep or flip through it in the middle of an overwhelming workday. As you read, I hope to give you the sense that I am right there with you as your cheerleader and stress coach, encouraging you, honoring the legitimacy of your experience, and supporting you with practical ways to make difficult moments easier.[3] As my friend

---

2 I don't want you to write off the power of relationships! Later in this book, we'll focus on asserting yourself so you can improve the likelihood of getting the support you crave.

3 Even if I don't know you, I can empathize with what stress and challenges feel like because of my experience working with so many people and living a full life myself. It can be frustrating to go through a lot without people necessarily noticing. As best as I can, I would like to give you the sense that your feelings are valid and I want to help.

and colleague Dr. Cory Newman, a professor in psychiatry and the director of the Center for Cognitive Therapy at the University of Pennsylvania, says, "You can reduce stress by 50 percent immediately, at no cost, without even trying. Just don't make things worse." By not reacting impulsively, you dramatically deescalate your situation. In the pages to come, you'll learn both how to not make things worse and, even better, ways to improve your circumstances.

How to Use This Book

When I sat down to write *Stress Resets*, I dreamed of creating a book that would feel like the ultimate care package I could gift to clients so they could remember key takeaways as well as offer to the countless people needing support these days. Think of it as a recipe book for your well-being—in other words, accessible, easily digestible strategies with clear instructions that you can pick and choose from, depending on your taste and needs. In a time of so much collective inattention, a book about stress shouldn't feel stressful to absorb.

If you first want to make sense of your stress and gain a better understanding of how to improve your mindset, mental habits, and ways of coping, begin with Part One (page 1), which will also help orient you as to how the tips ahead will help. But if you're feeling overwhelmed and don't have the bandwidth to read a lot right now, skip to Part Two (page 56), where you'll find quick exercises to help you reset when you're experiencing high stress (though please do come back to Part One when you can!). Finally, in Part Three (page 130), you'll discover stress resets for the long term, or *buffers*, as I've dubbed them: strategies for when you have more space and clarity, allowing you to create a life that feels less stressful and increasing your confidence that you *can* bounce back after tough situations. Instead of frantically jumping from one intense moment to the next, you'll discover that it's possible to adopt ongoing coping habits to nourish yourself.

As you get started, it's important to commit to truly leaning in to these ideas with your heart, mind, and body. Studies show that acquiring new skills is what makes psychotherapy beneficial. Merely reading and thinking about these strategies won't be as effective as actually trying them and developing new ways of responding. So when you're ready, choose a few stress resets and buffers and give them a chance to empower you, knowing that a new perspective lies just on the other side. In the pages ahead, there are suggested charts and diagrams you can use to track your own experience; feel free to copy them into your notebook or planner. Once you find the tips that help you most, flag them so you can easily revisit them. Try practicing and using these ideas in a wide range of contexts—at work, at home, with others—so you'll feel increasingly confident in your ability to manage your emotions, regardless of what pops up in your life.

I do want to take a moment to acknowledge that if you're already feeling overwhelmed, it may feel extra hard to pick up a book like this. That makes it all the more inspiring that you're trying to work on living better. At the risk of sounding like a stereotypical therapist, I'd like you to take a moment to give yourself credit and a heartfelt pat on your shoulder.[4] I also need to mention that if you're experiencing a crisis, the best thing to do is to get professional help (for resources, see page 198). The strategies in this book aren't a substitute for therapy if you're facing an emergency, nor are they meant to fix life's most difficult challenges. What they *are* meant to do is show you that at any moment, whether you're feeling stuck, stressed, or panicked, *you* have the power to improve how you feel. You *don't* have to continue down a path you'll regret. All it takes is a few minutes to shift your mindset and behaviors. The more you practice regulating intense feelings, the more you'll experience a growing sense of possibility and be able to tap into something we all need these days: hope. Hope isn't just a transient feeling. It hinges on having a clear life purpose and willingness to persist in moving toward that purpose. I'd chase that over any short-term alternative, wouldn't you?

---

4 If your mind is starting to judge this suggestion, that's okay! That's what minds do. But hey, don't you think you'd feel less stressed if once in a while you caught yourself doing something right rather than being your biggest critic? My goal in writing this is to reach people who may not have the opportunity to see a therapist, so I write in a tone that is similar to the way I'd speak if we were meeting face-to-face.

PART ONE

Befriending Stress, Living Better

1

Turning Your Knots into Bows

STRESS, UNFORTUNATELY, DOESN'T HONOR "Do Not Disturb" signs. We all experience pesky thoughts and feelings that slow us down, work us up, and interrupt us. I can testify to this through my own experiences and those of the many people I see who are looking for ways to feel more effective. I'll be using some of their stories—with names and identifying details changed to protect privacy—along with my own in hopes that you'll feel less alone and see how life can get better when you face stressful situations differently.

Laurie, for one, is a client of mine in her fifties who started a new job working remotely for a technology firm in an era of rampant layoffs. She'd been excited about changing companies, but it turned out that the switch brought on more stress than she'd felt in years. Instead of feeling liberating, working remotely felt isolating—it was tough to get to know her colleagues, and she was concerned about how they viewed her. And because she connected with her manager only through a screen, Laurie wondered what she thought about her performance, even though no one was complaining. "My review is once a year, but I'm stressing about it embarrassingly often," Laurie said. After she mentioned that she knew others at the company who had been fired without cause or warning, her concerns made more sense to me.

By the time Laurie saw me, she told me she'd given up activities she loved, like hiking and participating in a book club, because she was too stressed to deal with anything besides work. No wonder, given that she'd been suffering from migraines and stomach issues, symptoms that she blamed on her new job and were taking over the rest of her life. She also worried that stress was affecting her sleep and even shortening her life span. When friends casually asked, "How's the new job?" she felt too self-conscious to talk about what she was feeling. Her partner, frustrated with her anxiety, repeatedly said, "It's just not worth the stress! Quit!" which was clearly not helpful. When he gave her a book on eliminating stress as well as some "Keep Calm" swag, she felt even more hopeless. "Stress isn't making me occasionally antsy—it's getting in the way of me living my life and making me feel out of control," said Laurie.

Unpacking Stress

The word "stress" is a catchphrase we use to describe everything from a frustrating experience—something acute, like a major argument or health scare, or more chronic, like Laurie's work situation—to how we feel about and respond to those events. When I talk about stress in this book, I'll be focusing on what often feels like a mismatch between our resources and the various demands we are dealing with. This explanation, first described by psychologists Richard Lazarus and Susan Folkman at the University of California, Berkeley, encompasses 1) thinking that you're facing a threat and 2) believing you can't manage it, either emotionally or logistically. If, like Laurie, you find yourself thinking, *It's too much . . . I can't!*, those are the types of moments we'll be remedying.

I also want to clarify that stress is different from anxiety. Stress is when our sense of physiological or emotional balance is disrupted. Anxiety is more prolonged worry that is disproportionate to the cause, but it can also be a response to stress. Granted, the difference between anxiety and stress is a bit blurry because so much of our stress, like anxiety, is *anticipatory*, or not directly related to what is happening in the moment. But there are ways to tease stress and anxiety apart, starting with how each is measured.

There are tons of ways to measure stress, from degree of upheaval to how long stress lasts to the amount of control we feel. The most popular way mental health professionals assess stress is by using the Perceived Stress Scale. (The title alone highlights the fact that so much of stress lies in our perception.) This includes a questionnaire that asks people whether life feels overwhelming and to indicate how confident they are that they can cope. In contrast, measures of anxiety that experts commonly use, such as the Beck

Anxiety Inventory, focus on how much a person worries and the physical symptoms they experience, such as panic or a racing heart.

Another differentiation is that stress initially arises from external circumstances. Anxiety, on the other hand, may not have a clear outside impetus and can linger, especially if you struggle to accept uncertainty in life and avoid situations that elicit your fears. In Laurie's case, her stress was sparked by the new job and morphed into anxiety. I was thrilled she'd reached out to start therapy, as intervening early would prevent her stress from turning into a prolonged struggle with an anxiety disorder.

One thing I made a point of telling Laurie is that stress doesn't have to be bad. If you're facing something daunting but you believe that you're able to manage it, stress can feel like a potentially positive *challenge*. However, if you believe that what you're facing is more than you can handle, stress becomes a *threat*. As you may expect, researchers have found that the situations we deem threatening increase our physiological response, ratcheting up heart rate and blood pressure, intensifying negative moods, and reducing cognitive performance.

This is not to say that stress is all in your head or merely a matter of perception. So many of us are feeling exhausted and that the stress we're facing is too much to handle. Good health (or insurance) isn't a guarantee, our jobs and relationships may seem shakier than ever, and tragedies like mass shootings, poverty, and inequality can make us feel hopeless. And because we have more ways to communicate than ever, it can be tough to get a moment of quiet. After all, it's easy to get sucked into believing that we must be "on" and responsive constantly, which is draining, to say the least. On top of that, the ways we choose to unwind aren't necessarily replenishing. Scrolling on social media for an average of two and a half hours a day (as studies show most people do) leaves us saturated with messaging that we need to be physically stunning, on trend, successful, and always having fun, which creates pressure to not miss out and to be perfect, which is . . . stressful![1]

---

1 This book isn't designed to be a nice idea as much as it's meant to actually free you up. If you're ready to jump into taking actions to improve your contentment, would scaling back on social media help you? Want to take a look at your screen time? What would be the upside of removing social media apps from your phone?

But stress doesn't need to become all-consuming. I know from experience that it's possible to learn to *not* make things worse and to act strategically so that life gets better, even if your circumstances feel especially taxing.

Accepting Stress Is Empowering

One essential point to keep in mind is that the goal of this book is not to get rid of stress entirely. That's impossible, because stress is part of the price we pay for living a life that matters. As Dr. Roy Baumeister, a renowned social psychologist and professor at the University of Queensland in Australia, describes, "Meaningful involvements increase one's stress." Think about it: To design a life with zero stress, you'd have to shrink the scope of what you do, willfully denying life's realities and avoiding anything remotely challenging. In other words, you'd have to lead a life that was boring and detached—and depressing. Moderate exposure to stress and hardship is actually good for us, boosting resilience. After extensive research, Dr. Mark Seery, a professor at the University at Buffalo, SUNY, writes, "A history of *some* lifetime adversity predicts better outcomes than a history of *high* adversity and a history of *no* adversity."[2]

In other words, all of us can use stress to evolve and grow, despite its terrible reputation.[3] That starts with looking at it as a normal, often helpful reaction to anticipating or facing obstacles as you pursue your goals, which I pointed out to Laurie. She also tended to stress about her stress, beating herself up with questions like *What's wrong with me? Who takes a good thing and makes it a problem? What if my stress steals my focus and I get fired?*

The hopeful news is that depending on how you approach stress, you can make it work for you instead of hold you up. Laurie and I talked about how it's natural to experience stress, especially when starting a new job, not to mention doing so in a makeshift home office. But experiencing stress is

---

2 This fact isn't meant to encourage you to seek adversity but to accept the stress that comes up as you try to meet your life goals.

3 Similarly, when I'm describing stress here, I'm referring to facing challenges in your life that align with your values (e.g., Laurie's job), not stress that you have a part in creating and that isn't helpful (e.g., overthinking and perfectionism).

different from letting stress define you. It's also nothing to be ashamed of. When Laurie said things like "I need to get over myself—what's my problem?" I had to remind her that she didn't need to apologize for what she was feeling.

I was excited to tell Laurie about clinical psychologist Alia Crum's pioneering work on the *stress mindset*, or seeing stress as potentially useful. As the principal investigator of the Stanford Mind & Body Lab, Dr. Crum has studied how adopting a "stress is bad for me" attitude can backfire. She recommends taking a fresh look at what we make of stress. While thoughts may come and go, a mindset describes how we perceive things more broadly, which means that revising our overarching attitudes can be a powerful way to improve our worldview.

In one study, Dr. Crum and her colleagues created a three-minute video promoting stress as a positive thing in life, complete with upbeat music and messaging and salient facts about how stress relates to peak performance, raises oxygen levels, improves focus, enhances decision-making, and helps people become leaders. Participants who viewed the clip were able to think more flexibly and experienced more positive emotions after doing stressful things like sitting down for a mock interview and giving a short speech.

Rather than judging your stress, engaging in problematic behaviors to reduce or avoid stress (such as turning down a work opportunity that would put you in the spotlight), or turning to destructive behaviors (like drinking too much), Dr. Crum and her colleagues encourage *optimizing stress* by leaning in to opportunities you care about, allowing yourself to feel whatever you feel without judgment, and appreciating that stress can

All of us can use stress to evolve and grow, despite its terrible reputation.

be good for you. The point is to do things to pump yourself up rather than back out, especially when approaching challenging opportunities that align with your life purpose. How, for instance, might you face intense moments if you perceived them as chances to flex your values and level up? Through that lens, even ongoing stressful situations, like caring for a loved one, can be viewed as akin to chiseling and polishing your virtues.

Laurie, like many of my clients, was skeptical when I talked about the possibility of embracing stress. "Doesn't stress accelerate disease and death?" she asked. In an incredible study of more than 28,000 people led by Dr. Abiola Keller, an assistant professor at Marquette University College of Nursing, researchers found that individuals who experienced a high amount of stress *and* believed stress affected their health were indeed at greater risk of premature mortality (by 43 percent!) than those who were stressed but didn't associate it with poor health. Worrying about negative health outcomes from stress doesn't prevent them; it escalates them.

One afternoon, Laurie told me her agenda for our session was to learn how to calm down before big meetings and focus less on how she was being perceived by others. She looked at me quizzically when I suggested she swap the words "calm down" with "get excited."[4] In research by Dr. Alison Wood Brooks, an associate professor at Harvard Business School, 90 percent of participants believed calming down was essential before an anxiety-provoking performance, a belief that was actually causing them stress. If you reflect on your own efforts to unwind on command, you may notice that rigorously trying to relax is both exhausting and impossible. To resolve this, Dr. Brooks recommends *reappraising*, or letting go of the urge to dramatically change how you feel and instead allowing those intense emotions to exist while reinterpreting them as excitement. Instead of suppressing your sensations, you're honoring them while also shifting their emotional impact in a more positive direction.

In a different study led by Dr. Brooks, participants who announced "I am excited"[5] before singing Journey's "Don't Stop Believin'" in a karaoke performance sang more accurately and confidently than those who didn't say the phrase. In another one of Dr. Brooks's experiments, participants who reframed their jitters about performing a two-minute speech as excitement felt more enthusiastic—so much so that they spoke for longer! Those who reframed their stress as excitement were also perceived by others as more confident and competent.

---

4 I would never invalidate you by suggesting that you reframe all of your stressors as opportunities to get excited. This tip is specifically helpful with performance and social worries.

5 I initially joked with some close friends that I was stressed about writing a book about stress, but since writing about Dr. Brooks, I've noticed that saying "I'm excited!" has felt both accurate and uplifting.

Laurie realized that once she let go of judging her stress, she could get back in touch with her enthusiasm about her new job. Plus, when she stopped berating herself for being worked up and pressuring herself to calm down, she had more bandwidth to focus. The truth is, to do well, you need a certain level of energy rather than tranquility. Laurie similarly applied her excitement to causes that mattered to her outside of work. "Getting excited has given me my brainpower and energy back. I'm happy to say that I rejoined my book club and I began volunteering with a program to help domestic violence survivors with their résumés," she told me.

Now it's your turn. Experiment swapping "calm down" with "I am excited!" in your life. You may be thinking, *Fine, I can tell myself stress is okay and even exciting, but what happens when my body isn't cooperating?* Dr. Jeremy Jamieson, a professor in psychology and stress researcher at the University of Rochester, and his colleagues coauthored a paper with the amazingly descriptive title "Turning the knots in your stomach into bows."[6] In their study, they encouraged one group of participants prepping for the GRE, an exam that is a prerequisite for admission to many graduate schools, to reappraise any physiological symptoms of stress they experienced. The participants were asked to simply remind themselves that their physical signs of stress, whether heart palpitations or butterflies, could be helping them do well rather than signifying struggle. Students who did this performed better on the math section of the test compared to a group that wasn't told to think of stress this way.

In another study, this one looking at a group of community college students taking a math course, Dr. Jamieson and his colleagues noticed that teaching the students to reappraise arousal sparked by stress not only improved their math scores but also increased their likelihood of completing the course and lowered their cortisol levels, a physiological sign of stress. In a different study, where participants were invited to try public speaking, psychologist Miranda Beltzer and her colleagues at Harvard found that thinking of butterflies in the stomach as beneficial and a sign that oxygen was being delivered to the body led to improvements in performance "across

6 When I asked Dr. Jamieson if I could borrow a version of his fantastic title for this chapter, he enthusiastically and humbly said the title is all thanks to his coauthor, Dr. Wendy Berry Mendes. Big thank you, Dr. Jamieson and Dr. Mendes.

the board," ranging from less shame, anxiety, and fidgeting to cognitive and cardiovascular benefits. What we tell ourselves significantly affects how we approach and feel about situations—and how we perform.

Even more surprising is that improving your view of stress can also reduce stress in those around you. Research spearheaded by Dr. Christopher Oveis, a social psychologist and an associate professor at the University of California, San Diego, Rady School of Management, showed that when individuals on a product design team learned to reappraise their stress, their teammates also felt less stressed.

One of the challenges of reappraisal is applying it to different situations. While participants in studies can actively rethink their stress responses in specific situations, like taking a test or giving a talk, they are not necessarily able to do the same when it comes to navigating a difficult relationship or worrying about a health issue. As Dr. Jamieson put it, "What we're running into is a transfer problem." To truly internalize adaptive mindsets across various areas of your life, one of Dr. Jamieson's collaborators, Dr. David Yeager, a developmental psychologist and associate professor at the University of Texas, Austin, recommends adopting a *synergistic mindset* by merging a *growth mindset* (the belief that challenges can be positive if you approach them thoughtfully and seek help along the way) with a *stress-can-be-enhancing mindset* (appreciating that our physical stress responses can mobilize us). By believing that you're capable of growth *and* that your body is serving you, you're more likely to flexibly approach all sorts of stressors. In a sample of more than 4,000 students ranging from eighth grade through college in six different experiments, Dr. Yeager and his colleagues discovered that taking a thirty-minute online training session on the synergistic mindset reduced students' cortisol levels and correlated with fewer mental health symptoms. Those who received the training were also more likely to pass courses even a year later, narrowing achievement gaps.

We need to both allow ourselves to experience stress and have quick strategies for instances when we need to recharge.

In your own life, holistically improving the way you see your capacity to grow and learning to accept occasional discomfort (even knots in your stomach!) can lead you to take on new goals with more faith in yourself.

But like tiny wheels on a hefty suitcase that lighten your load, a moment of awareness and a doable strategy can make a big difference in how you feel, especially when paired with acceptance.

Together, Laurie and I worked on how she could broadly see herself as someone who was always improving and whose stress responses were serving her rather than getting stuck debating whether or not she was about to be fired.

Of course, to nurture a healthy mindset, it's important to be in a supportive environment. As Dr. Jamieson told me, you don't only need good seeds, you also need the right soil, because nothing is going to grow in sand. Laurie and I worked on how she could be more assertive with her partner, asking him to cheer her on rather than nudging her to calm down or quit her job. I hope you'll also talk to members of your support network about how stress can be enhancing and tell them to encourage you (when that's what you need) rather than judge your stress.

Laurie also learned to come up with a specific coping plan for times when she was struggling. The two of us worked on clarifying her values and pinpointing strategies to prevent overanalyzing. When she was especially stressed after getting an ambiguous email from her boss, she set a timer, then spent a few minutes sitting on a lawn chair in her yard and focusing on her breath and nature instead of sliding into her prior habit of overthinking. Once she was in a better state of mind, she sent a follow-up message to her boss to gain more clarity.

* * *

We need to both allow ourselves to experience stress and have quick strategies for instances when we need to recharge. In our complicated world, it's all too easy to reject seemingly simple solutions, like the stress resets you'll find in this book. But like tiny wheels on a hefty suitcase that lighten your load, a moment of awareness and a doable strategy can make a big difference in how you feel, especially when paired with acceptance.

I've personally discovered the benefits that thoughtfully easing stress can have, even in desperate situations. Years ago, I volunteered at a suicide hotline. One of the fascinating things I learned while engaging with people in their hardest moments was that good crisis counseling often depended on two core skills: 1) helping that person feel understood and less alone and 2) creating a coping plan they could use for the next few hours, like doing a crossword puzzle, watching a TV show, and reaching out to a friend. Such simple things, but they helped someone get through the night safely. "When people are headed for trouble, the limbic system is on fire and the prefrontal cortex shuts down," explained Dr. David Jobes, a professor at Catholic University who developed the Collaborative Assessment and Management of Suicidality, a leading clinical intervention to prevent suicidal crises. That said, "People are really good at getting better if you give them the right tools," he told me, going on to explain that by understanding problematic patterns and leaning on relatively simple coping plans, it's possible to access the parts of the mind that facilitate moving forward. When I began training in DBT as a psychologist, I was surprised to come across the same basic strategies I'd used as a hotline volunteer, only now I was using them to improve a person's ongoing ability to manage and self-soothe. And while the goal of this book is learning how to better cope with stress, not suicidal thinking, this overlap speaks to the power of stress resets, even in a crisis.

As for Laurie, she noticed that when she started seeing stress as motivating instead of embarrassing while also having go-to strategies for putting work aside when it wasn't helping her, she was able to find more peace. I hope you're beginning to experience something that you might not have previously paired with stress: excitement. It's a vital part of improving your relationship with the stress that comes from living a meaningful life, helping you pivot from *It's too much—I can't* to *Yes I can, yes I will, and here's my plan* . . .

Regulating
Your Emotions

WHEN I MET MELANIE, a client in her forties, she described herself as an "intense person," explaining that her emotions, whether happy, sad, or irritable, tended to reach high peaks that lasted over time. In certain respects, she appreciated her ability to feel so deeply, recognizing that her emotional sensitivity contributed to her being an empathetic friend and person. But she also judged her emotions, especially sadness, anger, and fear. "From the time I was a child, my father liked to tell me that I was overreacting," she recalled.

Now, as a mother to a toddler,[1] Melanie was juggling a demanding job in journalism and a son going through the "terrible twos," all while being incredibly sleep-deprived. She was also worried about her irritability: "People on Instagram look so happy, but I'm often stressed and annoyed. I don't get it." She told me that just before our first appointment, she was rushing around her apartment, stepped barefoot on a small toy garbage truck (painful!), then, cursing, threw it across the room. (Luckily, her toddler wasn't in earshot.) "I'm sure I sound like a lunatic," she told me. "But in those moments, I fully believe my life is unfair. And don't get me started on my husband and football . . ." Despite her harsh self-assessment, I wasn't judging her. Melanie seemed kind, and as a mother of three young children

---

1 If parenting isn't a relatable example, consider any demanding and meaningful endeavor you're pursuing.

myself, I empathized with how unpredictable and endless her days sometimes felt to her.

"I just want to feel like a decent human, be a good mom, and not hate my husband," Melanie said. I offered her the opportunity to join a group I lead that focuses on learning concrete tools to manage emotions. The goal of emotion regulation is to be able to experience your feelings almost as if they're on a dimmer instead of a light switch—you aren't turning them on or off, but simply getting rid of the harsh glare. I asked Melanie to consider what changes might result from her learning to better navigate her emotions. She told me that she'd likely feel less thrown by stress and unexpected upsets, because she had noticed that the demands of being a working parent contributed to her feeling short-tempered—and feeling short-tempered made her feel ill-equipped to deal with challenges.

Melanie was onto something: Stress and emotions are interconnected. When you're physiologically aroused (a common reaction to stress reaching a peak), it's easy to feel emotionally reactive, too. Conversely, learning to manage your emotions improves your ability to manage stress. In fact, when I asked Dr. Wendy Berry Mendes, a professor at the University of California, San Francisco, who researches both emotion regulation and stress, about the differences between the two, she explained that stress and emotions are remarkably similar. However, while an emotion may rise quickly, like a flash of anger or a wave of disgust, managing stress is something you have to do over time; it requires ongoing skillfulness. But "interestingly, when we consider ways to regulate and manage stress or emotions, the same processes are at our disposal," Dr. Mendes said. Essentially, you can consider regulating emotions to be synonymous with navigating stress.

Where to Begin

In the same way that improving your relationship with stress calls for not judging the experience, an essential first step in regulating your emotions is noticing if you're criticizing what you're feeling. Melanie told me that she was often angry at her husband, Brett, for not co-parenting their son as much as she hoped he would. But instead of staying with that emotion, she quickly began thinking that feeling angry made her a bad person, which made her feel even worse. By jumping from feeling angry about a situation or event to feeling angry about being angry and throwing in a splash of shame, Melanie was creating a veritable web of negative emotions. When your emotions are based on facts (as opposed to negative thoughts), they can teach you something, motivate you, and send a message to others. For example, at the right level of intensity, fear/anxiety can fuel urgency to act, sadness can be a wake-up call to make positive changes in our lives, envy can drive ambition, jealousy can protect relationships, guilt and regret can help us do better and repair our missteps, and disgust can prevent us from contamination. But when you go from *primary emotions*, or what you're initially feeling, to *secondary emotions*, what you feel once you judge your initial emotions, you lose sight of what's making you feel upset in the first place. It's almost like going to the store to pick up something essential, making some impulse purchases, and then leaving without getting what you actually needed.

I explained to Melanie that if she could learn to accept her anger without judging it, she might be able to see it as a signal that her needs weren't being met and ask her husband for more help. Instead, her secondary emotions—feeling both angry about and afraid of feeling angry—compelled her to snap and yell, which didn't exactly inspire Brett to jump in and help.[2] She also felt guilty about and ashamed of her anger, which sometimes led

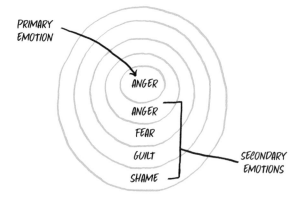

PRIMARY EMOTION

ANGER

ANGER
FEAR
GUILT
SHAME

SECONDARY EMOTIONS

---

2 Beyond judging our emotions in negative ways, it's also useful to notice if we have positive beliefs about emotions. For example, on some level Melanie believed, *If I show him how angry I am, he'll finally listen!* She wavered between assuming she'd somehow get through to him and worrying that she was becoming permanently unlikable. The complicated thing was that every so often Brett *did* listen when she was livid, which meant her anger was being reinforced, making it harder to break the cycle.

to her suppressing her emotions, escalating their intensity. And as you may know from your own experiences, suppressing emotions is stressful. Across cultures, researchers have found that covering up feelings increases blood pressure.

Melanie was relieved to discover that she could learn to use her emotions as a guide to life and herself, but she worried that her primary emotion—anger—was possibly too intense to manage and communicate effectively. I told her that, just as with stress, how she viewed her emotions mattered deeply. In a study led by Dr. Maya Tamir, a professor at the Hebrew University in Jerusalem, researchers followed the emotional ups and downs of Stanford University students during the often stressful period of transitioning to college. They found that students who viewed emotions as fleeting and felt confident that they could navigate those emotions were not only better able to regulate their emotions but also had more social success and a deeper sense of well-being. No wonder Dr. Tamir and her colleagues concluded their findings by quoting the Buddha: "He is able who thinks he is able."

That's why it's essential to adopt a growth mindset as you practice emotion regulation, just as it is when you're coping with stress. But daily habits matter, too, as it can be more difficult to regulate emotions if you're feeling exhausted, hungry, or lonely or aren't exercising regularly. As we discussed what her life was like beyond her child, husband, and work, Melanie shared that she had barely done anything social in months. Just as unhelpful, the typical ways she relaxed, like staying up late at night playing addictive games, set her up for more stress the next day. I know this sounds clichéd, but just as you'd go out of your way to fill up your gas tank rather than risk stalling on a highway, it is essential to set yourself up for better coping by practicing good sleep habits, steering clear of substances that negatively impact you, and making sure you're engaging in activities that boost your resilience, like nurturing friendships, eating nutrient-rich foods, and finding ways to move your body. Melanie was surprised that experimenting with minor tweaks to her schedule, like going to bed an hour earlier and making sure she had at least one social plan a month, made it easier for her to implement emotion regulation.

It's also important to notice if you have any undiagnosed health issues that might be impacting your well-being. After seeing her primary care physician at my suggestion, Melanie came to discover that some of her irritability was due to hormonal changes and perimenopause, which opened the door for more self-compassion.

Of course, there will always be times when you feel more reactive—say, if you've had a bad night's sleep. Reminding yourself that you may be more susceptible to intense emotions like frustration when you're tired can also motivate you to slow down before taking action, putting off a big decision until another day.

The ARC of Our Emotions

Understanding the components of an emotional experience can help you recalibrate and improve how you feel at various points rather than feeling like your emotions and stressors hold you hostage. The first thing to know is that emotions follow a predictable pathway known as an *ARC*, an acronym that stands for Antecedent (a prompting event); your Response (including thoughts, physical sensations, and behaviors); and Consequences (both short-term and long-term).

To track how emotions unfold, start by noticing your common antecedents and whether they arise from something external, like someone disappointing you or a deadline you're not prepared for, or internal, such as experiencing physical pain or upsetting thoughts. (It's also possible for certain antecedents to pop up out of nowhere, like receiving a summons for jury duty.) As you notice your initial stressors, make a point of not beating yourself up, and instead, consider whether there is something you can do better going forward. Even if there's nothing you could have done to prepare—after all, like stress, emotions are unavoidable—simply bringing awareness to your own antecedents can help prevent a stress spiral.

Next, bring your attention to your response, which consists of thoughts, physical sensations, and behaviors—these combine to build emotions. When you take a moment to reflect on the various parts of your reaction, you can create exit doors at different stages of the cycle, mitigating the intensity of your emotion rather than getting stuck along the way.

It's also important to look at the consequences of your response, or, more specifically, your *emotion-driven behaviors*, like Melanie tossing her son's truck across the room. How did your action make you feel? For instance, maybe throwing the truck and cursing felt natural in the moment, but when Melanie reflected on what would have happened had her son seen her lose it, she felt motivated to make a better decision next time.

Now it's your turn. Break down a recent emotion you experienced into an ARC:

ANTECEDENT	RESPONSE			CONSEQUENCES (short-term and long-term)
	Thoughts	Physical Sensations	Behaviors	

Revamping Your ARCs

Once you're clear on what can contribute to your emotions spiking, there are steps you can take to improve how you feel along the way. Let's get right to them:

1. Anticipating antecedents

If the events that stress you out lend themselves to troubleshooting, coming up with a plan can reduce your stress and improve your mood. One example: If you're dreading a long weekend because you don't have much to look forward to, reaching out to a couple of people and scheduling some uplifting activities will feel better than trying to get unstuck once you're already feeling miserable. For Melanie, a recurrent antecedent was seeing her husband relaxing in front of the TV when she was "beyond exhausted" and hadn't had a break. After we talked about it, she felt inspired to work on a new response: communicating her needs *before* she became irate. She tried overtures like, "Hey, if you're going to watch a game, can I have an hour for me earlier in the day?" While she didn't love having to ask for that hour in the first place—*He should be offering!*—she was relieved to find that Brett was happy to help. Melanie also noticed that when she was clear about what she needed and carved out more downtime for herself, she had more patience to deal with upcoming stressors, like her son purposefully spilling the food she had just prepared for him.

2. Thinking flexibly

Practice observing your thoughts, because they can pop up so quickly and, like a mirage, seem real. Once you do that, it's also helpful to see if you're falling into any common categorical errors, such as *catastrophizing*, or taking something upsetting and making it exponentially worse. You may also be *jumping to conclusions*, or preparing for an unlikely worst-case scenario. For example, if a friend forgets your birthday (an antecedent), you may have a dramatic takeaway (*I can't count on anyone*) that will elicit a different emotional response than a more reasonable explanation (*she's forgetful*).

As you become a more mindful observer of your mental habits, it will be easier to see when they are unhelpful. Simply labeling them—*This thought isn't helping me*—can go a long way toward turning down the temperature when you feel overcome by emotions. You can also try seeing an unhelpful thought, such as *Things never work out for me, so why bother?*, from a distance, as you would read a message on a billboard, which dilutes its power. Another option is to do some fact-checking, systematically asking yourself questions such as: *Is this thought accurate? What are other possible interpretations? Could my thought be fueled by my intense emotions?*

We've covered how reappraising your stress and its physical sensations can flip them from something that hurts you to something that motivates you. The same goes for *cognitive reappraisal*, or rethinking the meaning of events. One example: If someone you're meeting with yawns, you can assume that you're boring or consider that they must be tired. After decades in the field, Dr. James Gross, a leading expert in emotion regulation and a professor at Stanford University, is clear that thinking more flexibly and adaptively is essential to regulating emotions. Too often we jump to pessimism when what we need is peace; if you believe the worst, your painful emotions won't budge. Brain studies show that compared with suppressing our feelings, when we reappraise our automatic thoughts, we reduce activity in the amygdala, the brain region responsible for emotions. Reappraisal takes willingness and effort, but as you'll discover, it's well worth it.

If you look back on your own experiences, you may find, like Melanie, that you have thoughts that don't prepare you to cope as much as they derail you. When Melanie struggled to think flexibly during tough moments, like when her son was sick and up all night, I reminded her that she'd had lots of practice thinking the worst; improving her thinking would take time. Eventually, she was able to see that extreme negative thoughts such as *My life is unfair!* were neither her reality nor her destiny.

Thinking more constructively doesn't mean you won't experience emotions. Those emotions, however, can feel less debilitating when you've adopted a healthier perspective. Lucy, another client learning the same skills as Melanie, shared that after going on disappointing dates, she often found herself thinking, *I'll never meet someone.* It's normal to feel sad, and maybe angry and anxious, after spending an hour with someone you don't connect with. But I also reminded Lucy that a bad date was hard enough without multiplying her distress by anticipating a future of loneliness. Another client of mine, Edgar, shared the thought *I'll never be able to afford a house*, which certainly sparked hopelessness in him. But the truth is, his career was just beginning and he was already putting money aside.

When you reflect on some frequent-flier thoughts in your brain, ones that may contribute to you struggling with emotions, what comes to mind?[3] Practice either seeing those thoughts from a distance or checking the facts.

3. Accepting physical sensations

Next, let's focus on addressing and improving the physical changes we experience during certain situations and the thoughts they elicit. Melanie noticed that her muscles tensed and her heart raced when she felt angry, which set the stage for more angry thoughts. Others also find that their physical sensations, like clenching, occur first and their negative thinking follows.

I taught Melanie to practice scanning and releasing tension in her body. Then I asked her to go home, watch a few minutes of political content that would likely cause her to feel tense, and practice staying present with that feeling and bringing acceptance to any uncomfortable sensations she was experiencing. "I told you I have a problem with anger and you want me to watch something I'm sure will enrage me?" she asked, surprised. I explained that while we can't always make ourselves feel better, we can learn to be

---

3 At this moment, the thoughts that have popped up in my mind include *This chapter isn't amazing enough* and *No one will read the book I'm working so hard on!*

better at feeling without reacting. Learning to accept physiological sensations by intentionally practicing them and staying present with them is freeing, and you'll come to realize that your body doesn't stay at peak intensity for very long.

"If you have patience and can remind yourself that your physiological hyperarousal will subside, you can make a better decision than if you act on it in the moment," said Dr. Cory Newman, a professor in psychiatry and the director of the Center for Cognitive Therapy at the University of Pennsylvania. "Eventually, you will feel differently, because physiologically, you can't stay at fever pitch all the time."

4. Acting opposite

The last part of the "response" in ARC is our behavior, which we can target by acting differently from how we feel. While it may seem natural and potentially cathartic to engage in emotion-driven behaviors such as snapping at someone when you're angry, canceling plans when you're anxious, or curling up in bed in the middle of the day when you're sad, doing so can amplify your feelings. Here's why: Thoughts and physical sensations set us up to behave in certain ways—and those behaviors tend to cement our emotions.

One strategy you can use to turn from destructive behaviors that stem from negative emotions is called *opposite action*. If there is an emotion you want to change, acting differently from how you feel can ultimately improve how you feel. Begin by labeling your emotion and noticing the behaviors the emotion is pulling you toward. Next, consider whether acting on the emotion will be helpful in the long term, and if not, act differently from how you feel. It's also essential to watch your thoughts while you're trying opposite action, because approaching something like trying a new hobby that intimidates you while thinking *I'm pathetic* won't feel like a pick-me-up.

I love this skill, which isn't to be confused with faking it. The point isn't to pretend you feel amazing but to choose to take actions that correspond with your ultimate goals while allowing yourself to feel your feelings. Remember, stay present every step of the way, even if you feel uncomfortable, because worrying about when you'll start to feel better or getting lost in negative thoughts will make it hard to benefit from this skill.

In group therapy one morning, Melanie shared that she felt too anxious to play with her son after work because of a looming work deadline. Instead of acting on that anxiety by constantly clutching her phone and halfheartedly attending to her child, she took a step back and realized that her level of anxiety wasn't fitting the facts. She didn't need to respond to messages right away outside of work hours, and trying to do so would only keep her feeling antsy. Instead, Melanie committed to setting a timer for fifteen minutes, stowing her phone, and acting as if her only focus in the world was playing with her little boy. She was surprised to discover that simply behaving aspirationally—even if she didn't think she felt ready for it—made a big difference. She also found that she felt less anxious and enjoyed playtime more when she stayed present, which she did again and again by noticing thoughts about work and acting opposite. Keep in mind that it may take repeated practice for you to start to enjoy the emotional benefits of this shift. The goal of opposite action isn't feeling better—it's *living* better.

To me, opposite action is the ultimate mental health hack. I use it often, especially when I'm tired but know I'll feel better after exercising. I also try to use it when I feel frustrated—by choosing to give others the benefit of the doubt and communicating with kindness. When someone recently snapped at me for being a few minutes late, rather than being defensive or prolonging the tension, I thought, *She's pressed for time and feels disrespected*, and warmly apologized. Once she felt heard, I was itching to dodge more uncomfortable conversations, but instead I asked if going forward, it would be possible for her to share her frustrations without yelling. See, opposite action isn't just one behavior—it's continuously doing what will help in the long run rather than what's most comfortable in the moment.

Interestingly, all behavior therapies for depression and anxiety hinge on acting differently from how you feel, because acting how you feel keeps you *mood dependent*, or in a position where your emotions, rather than your higher intentions, drive your life. Remarkably, people who feel depressed and hopeless can significantly improve their symptoms by practicing an example of opposite action technically referred to as *behavioral activation*, or creating a schedule that matters to them with activities they enjoy and opportunities to feel accomplished. In a landmark study led by Dr. Sona Dimidjian, a psychologist and professor at the University of Colorado, Boulder, behavioral activation compared favorably with antidepressant medication, even for individuals experiencing severe depression. That's because acting differently from how you feel can spark an "upward spiral" where you create experiences conducive to positive emotions and chip away at negative narratives. The ultimate way to change your mind is by changing your life.

5. Considering consequences

That brings us to the *C* in ARC: "consequences." In order to rally the motivation to try other courses of action, it's helpful to track the outcomes of your responses. Gather your own data and see if you notice any trends. Here's my prediction, based on what I see with clients and in my own life: Acting in emotion-driven ways feels good in the short term but feels unpleasantly sticky in the long term, intensifying your emotions and potentially adding shame and guilt to the equation. On the other hand, choosing to use skills like thinking more flexibly or acting differently from how you feel may seem like a reach at first, but doing so promises more lasting rewards. Melanie reminding herself that Brett can't read her mind and then consciously relaxing her face and asking him for a hand may take effort, but it creates enduring feelings of pride and relief. It's easy to seek instant gratification, but remembering consequences can help.

Because experience is your best teacher, you can use a chart like this to help you experiment with and reflect on revamping your ARCs:

ANTECEDENT	RESPONSE			CONSEQUENCES (short-term and long-term)
	Thoughts	**Physical Sensations**	**Behaviors**	
How can I prepare?	*What are more helpful ways to think about this situation?*	*What did I notice in my body? How can I add acceptance?*	*What opposite actions can I take?*	*What did I learn?*

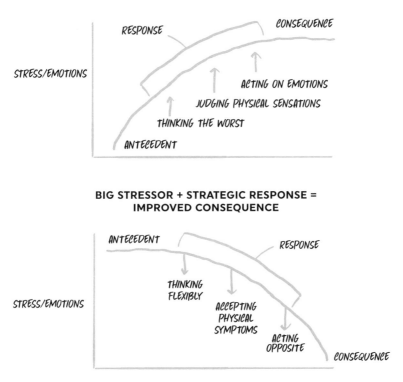

SMALL STRESSOR + ESCALATING RESPONSE = HEIGHTENED CONSEQUENCE

RESPONSE — CONSEQUENCE

STRESS/EMOTIONS

ACTING ON EMOTIONS
JUDGING PHYSICAL SENSATIONS
THINKING THE WORST
ANTECEDENT

BIG STRESSOR + STRATEGIC RESPONSE = IMPROVED CONSEQUENCE

ANTECEDENT — RESPONSE

STRESS/EMOTIONS

THINKING FLEXIBLY
ACCEPTING PHYSICAL SYMPTOMS
ACTING OPPOSITE
CONSEQUENCE

Practice Wherever You Can

When Melanie had to work on her taxes when she already felt spent, she practiced noticing her thoughts, such as *I can't handle this*, and doing some fact-checking: *I can work on this for thirty minutes*. By thinking more flexibly, not judging the tenseness in her body, and starting what initially felt like an impossible task, Melanie was able to get over her initial surge of anxiety more quickly and wrap up her work sooner.

As for me, I used to fear public speaking so much that if I had to film a three-minute TV segment, I'd be up the entire night before worrying. Clearly I needed to practice what I preached, so I signed up for a public speaking course, which was the opposite of what I wanted to do (never speak in public again, including in the class). Then I signed up for another, and another. Now I relish opportunities to speak in front of audiences. (But I do still feel some anxiety and excitement, which I find inspire me to prepare the best I can.)

To truly master a skill and thrive in high-stress situations, we need to regularly practice a range of techniques in a variety of contexts. I realized that I wasn't mastering public speaking as much as I hoped, because participating in interviews isn't something I do every day. One teacher told me that I need to introduce more variety in my tone of voice rather than talking in the calm, steady manner of a meditation teacher, so I decided to introduce vocal variety in at least one therapy session a day and one daily conversation, whether with a friend, a stranger, or one of my children. That way, when I'm in a high-stakes speaking situation, varying my tone of voice comes more naturally.

According to Dr. Amelia Aldao, a visiting scholar at Columbia University who has published dozens of papers on emotion regulation, we need to try different strategies in many situations across a range of emotions to build an enduring ability to manage them. "Having a wide range of tools at our disposal allows us to become more self-confident and grounded," she said. "When I only have one or two emotion regulation skills, it better be the right one for a given context. But if I have many (and I'm willing to engage in a trial-and-error process), then even big challenges can be dealt with!" Dr. Aldao explained.

Dr. Steven Hayes, a Nevada Foundation Professor at the University of Nevada, Reno, who developed ACT, and a team of more than fifty psychologists came together to study hundreds of psychotherapy outcome papers to pinpoint the essential ingredients that help people change their lives for the better. They narrowed in on *psychological flexibility*, which Dr. Hayes considers to be "the most important skill set in mental health" and defines it as: *awareness*, or noticing; *openness*, or allowing yourself to process difficult thoughts and feelings; and *valued engagement*, or identifying what matters to you and moving in that direction.

We know how much physical flexibility can help our bodies navigate and reduce risk of injury, and the same holds true when it comes to psychological flexibility. I hope that seeing the messages in your emotions and practicing observing and improving your ARCs will help you change your relationship with your emotions and stress, allowing them to inspire you.

Rethinking
Overthinking

ONE OF MY CLIENTS, MAX, once overheard his college roommate describing him as having "no chill factor"—Generation Z lingo for being unable to relax. He told me that felt hurtful but accurate. Beyond feeling the shame of hearing himself labeled that way, Max told me that he struggled to enjoy ordinary moments, like lounging around on a Sunday afternoon, because his mind frequently drifted into stressful thinking. He'd been considering trying therapy for a while because his health benefits included ten free sessions. His roommate's words finally propelled him to reach out to me. I was so happy he did—overthinking isn't only a draining habit; it's also a risk factor for depression.

In our initial meeting, Max told me that if he had anything significant on his to-do list, like studying for an exam or writing a paper, or even any looming issue of importance, like an ongoing conflict with a friend or a decision to make, he couldn't get it out of his mind. It didn't matter if he was trying to do something else, like watch TV or fall asleep. "I've always been this way," he said, "getting lost in my own head and analyzing topics that are impossible to answer, like *What's the point of life?* and *Why do bad things happen to good people?*" When I asked him about what he'd tried to help him stay in the moment, he told me about a guided mindfulness practice he'd learned in his high school health class. "It was impossible—though it should have been easy," he said hopelessly.

When filling me in on his background, Max said his parents were incredibly loving and attentive and that his younger brother, Joey, had been diagnosed with autism and struggled to speak. When I asked about his life goals, he told me that his parents were immigrants who pumped every resource they could into his future and Joey's therapies, and I found myself moved by the way he described his dream of earning enough money to help his parents so they could comfortably retire and still support Joey. Since middle school, Max regularly wondered if he was doing his best and felt stressed about finding a career that paid well but wasn't "soul crushing." These were valid concerns, but Max's thinking tended to be repetitive and passive, extending beyond useful strategizing. Clinically speaking, he was *ruminating*, a term psychologists use to describe repetitively thinking about concerns or feelings. (The word "rumination" stems from "ruminari," a Latin word that means to chew the cud, or to slowly chomp on partially digested food. Think of it this way: When you ruminate, you're chewing without digesting or fueling yourself.)

Humans have the unique ability to replay and anticipate stressful experiences. In doing so, we run the risk of creating chronic stress. Ruminating doesn't only affect us—it affects the people around us. I'm guessing if you come home a couple of hours late, your dog lovingly licks your face; however, your thoughtful partner, who may have been stewing, might struggle to let it go. Someone can give you a slight tilt of an eyebrow (that may be as innocent as dust in their eye!) that leaves you overanalyzing, creating awkwardness where none existed before. It's hard to have a mind that creates and responds to so many false alarms.

The first thing I told Max is that it's normal to get stuck in our head, especially concerning unresolved goals that matter to us. Overthinking tends to be an ingrained habit. That's why you need to understand why you do it, when you do it, and how it affects you and repeatedly experiment with a range of alternatives to help you more effortlessly return to the present.

Why Overthinking Comes Naturally

On some level, overthinking can feel like a responsible move. It's easy to assume that by keeping problems we can't immediately work out at the top of our mind, we're inching toward understanding, motivating ourselves, preparing to problem solve, and saving ourselves from making mistakes. Some clients even describe an element of magical thinking, assuming that if they worry about something, it will work out, because many of the things we stress about coincidentally turn out okay. But the truth is that obsessing too much over anything doesn't magically affect the future—and it can keep us stuck in mental ruts.

Ironically, the first step in breaking free from this pattern is to reflect on your thoughts about your thoughts, or your *metacognitions*. Once you start reflecting, you may notice that you have various beliefs about your overthinking, from *Overthinking is making me unstable and I can't control it!* to *Focusing on why this happened is going to save me from humiliating myself in the future.* Another tactic is to notice the costs and benefits of your overthinking. I'm hoping you can set a timer for two minutes and jot down some of the negatives (*Keeps me stressed*) and positives (*Maybe I'll realize something I didn't before?*). Putting your unique experiences down on paper will reveal more about the ramifications of this habit and motivate you to be more mindful.

When I tried this exercise with Max, his list was all over the place. He found his overthinking stressful, annoying, and guaranteed to steal his joy, yet he also imagined that it kept him on track when it came to his goals. To better gauge that theory, we tried a behavioral experiment for a week. We created a detailed schedule for Max, slotting in time for work and pleasure, with the goal being to let go of thinking about all he needed to do when he wasn't doing those tasks. Not surprisingly, Max reported that he was significantly more productive when he focused on whatever was in front of him rather than obsessing over his long-term plans. Getting clear on the costs and benefits, systematically testing his metacognition (i.e., that over-thinking was keeping him moving toward his goals), and creating a plan to problem solve, including working from the library instead of at home with his loud roommates, allowed Max to discover that he didn't need to over-think to motivate himself. Ruminating only fueled more anxiety, which led to procrastinating—and the negative cycle continued. And while it's possi-ble for bursts of stress to inspire us (like a looming deadline), constant stress is depleting; dwelling on your concerns actually gets in the way of thinking pragmatically and taking constructive next steps.

Overthinking is also isolating—even generous friends can feel frustrated when they hear you repeatedly ruminate out loud. Within friendships, there's also a risk of getting stuck in *co-rumination*, or repeatedly focusing on upsetting topics with others, which can result in losing the benefits of social support. Plus, endlessly venting to someone else is no more cathartic than cycling through the same thoughts on your own. A study led by researcher Dr. Cristina Ottaviani, an associate professor at the University of Rome, found that people had a just-as-intense cardiovascular reaction when they they talked about something upsetting in detail as when they ruminated about it.[1]

No wonder overthinking often lies at the core of so many psychological struggles, including anxiety and depression, insomnia, binge eating, substance abuse, problems in relationships . . . and the list goes on. Overthinking, as we'll soon explore, also tends to be the culprit behind many physical symptoms we might blame on stress.

On a personal note, I wasted thousands of hours wondering whether I'd get into psychology graduate school and succeed as a psychologist, even though I was doing all I could to make it happen. On the romantic front, I tended to rehash and dissect the mixed messages from guys I was casually dating, a habit that never gave me peace or power. But then I came upon academic papers on rumination by Dr. Susan Nolen-Hoeksema, a psychology professor at Yale University until her untimely passing in 2013. Rather than bleakly attributing people's struggles to chemical imbalances or unfortunate circumstances, Dr. Nolen-Hoeksema clarified that our mental habits may be at fault for our suffering. In reading the papers, I had an epiphany: I was a ruminator, and it wasn't doing me any good.

Simply having a name for the process and knowing its downsides gave me a new feeling of clarity—and choice. Like Max, part of me assumed that always keeping my concerns close kept me conscientious. Another main reason I ruminated (and why so many of my clients struggle with this) is because I was confusing overthinking with *self-validation*, or compassionately normalizing my inner experiences. We all want to feel like our feelings are legitimate—that's why it's such a gift when people listen attentively. Many of my clients who struggle with the invisible wounds of chronic pain, grief, trauma, or injustice tell me that it feels especially hard not to ruminate when others aren't honoring their experience. But eventually, they come to notice that ruminating is only prolonging their suffering and that there are more empowering ways to face painful experiences.

---

1 Does this mean you should never share what you're going through with a therapist or friend? Absolutely not! It's a matter of sharing what feels helpful as opposed to what keeps you stuck.

Overthinking Keeps Stress in Your Mind and Body

How can any of us know that overthinking is the culprit when the demands and stresses of life are so heavy? Max, for one, wondered if his thinking habits reflected the fact that his life felt hard because of his experiences and responsibilities. To answer, I shared one of Dr. Nolen-Hoeksema's studies with Max. When she measured the well-being of students who had experienced the 1989 Loma Prieta earthquake, which was recorded as a 6.9 on the Richter scale, she found that those who were prone to ruminating and responded to the disaster by overthinking were likelier to develop psychological problems, even heightening the risk of PTSD.

In fact, *perseverative cognition*, the phrase stress researchers use to describe ruminating and worrying, turns acute stress into prolonged stress. "You can have chronic stressors that *don't* have a lifelong impact, and you can have acute stressors that *do* have a lifelong impact," explained psychologist George Slavich, a professor at University of California, Los Angeles, who leads the Laboratory for Stress Assessment and Research. "The thing about these stress pathways is that they don't seem to care too much about whether a stressor is actual or imagined, meaning we all have the ability to activate or engage those pathways," Dr. Slavich told me. That's even the case if nothing stressful is happening around us. "We can still be reexperiencing that acute stressor," he said. That reminds me of an anecdote I heard from celebrated mindfulness teacher and author Sharon Salzberg about a friend who was trekking in Nepal and developed a blister. The man complained of pain with each footstep, anticipating it before, bemoaning it as he stepped down, and replaying it afterward. His guide said to him, "You can experience the pain once per step or three times per step."

Blisters aside, there's no doubt that all this stressing can impact your physical health; worrying by day can compromise restful sleep by keeping us "on," which diminishes the brainpower and energy we get with a good night's rest. Ruminating and the stress it causes can also affect heart health. In one study, psychologist William Gerin, a now-retired Penn State professor, asked people to think back to something that incensed them while researchers recorded their cardiovascular activity. Even thinking about events that occurred decades ago spiked their blood pressure. "Representational threats become very real" to our bodies, Dr. Gerin said. "When you ask someone, 'What's the worst thing that ever happened to you?' what comes up is not just the memory—it's the whole package. They reexperience the full effect of the event."

Dozens of studies confirm this, but the flip side is that if you can develop ways to keep yourself from reliving stressful moments, you can shift prolonged chronic stress into a more fleeting experience. In a frequently cited study by Dr. Matt Killingsworth, a psychologist and senior fellow at the University of Pennsylvania, people were asked to record what they were doing and thinking about in the moment and then rate their own happiness. His team found that nearly half of the time, participants had thoughts that were unrelated to what they were doing. But when they were present and in the moment, they were more likely to report being happy, whether they were sitting on a beach or waiting in line at the post office. As Dr. Killingsworth concludes, "A human mind is a wandering mind, and a wandering mind is an unhappy mind."

Increasing your sense of peace by becoming more present is possible even for people facing devastating circumstances, according to Dr. Gerin. There is something freeing about realizing the serenity you can access while you're waiting for circumstances to improve. Sharon Salzberg shared another story that I've been retelling since I heard it. When she was visiting Texas with renowned meditation expert Joseph Goldstein, a man told them he was itching to go to Wyoming to enjoy more open space. In a delivery you might expect from a meditation teacher, Mr. Goldstein responded, "Did you know that there's a Wyoming in you?" We don't need to wait for things to go our way to enjoy more contentment right now.

One of my clients, Cara, came to see me when her mother was receiving hospice care after years of struggling with cancer. She told me that just the sound of her phone ringing was an acute stressor, leading her to panic that she was going to receive bad news. Visits with her beloved mom were also sources of extreme sadness, yet for much of the day, Cara was able to interrupt the tape of visualizing her mom on her deathbed by participating in her life and focusing on interesting work she was doing, running, or meeting up with friends. Her deliberate investment in staying present wasn't avoidance—she certainly felt her feelings—but she allowed other experiences to replenish her so she could respond to crises without burning out.

Your Abbreviated Guide to Breaking Up with Overthinking

If you want to reduce your overthinking so you can focus on what's actually in front of you, here's an overview of the techniques that Max found helpful. I use them myself, of course, and with many of my clients. Incidentally, all of the stress resets and buffers ahead are also designed to help you break free of ruminating.

1. Clarify your goal.

To change your relationship with overthinking, it can help to break down your goals into smaller steps. Maybe you want to start with not overthinking what you did or said during a social event. Then you can work through bigger worries that seem stuck in your head, like *Will I find someone who will love me forever?* or *Will I ever earn enough money to achieve the lifestyle I want?* Given how overwhelming it can feel to try to stop overthinking, it's easier to start with a specific and reasonable plan to reduce ruminating.

2. Pinpoint your risk factors.

I like a strategy called *functional analysis*, which Dr. Edward Watkins, a professor of psychology at the University of Exeter in the United Kingdom, who developed Rumination-Focused Cognitive-Behavioral Therapy for Depression, turns to when treating overthinking. Focus on spotting what seems to push you into overthinking. For example, are there certain times of the day when you get lost in worries, such as first thing in the morning or while lying awake at night?[2] Are there physical cues you perceive, such as scowling, or are there mental signs, like tuning the world out? Are there certain themes that come up again and again, or people who bring out the behavior? Once you've made note of these patterns, reflect on the times when you're *less* prone to overthinking, even after something difficult happens. For example, do you

---

2 A huge issue for me is checking my iPhone when I'm trying to do something fun, especially if I get an upsetting email that I can't immediately reply to or stumble upon distressing news. On the flip side, putting my phone in airplane mode helps me enjoy my outing.

struggle less when you commit to doing something to unwind after work, like exercising or listening to a funny podcast on your commute home?

As Dr. Watkins noticed, there is no one-size-fits-all hack to fix overthinking, but gathering details from your life can help you design a few strategies that work for you. He suggests brainstorming "If-Then" plans. For example: **If** *I'm being self-critical,* **then** *I need to slow down, relax my shoulders, and engage in an activity that gets me into a flow state, like reading fiction for fifteen minutes.*

3. Recognize the power of language, then rise above it.

Another way to sidestep mental quicksand is by reflecting on the distress that language can generate. In a matter of seconds, language can spark real feelings. If you think of the word "cockroach" while in a doughnut shop— that spoils your appetite, right? Practice detaching from your thoughts and seeing them as just that—mere thoughts. If that sounds too abstract, imagine someone juggling colorful balls (the balls being your thoughts) without getting fixated on a particular ball or judging the balls or the juggler. In other words, you're focusing on the process of thinking rather than the specific content of your thoughts. Doing this takes practice, but eventually it will become easier to recognize that familiar, unmotivating thoughts are patterns, not predictions.

4. Experiment with self-distancing.

A big reason why overthinking when we're upset backfires is because it deeply immerses us in whatever we're going through, explained Dr. Ethan Kross, a professor in psychology at the University of Michigan. Similar to rising above language, try taking a step back and seeing the bigger picture, a strategy known as *self-distancing.* To be clear, self-distancing isn't meant for situations where you're looking back on a mistake and need to apologize. It works best when you're losing yourself in overthinking. Revisit and observe whatever difficult experience you're ruminating about as if you're a fly on a wall rather than directly involved.

Another option is shifting from "I" to "you" in your self-talk—for example, switching out *I made a huge mistake* with *You think you made a huge mistake.* Compared with our own challenges, it can be easier to think more clearly about what others are going through. My personal favorite technique is mental time travel: considering how you'll feel about a current stressor in a week or even years from now. (Maybe you won't remember it!)

5. Swap *why* with *how.*

The simplest way to replace negative thoughts with more constructive thinking is to shift from asking *why* questions (*Why me?*) to *how* questions (*How can I move forward?*), always with an element of self-compassion. Essentially, you're changing your processing style from unproductive ruminating to empowered planning. For instance, if you went on a date and the person didn't message you after what you thought was a great time, rather than ponder why, focus on how you can have a relaxing night despite that fact. Notice the difference—"why" is a dead end, but "how" leads to action.

6. Problem solve what you can control.

It makes sense that the topics that take up mental space in our brain reflect areas in life that matter to us. But the more you ruminate and focus on causes and consequences, the less likely you are to initiate useful actions to move forward. As I joke with my clients, no one benefits from analysis paralysis. So if there is something you care about that you can act on, replace circular thinking with taking steps to find a solution (while simultaneously accepting discomfort and uncertainty). For example, if you worry about your health, then actions like tracking your steps and improving your cholesterol will help you more than pondering whether you'll face a sudden catastrophic medical crisis.

7. Write it out.

When you need to process your feelings or an experience, instead of overthinking, try *expressive writing*, a technique pioneered by Dr. James Pennebaker, a professor of psychology at the University of Texas at Austin. In a study led by Dr. Denise Sloan, who was inspired by the benefits of expressive writing, college students answered questionnaires on rumination and depression and were then asked to try the technique. The first day, students in one group were asked to use a pen and paper to write about the most stressful or traumatic experience of their lives with as much emotion as possible for 20 minutes. (Don't worry, I'm not going to ask you to write about your most traumatic experience.) For their next session, the students were instructed to write about how the experience related to other aspects of their lives. Finally, on the third day, they were told to wrap up their writing by describing how the experience related to their current lives and future. Compared to students in a control group who journaled in an unemotional way about how they spent their time, students in the first group whose questionnaires indicated a tendency to ruminate reported significantly fewer depression symptoms at the follow-up five weeks later. Remarkably, those three 20-minute sessions of writing led to improvements in depression for those same ruminators even six months later!

If something is plaguing you, try spending three to four consecutive days writing about it for at least 15 minutes with a pen and paper. By writing, you create both an end point and distance. You'll find writing prompts to guide you through specific steps on page 140.

8. Make space to feel.

Surprisingly, ruminating does not equal experiencing your emotions; in fact, for many it can be a way to stay in your head rather than allow yourself to feel. Dr. Watkins, the expert who developed Rumination-Focused Cognitive-Behavioral Therapy, told me that a participant in one of his therapy trials, a woman who'd gone through a complicated divorce, complained that she wasn't feeling better, even though her scores on questionnaires measuring rumination had plummeted. What happened? Turns out that she was actually sitting with her emotions for the first time. Being present instead of ruminating doesn't mean you get to escape emotions; it means staying with whatever feelings are coming up. That can be helpful, because ruminating can creep up again if you don't give yourself the time and space to address and feel valid concerns. If that sounds challenging, remember that all emotions are transient, especially when we don't keep them going with overthinking.

All emotions are transient, especially when we don't keep them going with overthinking.

9. Reschedule ruminating.

To make your overthinking feel less compulsive (and therefore make you feel more powerful!), notice when you start to worry or overthink and postpone it until later—for example, giving it ten minutes of time at seven p.m. Afterward, move on. This strategy, which I describe in more detail on page 138, was developed by psychologist Thomas Borkovec, a professor emeritus at Penn State who spent decades researching anxiety. The goal is to turn overthinking from an all-day background buzz in your head to something more self-contained and transitory. This method can help you discover that it's possible to shift from feeling like you *have* to listen when the same old troubling thoughts come up to realizing that you can revisit them later. Another bonus: There's a good chance that you'll get so caught up in your day or evening that you'll forget to return to your worries. But even if you don't, you'll likely be able to see your thoughts with more perspective when you're conscious of them.

10. Get absorbed in something else.

Simply participating in something else can help you enter the moment, especially if you choose to do something that absorbs you. In a study led by Dr. Ottaviani, from the University of Rome, participants were asked to recall an event that made them angry and that continued to upset them afterward while pondering how they felt. Next, one group of participants sat quietly for ten minutes, while the other half distracted themselves by "eavesdropping" on an experimenter who was in an adjacent room with the door ajar. More than 90 percent of those in distraction mode stopped ruminating when they were listening in on someone else's conversation, while 100 percent of those who weren't distracted acknowledged that they were ruminating after the emotional recollection. The bottom line: Distraction can quickly shift your focus, especially if it's captivating.

A similar study led by Dr. Gerin showed that even simple visual distractions, like brightly colored cards and posters on a free-standing screen, reduced rumination and improved blood pressure in participants. Remember that a little distraction can go a long way; you don't want to endlessly run away. The goal is to take a quick break so you can return to what matters in a healthier frame of mind.

* * *

Using these techniques afforded Max the ability to get out of his head and the freedom that comes with it. He was relieved to realize that he could actually hang out with his friends and be chill. Like Max, too many of us have minds that berate us, insisting we need to do more and figure things out. That's why it's essential to give yourself mental breaks, as new events will continuously lure us into overthinking. If you want to be happier and less stressed, it's key to replace circular thinking with coping and strike a balance between analyzing and participating in your life.

4

Thriving
Without Substances

"I HAVE NO MOTIVATION AND I'M SO TIRED," Cameron, one my clients, told me. He had been diagnosed with attention-deficit/hyperactivity disorder (ADHD) as a kid, and now, in his thirties, he told me he was feeling "so bored all the time." He hoped to work on feeling less blah and find a way to stop languishing in both his career and social life. Another goal was to act with more consistency. "I am sick of being the flake who's always late," he said. Instead, he wanted to be the sort of person who could jump out of bed and work out in the morning. "I'll never be a seven a.m., seven days a week sort of person, but maybe I could pull off eight a.m., a few times a week?"

Cameron also felt on edge and stressed at his job in sales. After having a panic attack once on a flight, he always kept a low dose of the medication Klonopin—a benzodiazepine designed to immediately relieve symptoms of anxiety—on hand. Cameron found that just knowing the pill bottle was in his bag was comforting, especially if he was anticipating a meeting he felt unprepared for or started to feel his heart fluttering. "Klonopin makes me feel like I'm weightless, like I'm lying on a hammock," he told me, describing how the drug melted his stress away. His psychiatrist had prescribed it to help Cameron ward off panic and advised him to take it "just a couple of times a week." But he liked the feeling of calm it created and quickly upped his dosage to daily. Given work "sucked," Cameron admitted that he frequently looked forward to heading home, getting high on weed because the effects of the benzo had worn off, and sinking into distractions like watching hours of comedy specials with a pint of ice cream in his hand. In his mind, he'd found decent enough ways to self-medicate and manage, but he wasn't feeling especially fulfilled. Then his boyfriend, a therapist in training, told Cameron that his flakiness, memory, and focus seemed worse than ever and that he should get help.

So many people I come across—not only clients but also friends—don't think much about unwinding with a joint[1] or a prescription benzodiazepine like Klonopin or Xanax that instantly brings physical calm. And I know it can feel infuriating to hear someone suggest that you stop using something that seems like it helps, especially if other things you've tried don't. Like many of my clients, Cameron felt agitated when I asked him if his substance use may be working against him; he had several theories about cannabis helping his ADHD. He wasn't interested in talking about substances; he wanted to focus on being more productive, organized, and patient. But my job is to be radically genuine, with warmth and a nonjudgmental stance. I told Cameron that I'd be honored to help him build a life he was proud of, but that in my experience, the substances he was taking were only going to get in the way of him achieving his goals. I didn't want to waste his time if I didn't think I could help him with his focus and motivation. We finally agreed that he would try some techniques to increase his performance for a few weeks, but if those weren't making much of an impact, we'd have to look at the role substances played in his life. He could also find a different therapist who felt more confident in his progressing while continuing to use the drugs. Once I gave Cameron options, he perked up and wanted to hear more about why I wasn't "into benzos" and why I was, as he put it, "anti-weed."

* * *

1 Given that most people would agree that alcohol is a depressant and impairs judgment, excessive emotional eating affects health and self-worth, and cigarettes and illicit drugs have serious ramifications, I won't focus on those types of "escapes" that only create additional sources of stress. If you do struggle with any of those substances, please think about the impact they have on your life and check out the resources on page 199.

To start, I want to acknowledge that I *do* encourage some of my clients to consider taking psychiatric medications, especially for certain conditions where a prescription can be incredibly helpful, such as bipolar disorder. Medication can also be helpful at the start of therapy, particularly if someone is struggling to the point where it's affecting their ability to participate in treatment. In those situations, medication can help you move forward. Some studies suggest that a combination of medication and therapy is ideal; others find that therapy and medication on their own are each equally impactful. Still others suggest that therapy, without medication, can lead to enduring benefits. So much depends on you and what you're going through, so I always defer to whatever plan you and your treatment provider come up with. But I'll add that supercharging your coping skills can often help you reduce medication and prevent you from slipping back into unhelpful habits that negatively impact your mental health.

I put antianxiety medications, specifically benzos, in a different category. Benzos affect a neurotransmitter known as *GABA* that acts almost like brakes on a car, inhibiting neuronal activity. When a benzo binds to the GABA receptor, it amplifies its braking power, suppressing central nervous system activity, which results in a sedating effect. When someone starts taking a benzo, the brain reduces its natural output of GABA. If they then try to taper off the medication, they end up with heightened anxiety and withdrawal symptoms, because the GABA system is now out of whack. I've seen many of my clients become dependent on benzos and then have to detox, an experience that causes sweating, irritability, and nausea and is exponentially worse than their initial anxiety.

The history of benzos is just as disturbing. I learned more about this from talking with Robert Whitaker, a journalist and former director of publications at Harvard Medical School, who happened to stumble upon concerning studies of psychiatric medications and found himself in what he calls a psychiatric "minefield." Since then, he has become who I think of as the Erin Brockovich of psychiatric medications, consulting a countless number of people who have become dependent on antianxiety prescriptions, and currently he runs *Mad in America*, a webzine focused on science, psychiatry, and social justice. If, like Mr. Whitaker, you've ever wondered how this compound landed in the pillboxes of roughly thirty million adults in the US, he explained that it all started when a pharmaceutical company was developing medication to treat gram-positive bacteria. The company noticed that after the drug was administered to lab mice on the verge of being electrocuted, the rodents behaved passively. Even on a low dose, the mice remained calm as they approached a device that would administer a shock. In the 1960s, psychiatrist and pharmaceutical marketer Arthur Sackler, who you may have heard of in relation to the current opioid crisis, began advertising a version of this drug as "mother's little helper" to women who felt depleted by stultifying days at home as housewives. The problem is, no substance can cure you of an unsatisfying life—not Valium then, nor the variety of benzodiazepines available now. But, tragically, there are people who essentially become unable to function[2] due to their reliance on benzos, Mr. Whitaker warned, echoing what I've seen several of my clients endure.

Another problem: When it comes to navigating anxiety, facing your irrational fears rather than running away from them—or drugging them into submission—is essential to reclaiming your freedom. Having uncomfortable emotions and sensations is normal. Taking a sedative is about escaping those sensations and emotions, when what we actually need to learn is to accept them.

I explained all this to Cameron and asked him whether taking a pill that drained his energy could be contributing to him feeling "bored." "But what if I'm having a panic attack on a flight?" Cameron asked. I told him that Klonopin would help in the short term, but if he continued to take a pill to "calm down" in case of a nerve-racking situation like turbulence, he was setting himself up to become dependent on the pill instead of learning to navigate his anxiety. That's not an empowering mindset.

When I asked Dr. Tola T'Sarumi, an addiction psychiatrist and instructor at Harvard Medical School, if there are ever situations when benzos can help, she told me that she prescribes them in small amounts to people who have been hospitalized for an acute psychiatric problem, knowing that she'll taper them off this class of medication before they leave the hospital. But regularly using them to relax as you face routine stressors raises complications and dangers. As Dr. T'Sarumi explained, you can start taking a

---

2 If this topic interests you, the documentaries *As Prescribed* and *Take Your Pills: Xanax* chronicle people whose dependence on benzos has upended their lives.

benzodiazepine and it may work for six to eight months, but after a while, you may notice it's not working as well. "And so we increase it again. We keep increasing it. And then you begin to realize that you can't live without it." For this reason, Dr. T'Sarumi rarely prescribes this class of medication to people she is treating on an outpatient basis.

Addiction psychiatrist Arthur Robin Williams, who's also a research scientist and an assistant professor at Columbia University's division on substance-use disorders, put it this way: "Anything that quickly changes how someone feels is going to have abuse liability." And while the allure of a substance that can help you feel less anxious or lonely in minutes may be powerful, to Dr. Williams, the immediacy of symptom relief is a huge red flag for risk of dependence. "You don't want to become accustomed to using it, because that's not sustainable. Over time, that's going to lead to the quickest buildup of tolerance and the worst withdrawal."

> When it comes to navigating anxiety, facing your irrational fears rather than running away from them—or drugging them into submission—is essential to reclaiming your freedom.

Of course, many people assume they use substances—benzos or whatever tempts them—because they like them. They think of their use as *positively reinforcing*, or giving them something they desire, Dr. Williams told me. But they're actually *negatively reinforcing*, or removing something unpleasant, whether it's stress or panic or the withdrawal symptoms that occur when they try to stop taking the pills. This leads to a cycle of escaping negative feelings instead of mastering coping skills to enhance your life.

Another critical problem with these drugs is that people overlearn *using* as a coping strategy. In other words, leaning on benzos, as Cameron did, meant he wasn't trying other ways to deal with his anxiety at work or his fear of flying. That means if he were to try to discontinue his Klonopin habit, his stress response during early abstinence would be more intense while his body was recalibrating, and just as bad, it might seem as if nothing else could help.

The effort to quit is worth it. Though it may be difficult initially, my clients ultimately find that they have less anxiety and depression, because regular benzo use can increase both. Excessive benzo use can also cause aggressiveness and poor judgment and increase the risk of dementia in the long term. As Mr. Whitaker described it, prolonged use of benzos can cause an "iatrogenic brain injury," which means a medical treatment that causes a medical problem (it's one of the most memorable phrases I learned while studying psychopharmacology).

Wouldn't it be better to be able to react flexibly to life, to stay alert and engage with the world in all its variations? Once Cameron knew more about the very real risks of his daily Klonopin use, he worked on learning to sit with his feelings—and also using them as inspiration. We talked about how some anxiety actually helped him get stuff done, especially when he wasn't judging his stress. He also partnered with his physician—as many people do when trying to get off benzos—to gradually taper his use.

Cameron was less open to giving up cannabis. "It's a plant! And it's legal!" he argued. Certainly, in an era of boutique dispensaries, it can be especially difficult to see weed as anything other than a harmless recreational or medicinal substance. Studies *do* show that cannabis can be helpful for certain conditions, including chronic pain, seizures, muscle spasms related to multiple sclerosis, and loss of appetite in cancer patients. Yet when it comes to anxiety, there is no evidence that cannabis is an effective treatment. As Dr. Williams put it: "Many patients with anxiety, depression, insomnia, and post-traumatic stress disorder report short-term relief with cannabis use." But "if you look at people using benzos, alcohol, and cannabis and you follow up with them years later, they don't look better, they look worse—their anxiety and depressive symptoms are worse, and they're more likely to have progressed to opioids than people who aren't regularly using substances," he said.

And while cannabis intoxication may bring on relaxation, reduced anxiety, and even euphoria, alleviating some anxiety and stress, Dr. T'Sarumi also warned that over time, people may experience slower cognition, decreased motivation, memory loss, and, more rarely, psychosis. "I've seen people who don't want to get up, go to school, go to work," she said, describing the *amotivational syndrome* she sees in some of her cannabis-using patients. Her words made me think of a study of more than five hundred college students spearheaded by Dr. Andrew Lac, an associate professor in psychology at the University of Colorado, Colorado Springs, who found that students who consumed cannabis were less likely to take initiative and doubted their ability to reach their goals.

Another issue is that even with dispensaries and medical cannabis, it can be tough to know what you're getting—and how you'll react. "Cannabis is the Wild West," said Dr. Williams. The label may say 10 milligrams of THC, but the reality might be closer to 0—or 100. "This is especially true for edibles," he explained. Even if someone uses minimal amounts of cannabis daily, Dr. Williams is concerned that they might be regularly ingesting higher amounts of cannabinoids than they realize, given the unevenness of dosing.

In case you're reading this and shaking your head—yes, there *are* some people who can use cannabis intermittently[3] and never experience major problems, just as some people can occasionally have a drink and not run into problems. But becoming preoccupied about when you're going to use cannabis, using it earlier in the day, and turning to it with more frequency are all risk factors for developing cannabis use disorder, according to Dr. Williams. More than 30 percent of cannabis users—a number that has doubled in the last decade—meet the criteria, which include using more than you mean to, experiencing cravings, giving up activities like going out with friends to stay home and use, and needing more to get high.

If you want to take a step back from using cannabis and/or benzos and find other enduring and effective ways to manage your stress, professional treatment can help. A big misconception is that there aren't effective treatments for substance dependence, that it's all about willpower and personal choice. But getting help from a professional, especially early on, is the best way to cut down or stop using. "Waiting until you hit rock bottom is just for movies," added Dr. Williams, who suggested meeting with a medical doctor who specializes in addiction to help with a slow taper off substances. Your physician may also determine if medications are necessary to mitigate symptoms of withdrawal. Psychotherapy that is focused on behavioral strategies to improve coping is also key, as is building a support network.

I won't sugarcoat this: Cameron had a rough time giving up both benzos and cannabis. But he did it, quitting one substance at a time over a matter of four months, starting with Klonopin. In addition to working with me,

3 Keep in mind that it can be tricky for many people to infrequently use something they really like! Most of my clients realize that if they like weed too much, it's easier to *not* smoke than to give in a few days a week, because they then feel deprived on their "off" days.

Cameron met with a psychiatrist and joined Marijuana Anonymous. Along the way, he experienced a lot of uncomfortable symptoms, including anxiety, nausea, irritability, and insomnia. But as he progressed through weeks and months of tapering, he felt a sense of pride and even hope, and he was excited to realize that his memory was a lot better than he thought. About six weeks after he stopped using Klonopin and cannabis, he told me, "I feel like my brain is sharper and I've realized that some of the anxiety gets me going." I couldn't have said it better myself.

* * *

Once we removed the benzo Band-Aid and the cloud of cannabis, Cameron and I were able to work on improving what brought him to me in the first place: his poor time management, which was affecting his personal life and contributing to his stress at work and pervasive feelings of dissatisfaction. Given his struggles with attention and focus, we mapped out his day, creating blocks of time for work with planned breaks, which helped him feel less overwhelmed. We also introduced rewards, like taking an iced coffee break with a coworker after he started the hardest task of the day, which reinforced his desire to be productive. Beyond that, we set aside time after work for him to look for other professional opportunities that would feel more engaging.

Cameron came to see that levity wasn't all-or-nothing or something that he had to reach for beyond himself, but a mindset. He learned it was possible to find more ongoing joy by "navigating the world on the precipice of a smile," as Stanford University professor Jennifer Aaker and lecturer Naomi Bagdonas, coauthors of *Humor, Seriously: Why Humor Is a Secret Weapon in Business and Life (And How Anyone Can Harness It. Even You.)* and a popular TED talk on the topic, have advised. Cameron found that small changes, like smiling while buying an apple from a bodega and dancing a little when a good song played, started to steadily shift his overall mood throughout the day. I hope you're starting to consider some ways to seek and spread more joie de vivre, too.

As for his fear of flying, Cameron and I determined that facing it in a systematic way would be the best route: He learned more about the mechanics of turbulence, researched logistics on how safe flying is, and started with shorter flights. Eventually, Cameron worked up to longer trips. "Did you ever think I'd get to Hawai'i without being asleep for most of the flight? And I caught up on the movies I wanted to see!" he said. Benzos would have never helped him realize he could sit with his physical sensations and even semi-enjoy the ride.

Cameron also worked on changing some of his less helpful patterns of thinking. "You know TikTok, but do you know TIC-TOC?" I asked one day, when he mentioned how hard it was for him to deal with a particularly "annoying" project. TIC stands for task-interfering cognition (or thought), like *It's too much—I can't* or *I already wasted so much time.* We discussed how he could notice these thoughts and swap them out for task-orienting cognitions (TOCs), like *I got this—I can start now.* This mental shift, introduced by psychiatrist David Burns as a technique to short-circuit procrastination, helped Cameron improve his punctuality and get to the gym more regularly. (Getting off TikTok and sticking to a set bedtime helped him, too.) He noticed TICs like *I'll head out after I do one more thing* and *I'm too tired* and swapped them for TOCs such as *Sticking to my plan is the most freeing option* and *I know I'll feel better later.* Ultimately, Cameron noticed that regular exercise expanded his view of himself and improved his ability to focus, which is consistent with research that shows exercise improves neural functioning in people with ADHD. Boosting his sense of competence improved his mood and motivation, because most of us struggle to feel motivated when we fundamentally believe we can't make headway toward our goals.

Can you think of some TICs, including ones related to substance use, that hold you back and some TOCs that move you forward? Rather than coming up with a lengthy list, focus on improving one recurring thought at a time. Once that sticks, you can continue to remedy others. While we all have countless thoughts and improving them may seem tedious, the combination of shifting our mindset, knowing how to regulate our emotions, removing obstacles within us, and continuously thinking in healthier ways alters our inner architecture.

5

Focusing on Something Bigger

GARY, A RETIRED CONSULTANT IN his late sixties, told me that his granddaughter had nicknamed him "Grumpy Gramps." "It's probably appropriate," he said wryly. Years ago, a car accident left him in chronic pain,[1] putting an end to his retirement dreams of travel and golf after decades spent climbing the corporate ladder. Worse, he was now experiencing intense health anxiety, agonizing over irritating but harmless symptoms like tinnitus, a ringing sound in his ears. He checked his blood pressure more than his doctor recommended and frequently met with his cardiologist to request tests, "just to be sure I'm all right—heart disease runs in my family," he explained. He wished he could escape the pain in his body and the ongoing sense that his health was precarious. "I feel like I'm constantly on the lookout for suspicious symptoms," he said.

When I asked more about his background, Gary told me he'd grown up believing that the point of life was to make money, amass stuff, and have fun, relishing what life had to offer. "Carpe diem and capitalism were my family's religion," he explained. In raising his own family, Gary told me that he hadn't given much thought to what mattered to him beyond working to afford a nice life for his wife and daughters. "Moments when we could come together, watch the sunset, and eat s'mores by a campfire made me think I was a good dad and husband. You could even say I was content," he said.

---

1 If chronic pain isn't relatable to you, feel free to use pain as a metaphor for anything in your life that's difficult and that you can't immediately escape.

But now that he and his wife had been empty nesters for nearly a decade, his chronic physical pain and his preoccupation with it had created a wedge in his once-happy marriage. "I'm distracted by my body, so I don't have much to talk about beyond that. I know my wife is sick of my health complaints and negative attitude, and I don't blame her."

Gary no longer felt like an ideal dad and husband—the combination of no longer working and perceiving himself as a chronic patient rather than a provider and partner rocked his foundation. It also contributed to his stress, as does anything that makes you question your abilities. But despite his narrative of being on the verge of a health crisis, I could sense his vitality when he wasn't listing his aches and anxieties. Something about Gary's facial expressions and storytelling made me suspect that underneath his struggles, he had a great sense of humor and there was more to him than being "Grumpy Gramps." We just needed to guide him toward noticing what mattered to him rather than stressing about issues that were beyond his control.

* * *

Stress and daily hassles often narrow our attention to the point where all we can prioritize are immediate challenges. In contrast, truly thriving requires thinking more broadly and making time for the things that give us meaning and purpose. Gary was so focused on his physical concerns that he rarely considered his hopes and dreams, so I asked him to imagine that he'd woken up one morning to find that a miracle had happened and all his reasons for coming to see me—all his complaints—had disappeared. I then asked him to think of how he would answer the following questions, which I invite you to consider as well:

▶ *How would you know the miracle had happened?*

▶ *What would others around you notice?*

▶ *What would you do? How would you think differently?*

▶ *What would you see if you compared your before and after pictures?*

The "miracle question" is a solution-focused approach developed by social workers Steve de Shazer and Insoo Kim Berg and their team at the Milwaukee Brief Family Therapy Center. After spending thousands of hours observing therapy sessions, the two narrowed in on this specific technique because it proved most likely to nudge a client toward positive change. A key assumption of asking about miracles is that focusing on solutions is easier and more empowering than getting mired in complex problems.

After a few minutes of "I don't know"s and protests—"I'm a very rational person!"—Gary reluctantly responded that he'd obviously stop with the doctors' appointments; not be preoccupied with pain; exude more gratitude; bring more attentiveness to his relationships, especially with his wife; and find better ways to spend his time. I nodded appreciatively, then asked, "How close are you to your 'miracle' day? Are there any steps you could take right now that would inch you closer to that day?" He admitted he was pretty far from living that kind of day. "I know you're trying to get me to spit out some goals," he said, "but don't we need to wait until I'm feeling capable of managing to talk about ideals?"

As I explained to Gary, simply imagining what you want your life to look like can be surprisingly freeing. And though it may feel counterintuitive and even fruitless to focus on hopes in the face of significant concerns, so many of us can benefit from reflecting on the miracle question; think of it as a strategy for improving coping during times of stress. In a study led by Jenna Sung, a doctoral student in clinical psychology at Stony Brook University, clients facing waiting lists for therapy at an outpatient clinic were offered a single session with a counselor who focused on the miracle question. The combination of considering a miracle day, generating three concrete steps to work toward achieving that day, anticipating potential obstacles alongside related solutions, and the counselor writing the client an encouraging note expressing confidence in their ability to move forward[2] significantly improved participants' symptoms of hopelessness and anxiety. What comes to mind when you reflect on your miracle day? What sorts of obstacles are holding you back, and how can you start making headway toward it?

---

2 I love the idea of someone you respect giving you a handwritten note conveying "You got this!" You can also brainstorm other ways to get this dose of cheerleading, perhaps by pairing up with a friend, discussing your hopes, and sending each other texts of encouragement. Or, if that feels hard to do, experiment with acting like you wholeheartedly believe in your ability to persist with your goals.

I followed up the miracle question by asking Gary to tell me both how he wanted to spend his time and what virtues he wanted to embody, even when he hit inevitable obstacles. I pushed this line of questioning because beyond being able to picture what you'd want your miracle day to look like, it's also essential to reflect on your values, because these can further guide you to the life you want. One of the biggest sources of pain is living a life that doesn't feel meaningful. I reminded Gary that despite his physical issues, it was still possible for him to live according to his values. Truthfully, I had no idea if we could dramatically mitigate Gary's physical pain. I *was* confident that we could expand his focus beyond his body and remedy other facets of his life, like his relationships, so that one or two difficulties weren't sapping his entire quality of life.

Gary agreed that he wanted to live a life that felt more aspirational, but he was filled with doubt that he could do that with his nagging pain and health worries. Still, he agreed to give it a try. To start, we focused on distinguishing between his *goals* and his *values*. While goals are what you hope to attain, like pain relief or work success, values are more about how you behave in your life. You can't just cross values off your to-do list; rather, the intention is to create a life that reflects what you most care about. I find one study by doctoral candidate Eric Tifft at the State University of New York at Albany very telling: He showed that the reason behind why people began a meditation routine affected how much they got out of it. When they did it simply to lower stress, as opposed to wanting to be more mindful and accepting, they didn't report as many benefits.

Despite his struggles, Gary had strong values that he hadn't always given himself credit for. He had been a good dad and he still was, continuing to coach his daughters through some difficult decisions. Yet he was barely able to acknowledge those moments. "That's just what you're supposed to do," he said stoically. "Plus it's helping your kid, so it's pretty self-serving." How might you be missing chances to celebrate your wins?

Another question I raised in a later visit: "How do you hope to be toasted on your seventieth birthday?" Gary realized that he didn't want to listen to tales about him being Grumpy Gramps. He also didn't want people in his inner circle to have to be "fake nice," as he called it. His hope, we discovered after several discussions, was to be called a thoughtful partner, parent, and grandparent. I was elated that Gary was open to refocusing on his values, whether or not he found pain relief. The challenge would be to help him accept his discomforts yet continue to persevere in being who he wanted to be.

The same holds true for whatever stressors you're facing, whether they're financial pressures, difficult family members, the desire for a satisfying relationship, or chronic pain. While we don't always have control over those things, it's possible to expand the scope of your focus to bring attention to your values. A couple of months ago, I attended the funeral of my friend Alison, who died from cancer at the age of thirty-eight. In one of the many poignant eulogies, a friend recounted an early memory of her: When they were in high school and he and other senior boys were teasing classmates and younger students, Alison, who was younger than him, approached them and announced that what they were doing wasn't cool. Rather than getting lost in the stress of social worries and others' perceptions, she was committed to her value of kindness, which helped her exude confidence. I couldn't help but think of how often I shied away from taking risks in order to seem easygoing and avoid conflict. At any moment, we can choose to embody our values in a way that will inspire others and define our life.

That's why taking a few minutes a day (or every week) to look beyond your to-do lists and problems and reflect more broadly on the things that give you a sense of purpose can help lift you out of the stress trap. By diversifying what I think of as your "life pie," which is essentially what you want your life to consist of, you're more likely to shrink the less optimal parts of your day. (If you want to try this, see page 76 to get started.)

Considering your life purpose and revisiting it every so often takes time, but it can improve your health and resilience. Studies spearheaded by Dr. Jina Park, a psychologist at Florida State University, highlight that having a sense of meaning helps us bounce back in the face of stress. And a study led by Dr. Stacey Schaefer, a scientist at the University of Wisconsin, Madison, in which students looked at disturbing photos (such as a baby crying in pain) showed that those who felt they had a purpose in life recovered sooner from the upsetting images than participants without a clear sense of what mattered to them.

I'm endlessly fascinated by how people cope with the stress that comes from life's greatest hardships. So I was eager to hear how Dr. Hawthorne Smith, a clinical psychologist who directs Bellevue Hospital's Program for Survivors of Torture in New York City, assists his clients. Beyond experiencing significant traumas, so many of the individuals from across the world who participate in his therapy group are stuck in an affirmative asylum backlog and have been separated from their families for years. Dr. Smith told me that when survivors see their sacrifices through the lens of contributing to society, it sparks feelings of hope. "Knowing that they are doing this, that they are surviving for the benefit of their family and future generations, makes a huge difference," he said. Dr. Smith also shared that many of the survivors he works with often look at the skills he teaches, such as deep breathing and muscle relaxation, as ways to take back their power and endure trying moments. When I asked about his own stress management, Dr. Smith told me that in addition to playing the saxophone, finding meaning is imperative to him. As a descendant of slaves, he said, viewing his work as a way to try to pay forward the sacrifices that his own ancestors endured moves him, even in the face of witnessing so much pain.

Taking the time to get clear on your values can help you maintain a healthy sense of self, warding off that horrible feeling of personal disappointment and instilling faith in your potential. In a study looking at African American and Latino adolescents from financially marginalized homes, Dr. J. Parker Goyer and her colleagues at Stanford University discovered that those who completed a series of fifteen-minute writing exercises focused on values and why they matter saw improved academic performance and that this was even correlated with success a decade later. Dr. Geoffrey Cohen, a collaborator on the study and professor at Stanford University who has studied brief interventions for decades, explained, "Affirming our most important values fortifies us, which can help protect us from stress." In other words, seeing your values clearly can improve your persistence. That persistence pays off, and a positive cycle ensues.

In our weeks together, Gary and I worked on how to keep track of his commitment to his values. As a therapist, I find that tracking progress is key to maintaining positive changes. Luckily, there are many resources to help people track and persist in their values. One of my favorite exercises, the bull's-eye values clarification exercise, was created by psychologist Tobias Lundgren, an expert in ACT. It's an approach that focuses on values, even when difficult thoughts and feelings arise. I asked Gary to draw a picture of a target and divide it into four sections of importance: health, relationships, work, and leisure. We then talked about what values he wanted to uphold

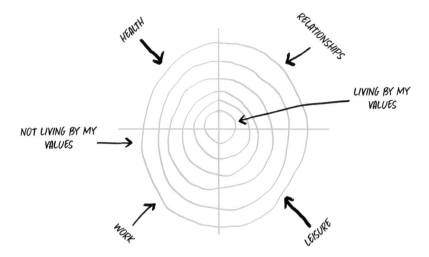

within each segment, where he was relative to his goal, and his ideas for how to move forward. Amazingly, he realized that when it came to health, he wanted to move from seeking reassurance to being able to accept uncertainty and discomfort. In the work area, Gary decided that besides focusing on bills, he wanted to do more volunteering and learning. When it came to relationships, he wanted to be more attentive. For leisure, instead of bemoaning what he couldn't do, he wanted to be more adventurous, starting with researching cities to explore that weren't too far away.

To maintain his momentum, we worked on another exercise known as the matrix, a technique developed by Dr. Kevin Polk where you take a piece of paper and draw two opposite-facing arrows (← →) representing "away" and "toward." Gary listed what he wanted to stay away from (e.g., ruminating on his health complaints, making unnecessary doctors' appointments, scowling) and what he wanted to move toward (e.g., speaking to his wife for five minutes a day about her hopes, helping his granddaughter with homework). Once he'd made a list detailing his dos and don'ts, it was harder to rationalize detours in the heat of the moment, as so many of us do. He also joked that he'd concocted a game in his head, envisioning that he lost points whenever he made a move on his "away" list and was rewarded with "cha-ching!" whenever he made a move on his "toward" list.[3]

---

3 We've now covered lots of exercises. I hope you choose a few to keep you heading where you want to go. I have faith in you!

These examples are just a few of the many ways to be more intentional about what you want your life to stand for, including how you want to show up for yourself and others. One person who inspires me in this way is Dr. BJ Miller, a physician specializing in palliative care and hospice who is also a triple amputee. He lost his limbs in a devastating accident as an undergraduate at Princeton University yet went on to graduate from medical school, despite grieving the loss of his sister to suicide in the middle of his training. I was eager to hear about how he managed to live by his values and help others do the same. Amazingly, his TED talk, "What Really Matters at the End of Life," has more than fifteen million views and counting.

He told me that after his accident, he felt like his slate was wiped clean. That was tragic in some ways, but it also allowed him to shrug off conventional expectations, to slow down and attend to the person he truly hoped to be. Arriving at his purpose didn't happen by thinking analytically or creating some sort of master plan, he explained. Rather, he got into the habit of constantly checking in with himself to consider whether his actions felt wise and staying open to whatever happened along the way. He recalled one night when he was in the hospital burn unit after the accident and a nurse smuggled in a snowball for him to hold. Feeling the cool snow in his burnt hand shifted his thinking and focus to the thoughtfulness of others. As the days and weeks and months passed, he found that fully savoring small wonders like these helped him continue to move forward, despite his physical pain and loss. Eventually he was able to consider ways to offer comfort and hope to others in dire circumstances, which ultimately drew him to the field of palliative care. In counseling the dying, he noticed that one regret came up again and again: people not truly being themselves or not loving more wildly and deeply. With that in mind, he has made sure to adopt a sense of awe and play in his own life, along with an ongoing practice of self-reflection and self-compassion.

You don't need to suffer a major loss or injury to do the same. Simply giving yourself kindness and allowing yourself to face difficult emotions—as opposed to seeking approval from others—can help you get clear on what actually matters to you. Said Dr. Miller, "I tell myself, 'You're still here. Now what do you want to do?'"

Living with a larger sense of purpose requires *self-regulating*, or managing your behavior in ways that help you in the long term. For Gary, that meant having weekly check-ins with his values charts and maintaining an ongoing awareness of what mattered to him so he felt as though he was working toward something and that he could count on himself, which was refreshing. Even if that seems like work, it's worthwhile, because self-regulating improves your well-being: A study by Dr. Michael Daly, an associate professor in psychology at Maynooth University in Ireland, found that people with high self-control were better able to manage their stress levels and had a lower heart rate and levels of cortisol.

Gary consciously changed his actions to better align with his values, instituting a ritual of sharing a morning coffee with his wife, where he was positive and attentive. He also had a weekly FaceTime with each of his five grandkids and sent his daughters an encouraging text message or meme each week. He began volunteering with seniors, helping them resolve technology issues. At meals, he was deliberate in practicing gratitude for the overwhelming number of bodily functions he had that were perfectly intact. His pain didn't go away, of course, and sometimes it distracted him. But he practiced acceptance by noticing the pain without rushing to complain, lie down, or search for answers. He also told himself that any heart symptoms he felt were most likely due to anxiety, not an emergency, given all his perfectly normal medical tests. In our meetings, we reflected on how his values-based behaviors started positive cycles. "Having to get up to make coffee and turn my attention outward makes me feel like a healthy person and good husband. I hadn't realized that my self-absorbed habits in recent years were weighing me down with guilt," Gary said. He discovered that it was inherently rewarding to focus on what he wanted (a more meaningful life and relationships) rather than what he was running from (pain).

In a world that can feel so precarious, embracing a values-driven life can also give you a dose of certainty.

I also encouraged Gary to consider his values around friendship. Studies show that repeatedly choosing to be a good friend has a beneficial effect on how we feel. Psychologist Sheldon Cohen, a professor at Carnegie Mellon and admired stress expert who developed the Perceived Stress Scale you read about in Chapter 1, discovered that the larger your circle of friends, the less susceptible you are to catching the common cold. Social support is also a huge buffer to stress and improves our resilience along with our immunity.

Gary was skeptical. "I'm too old to make new friends," he told me. But he agreed to reach out to some old acquaintances on Facebook and was surprised by how quickly so many of them responded, leading to an exchange of memories, photos, and podcast suggestions. "I felt like I was the only one going through stuff and no one else had time, but it seems like we've all been going through it. Most people seem oddly enthusiastic and happy to reconnect," he said.

In a world that can feel so precarious, embracing a values-driven life can also give you a dose of certainty. As Gary learned, there is a calmness that comes from knowing you can count on your inner compass, even when so much else—both within us and around us—seems imperfect. I hope you'll keep that in mind as you turn to the stress resets and buffers ahead.

PART TWO

Stress Resets for Intense Times

IN THE PAGES AHEAD, YOU'LL find evidence-based techniques for coping with life's stressful moments. Each one is intended to meet you where you are and move you toward a healthier state of mind. Again, think of this as your personal recipe book, except the ingredients are designed to satisfy your hunger for emotional well-being. I've given you lots of options on purpose. When you're feeling closed in, it can be nice to know there are various ways to improve how you feel that don't take long to do. Keep in mind that the goal here isn't to force stress or symptoms that you don't like to go away. Rather, the aim is to practice more self-compassion and flexibility in challenging situations.

If you don't know where to start, turn to any page and experiment with whatever reset you land on to improve your present focus and peace of mind. Ironically, the most effective ways of coping with stress may feel like they take a lot of effort. And at first, none of these tools may feel as immediately satisfying as your go-to ways of comforting yourself. I get that. It's all too easy to cling to unhealthy habits even though they contribute to our stress. But soon you'll begin to figure out which resets are most useful to you based on what you're experiencing, because different techniques work better (and are more appealing) for different people. As you work through them, think about pausing your less helpful ways of coping and opening yourself up to the fact that one good change often leads to another. These resets will also boost your feelings of self-efficacy, which will make it easier to stick with more empowering habits and replace negative spirals with a positive chain reaction. Realizing that you have the ability to take good care of yourself—and live better—will also make you more open to the effort required to initiate these changes.

I mention the possible difficulties that may arise because having this knowledge will help you loosen the grip of resistance that can take hold when we're trying to shake free of instincts that aren't serving us. If you're anything like me or my clients, there's something about facing intense stress and heightened painful emotions that can elicit a *hell no!* reaction, also known as *willfulness*, which tends to keep us stuck. *Willingness* is the opposite—the equivalent of saying *hell yes!* to life.

When you're struggling, it can also feel tempting to write off suggestions as too simplistic or tell yourself you just don't have the energy. When that kind of hesitation creeps up, remind yourself that the strategies in the pages ahead will take only a few minutes and are proven by research to be effective. Try to let go of any expectations or preconceived notions about what will work or how quickly you *should* feel better. These can get in the way of your success, like when someone invites you to try a new hobby and you preemptively say it's "not your thing," missing an opportunity for fun and growth. Feel free to track what you've tried using a format like this (simply labeling your thoughts and emotions can improve your coping!):

SITUATION	THOUGHTS/ FEELINGS/ URGES	EMOTION(S) AND INTENSITY	WHAT I TRIED	SHORT-TERM IMPACTS	LONG-TERM BENEFITS

I've divided the tips ahead into those that affect your *thoughts*, those that impact *physical sensations*, and those that change your *behaviors*. The purpose of these categories is to make it easier for you to home in on the strategies that feel right for you in any given situation, though the benefits do overlap: Techniques designed to improve your thinking can also help calm stress-related physical sensations. In Mind Resets (page 60), you'll untangle yourself from thoughts that make whatever you're dealing with exponentially worse. In Body Resets (page 86), you'll shift from worrying about your physical response to stress to trusting your body and all its capabilities. Finally, in Behavior Resets (page 103), you'll focus on actions to manage and move toward your goals.

RESET CYCLE

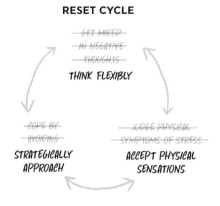

Begin by flagging a few to keep top of mind over the course of this week or month, then add more if you need to, repeating them until they become habits. Some of these suggestions may be hard to remember in trying moments, similar to how it's hard to find something right under your nose when your space feels messy. As I often tell clients, these skills can be akin to putting some air in your tires or doing some mental decluttering. The point of each reset is to help you recharge. Once you gain a bit of nourishment, you can move forward with clearer thinking and the ability to problem solve whatever was stressing you out in the first place. Peace of mind isn't life feeling easy; it's knowing you can manage, regardless of what comes up.

No. 1 Dig your heels in and anchor yourself.

WHEN: Your thinking is all over the place and spinning you into a crisis.

HOW: Take a moment to come back to what is happening *right now* with a simple anchoring technique. Start by experiencing the sensations of digging your heels into the floor, which will help you feel more grounded. Then ask yourself:

> ▶ *What am I thinking?*

> ▶ *What am I feeling in my body?*

> ▶ *What am I doing right now?*

Next, consider:

> ▶ *Are my responses helpful?*

> ▶ *Are they aligned with my long-term goals?*

> ▶ *Are they related to future worries or past pains?*

You can write the six prompts above (or just the abbreviation "TFD," for "thinking," "feeling," and "doing," as well as the question "helping?") on a Post-it and stick it to your computer to remind yourself to check in and center yourself whenever your mind drifts toward stressful negativity.

WHY: Stopping to take inventory of your mind, body, and behaviors at any given moment creates space for you to choose helpful next steps, especially if your thoughts are going around and around. At any time, you can bring your mind to where your feet are and anchor yourself to the present moment, which can also help you savor positive experiences.

No. **2** Acknowledge your state of mind.

WHEN: Your frame of mind doesn't match the task or situation at hand. When we need to access our reason to solve a problem, too often our emotions prevent us from seeing things clearly, like when you're feeling hopeless and tell yourself that there's no point in trying. There are times to let yourself be led by your emotions, of course, such as when you're watching an evocative movie or celebrating with a friend. But there are also situations that call for reason (like budgeting) as well as decisions that call for integrating your head and your heart (like choosing a career or a partner).

HOW: To figure out your state of mind, start by asking yourself three questions:

▶ *Are my emotions currently controlling my thoughts and behaviors?* If so, you are in "emotion mind."

▶ *Am I currently grounded in facts and logic?* If so, you are in "reasonable mind."

▶ *Am I synthesizing my emotions, logic, and intuition?* If so, you are in "wise mind."

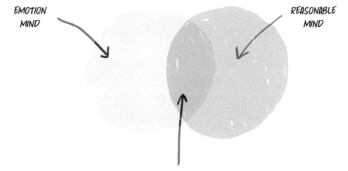

EMOTION
MIND

REASONABLE
MIND

WISE MIND

Next, consider if your state of mind is optimal for what you're facing. If you're sleep-deprived, overworked, or lonely, it's especially easy to land in emotion mind. But taking a moment to recognize that you're in emotion mind can help you recenter before slipping into habits that won't help. If you tend to be overly rational in ways that affect your well-being—say, continuously engaging with a relative who is critical of you because *they're family* and you think you *should*—you can step back, notice that you're in reasonable mind, and nurture yourself a bit, tending to your emotional needs.

WHY: Noticing what state of mind you're in and whether it's helping the situation can offer you a quick dose of clarity. By recognizing when you're in emotion mind, you can interrupt *emotional reasoning*, which is the tendency to assume that because you feel something, it must be true. During these times, thoughts like *I can't get anything right!* or *No one cares about me* may feel valid, even though they are just consequences of feeling sad or lonely rather than accurate portrayals of your life. Acknowledging that you're in a state that's not ideal for whatever you're doing can help you see that you *can* manage and that the stress you're experiencing will not persist.

No. 3 Find your "wise mind."

WHEN: You're struggling with a decision, doubting yourself, or feeling tempted to ask others for unnecessary reassurance.

HOW: Giving yourself the opportunity to access your wise mind helps you find insight within *you*, integrating your knowledge, your emotions, and your intuition. Try each of the following exercises for a minute and see which is most helpful. Consider practicing your go-to exercise whenever you need it.

▶ *Breathe in and out, thinking* wise *as you inhale and* mind *as you exhale.*

▶ *Try focusing on your breath as you naturally breathe in and out. Let your attention settle into your center, keeping your focus on your gut as you continue to breathe in and out.*

▶ *Drop into the pause that naturally happens between inhaling and exhaling. Breathe in, then, at the top of your breath, notice the brief pause before you exhale. After you exhale, notice the space before you inhale.*

▶ *In situations where you're about to do something you're not sure you should do (e.g., you're about to cancel a commitment), ask yourself,* Is this wise mind?

▶ *If you're a visual person, you can find your wise mind by imagining a small stone slowly sinking into a beautiful, clear lake, almost as if you're descending into the depths of wisdom within you.*

WHY: Harnessing your inner wisdom can keep you focused on and hopeful about attaining your ultimate goals. We often have the answers we seek; we just need to tune in to hear them. In my therapy practice, my clients notice that, with repeated effort, they're able to boost their ability to access and trust their wise mind. That's why, when clients ask me what I think, I defer to their wise mind. Tapping into what we know, how we feel, and our natural intuition allows us to discern our own incredible insight and increase our trust in ourselves.

No.

4 Sing your thoughts.

WHEN: You're having trouble shifting away from thinking that exhausts and demotivates you.

HOW: Try singing your thoughts in a playful way, which will change your relationship to them and help you take them less seriously. Here are a few ways to practice:

▷ *Pick an upbeat tune and sing whatever negative thought is repeating in your head. You might sing "I'm an awkward imposter" to the tune of The Lovin' Spoonful's "Do You Believe in Magic" or "I'm not enough" to the tune of Rihanna's "We Found Love" (my personal favorite tunes to shift away from sticky, negative thoughts).*

▷ *Try singing a song that refers to* all *thoughts, such as "What are thoughts? Thoughts can't hurt me, can't hurt me, no more" to the tune of Haddaway's "What Is Love."*

▷ *Check out the Songify app, which allows you to plug in your thoughts to create a silly jingle.*

WHY: Roughly 80 to 99 percent of people admit to having repetitive unhelpful and negative thoughts, whether about their appearance, work, or ability to cope. Practicing *cognitive defusion*, which means taking thoughts less literally and seriously, reduces the frequency and believability of those thoughts, transforming them into your own inside jokes.

No.**5** Radically accept.

WHEN: You're fighting against something, whether uncertainty or frustrations, large or small.

HOW: *Radical acceptance* means recognizing your emotional or physical distress and wholeheartedly allowing this moment, exactly as it is, right now. Here's why it's important: Pain on its own is difficult, but pain and nonacceptance together lead to suffering. While radical acceptance takes practice, it starts with being more open.

"Accepting is hard enough—what's with the pressure to make it *radical?*" many people ask me. This is a valid question. Acceptance has to be wholehearted, because half accepting, like making a kind gesture while having resentful thoughts, just doesn't help as much as going all in. Here's how you can practice:

1. Rate your level of acceptance of whatever you're facing on a scale of 0 to 10, with 10 being entirely accepting.

2. Scan your mind for judgmental thoughts, like *Why me?* or *I can't take this!* Try thinking more factually by describing what is actually happening.

3. Notice what's happening in your body and release tension in your forehead, lips, teeth, shoulders, and hands.

4. Allow yourself to experience your emotions and sensations by seeing and normalizing what you are currently feeling in the moment. The alternative—suppressing or amplifying your emotions by imagining they'll last forever or thinking they're weird (e.g., *I'll never feel better!* or *Why do I react like this?*)—will make whatever you're experiencing much heavier.

5. Ask yourself what you would do if you were to accept what is, whether that's getting started on a difficult task or not overanalyzing the actions of a person you find challenging. Then practice doing just that.

6. After practicing the previous steps, re-rank your level of acceptance on a scale of 0 to 10.

If you revert to struggling, work on returning to openness. As I tell my clients: Acceptance is more like a revolving door than boarding a plane— you can always come back.

WHY: When I ask my clients what they've found most helpful in therapy, they inevitably mention radical acceptance, even if they roll their eyes when I first introduce the concept. They're not alone—therapies that promote radical acceptance are proven to reduce stress, substance use, anxiety, and chronic pain and improve relationships and well-being. If you're skeptical, bring a stressful situation to mind and tense your face and body while judging whatever you're dealing with as *unfair*. You'll quickly notice that nonacceptance can lead to more suffering. (I find doing this gives me a tension headache.) Then sit with the same stressor while relaxing tension in your body. It's a little easier, right?

Whatever you're dealing with, learning to accept *this* moment and the emotions that come with it can help you manage and thrive. "Life regularly and inevitably involves emotional stress, anger, fears around health, shame around failed relationships," psychologist and mindfulness expert Tara Brach, author of *Radical Acceptance*, told me. "But anything short of fully accepting our human experience will keep us caught in those emotions."

If becoming more accepting seems like a complete makeover of your personality, research suggests that exercises like the steps listed in this reset can improve your peace of mind, conserving your energy so you can move forward. The thing to remember is that accepting something doesn't mean staying complacent; acceptance actually facilitates change.

No. 6 Name that emotion.

WHEN: You're feeling a negative emotion.

HOW: Start by reviewing this emotion wheel:

Next, slow down, then notice and name what you're feeling. You can say the emotion(s) out loud or list it on a mood-tracking app or in a journal, but it's important to be precise about what emotion you're feeling instead of merely labeling it as "bad."

Finally, label the intensity of your emotion on a scale of 0 to 10, with 10 being most intense. Try to get into the habit of doing this regularly instead of waiting until your emotions feel overwhelming and unpleasant. It's also helpful to notice positive emotions so you increase your awareness of what brings you joy.

WHY: It's easy (and common) to feel engulfed by emotions rather than to observe them at a distance with openness. But by taking a moment to label your specific emotions, you reduce their grip on your brain and body. *Affect labeling*, as it's called, disrupts activity in the limbic system—the emotional part of your brain—and activates the right ventrolateral prefrontal cortex—the rational part of your brain—which reduces the intensity of your feelings. Studies have shown that when people viewed upsetting images and labeled their emotions, they experienced significantly less distress. Another study found that naming feelings of anger actually decreased heart rate and cardiac output. And the benefits last: A study found that people diagnosed with arachnophobia (fear of spiders) who labeled their emotions as they approached a caged tarantula experienced fewer negative emotions when they saw the spider the following week compared with people who either tried to distract themselves or rationalize their fears away (e.g., "Looking at a spider isn't dangerous").

No. **7** Self-validate.

WHEN: You feel stressed about feeling stressed or you feel dismissed and crave support. You can also try this if you tend to make self-deprecating remarks, minimize your wins, or jump from accomplishing something to worrying about whatever's next.

HOW: Self-validation can help you find more moments of comfort, even if the people around you aren't making you feel understood. To practice, start by paying attention to your thoughts, feelings, and actions as well as the situation you're in. Then acknowledge what's legitimate about what you're experiencing, e.g., *It's hard to work for someone so demanding given how conscientious I am; my stress makes sense*, which is different from *I can't get anything right and I'm not normal.* Another example: *I worked really hard* versus *I'm just lucky.* Going forward, when you notice yourself slipping into self-invalidation or nitpicking your understandable feelings, transition into self-validation.

WHY: While it's easy to notice when others are dismissing you and your experiences, you may be overlooking the ways *you* reflexively discount what you're going through. Simply taking a moment and giving yourself a dose of understanding (*This wasn't what I expected; of course I'd feel this way, given . . .*) can ease the sting of whatever you're facing. An example: One of my clients told me he was worried about feeling more depressed. But in the last six months, he'd experienced a breakup, lost a friend to suicide, changed jobs, and moved apartments. Of course he was struggling with his mood—he valued relationships, and so much of his life felt unsettled. Once he realized that his feelings were understandable and gave himself permission to feel them, he went from feeling depressed and stressed to appreciating his humanity and opening himself up to more self-compassion.

If you're not sure how to develop a comforting inner voice, think about what a close friend, an exceptional therapist, or even Mr. Rogers might whisper in your ear if they were with you. Some people worry that self-validation will lead to going too easy on yourself, but that's not the reality—self-validation will improve your self-compassion so it's easier to thrive. When it comes to positive experiences, acknowledging and savoring  your accomplishments will prove more motivating than imagining that the pendulum is going to swing the other way and your peak will soon plummet.

No. **8** # Lay out the pros and cons.

WHEN: You're experiencing an internal tug-of-war, obsessing about a decision, or fighting an urge to do something.

HOW: Instead of exhausting yourself or indulging in something that won't help, lay out your options to make an empowering choice. On a piece of paper, draw four quadrants, labeled "Pros," "Cons," "Urge," and "Alternative," like the one on the opposite page. Then map out the urge or decision that you're struggling with, factoring in how you'll feel in the short and long term (e.g., *I'll feel regretful tomorrow if I give in to the urge today*). You can mark the long-term pros and cons with an asterisk.

The more explicit you can be when specifying your options—for example, giving in to the urge to procrastinate and the pros and cons of that decision versus sitting with your stress and starting and the pros and cons of that choice—the better equipped you'll be when you're tempted to do what's immediately gratifying. Save your list as a reminder for future instances.

To help you get started, here is an example.

	PROS	**CONS**
URGE *Send an aggressive text*	▸ *Feel like I have a say* ▸ *Make someone feel the way I do* ▸ *Don't have to sit with my feelings*	▸ *Go from being clearly right to contributing to the problem* ▸ *Feel angrier when I send hostile texts* ▸ *Never get the response I want* ▸ *Leaves me believing I'm too much**
ALTERNATIVE *Notice I'm angry and listen to a few minutes of a podcast I love*	▸ *Find myself distracted in a good way* ▸ *Know I can have a better conversation and outcome if I approach this when emotions aren't as high** ▸ *Easier to move forward with my day** ▸ *Feel like I can manage my emotions/life**	▸ *Feels unnatural (initially)* ▸ *Have to continuously pivot from the urge to snap* ▸ *Don't enjoy the podcast as much as I normally do*

* = long-term

WHY: Listing pros and cons helps prevent you from falling into risky or stress-fueled habits by making it easier to access your better judgment. When we're stressed, we tend to forget to look at all our options in a balanced way. Plus, stress can skew our perception, making it tough to resist the lure of quick fixes. I can't tell you how often clients who struggle with compulsions have told me, "I never realized that the pros of the behavior I want to change last for maybe five minutes and the cons, like the guilt and shame, last for days." Stress is less stressful if we don't engage in behaviors that ultimately punish us.

No. 9 Bring on the love (especially if just reading this title feels cringey).

WHEN: You make a mistake; notice you're feeling burned out or socially anxious; are approaching a challenging situation or temptation; or find yourself defaulting to some version of *I'm such an idiot!* You can also use it any time you find yourself ruminating.

HOW: It's easy to be tough on yourself, especially if, on some level, you think that toughness will whip you into shape. But there's evidence that developing a competing skill—the ability to swap out self-criticism for self-compassion—is a more beneficial way of relating to yourself. Loving-kindness meditation (LKM), a favorite exercise I learned from mindfulness teacher and author Sharon Salzberg, will help you be kind to yourself when you need it most.

Sit up with your eyes closed or, if you prefer, open and focused on a set point. Spend a few minutes thinking about people who fit into the following categories, then pick one person to focus on in each category:

▶ *Someone who naturally inspires loving feelings in you*

▶ *Yourself*

▶ *Someone you know who is having a hard time*

▶ *Someone you're acquainted with but don't know well (e.g., the person who regularly helps you at a local store)*

▶ *A moderately difficult person*

▶ *All beings*

Bring the people you've chosen to mind, then offer each of them these statements of loving-kindness:

- ▶ *May ＿＿ be happy.*
- ▶ *May ＿＿ be healthy.*
- ▶ *May ＿＿ be safe.*
- ▶ *May ＿＿ live with ease.*
- ▶ *When you're directing the meditation to yourself, you'd say, "May I be safe. May I be happy. . . ."*

Spend at least a minute on each person. To get the maximum benefit, imagine that you are delivering these well wishes as gifts to both yourself and others. Consider practicing this meditation on a regular basis, perhaps after your morning coffee or before bed, and sticking with the same list of people for at least a few weeks so you can fully immerse yourself in building up positive emotions. You can also try this as you go about your daily life, whether you're walking into a situation where you fear being judged or commuting home after a rough day.

WHY: Dozens of studies have shown that LKM can create positive emotions in people who are self-critical or who simply want to feel happier. There is also evidence that it enhances your connections to others. You can use this practice to help you be nicer to yourself just because, rather than waiting until you feel you've done something worthy. You'll find that it will boost your motivation to persist in self-improvement rather than letting self-criticism deplete your efforts.

No. 10 Make a pie chart of your life.

WHEN: An upsetting event becomes all-consuming and you need a dose of perspective.

HOW: To improve your ability to take a holistic look at your life, start by reflecting on and listing the areas of your life that matter most to you—health, friendships, family, personal growth, career, financial security, spirituality, hobbies, giving back. Next, think about the specific virtues you want to bring into each aspect of your life that you listed and write them down (e.g., "bring effort and forgiveness into relationships and reach out to a friend a week"). This ensures that your aims aren't just aspirational but doable.

Imagine you had to fit the areas that matter to you into segments within a circle, like slices of a pie. How much relative weight would you give each facet of your life? For example, what percentage goes to health? Where does that leave work?

Finally, draw a circle with segments of different widths that reflect your priorities. You've just created a pie chart of your life. Feel free to take a photo of it as a way to maintain balance and remind yourself to diversify your life portfolio. Also know that your priorities may shift depending on what's going on in your life. Every so often, revisit your various values and how much they matter to you.

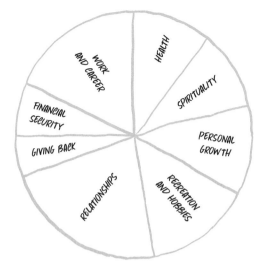

WHY: Once you analyze and specify what matters to you and how much, you'll have an easier time pushing annoying but relatively transient events, like a disappointing first date, offstage. You'll also create a bit of distance in the aftermath of a more significant source of pain, such as a less-than-stellar review at work. Think of it as zooming out to see the full picture (rather than zooming in and magnifying a flaw). This visual can also remind you what you should be paying attention to. Another perk: By breaking down what's within your control, like being patient and communicating with kindness, you'll feel more hopeful than you would if you were focusing on loftier goals that may feel daunting (e.g., meeting your soulmate).

No. 11 Catch yourself catastrophizing.

WHEN: You are stuck in worst-case-scenario thinking. This practice can also help when you're struggling with intense emotions, because the way you think can often exacerbate your distress. That's why your interpretation of an event, like thinking *I'm unlovable and things will never work out for me!* after being rejected, can affect you more than the event itself, with your mind escalating and prolonging your pain.

HOW: Rather than confusing your negative thoughts with absolute reality, take a moment to fact-check your thinking using the strategies below:

▶ *Ask yourself:* Is this thought helping me? *Merely realizing that a particular thought isn't useful can help you let it go. I like to think of this as creating your own personal "thought spam" folder.*

▶ *If you're so upset that you're having trouble deciding if your thoughts are baseless, try planning useful next steps (e.g.,* I'll fail at this! → I can try my best for fifteen minutes*).*

▶ *If you're continuing to think about the worst-case scenario and want to approach it more strategically, ask yourself:* Do I know for sure that this is true? Am I assuming a threat? How likely is it, realistically? What are other possible interpretations and outcomes?

If writing helps you create distance, try a format like this:

Prompting event	Thought	Is this helpful?	How likely is the worst-case scenario?	What are more realistic and helpful thoughts?	What is an empowering next step?

Example: If you're highly stressed and fearful after reading about a mass shooting at a grocery store, these questions may help you see that as horrifying and upsetting as these events are, the odds are overwhelmingly unlikely that a shooting will happen while you are running errands. The goal is not to brush off tragedy but to prevent you from focusing on worst-case outcomes and instead widen your attention to more realistic ones. You might tell yourself, *Choosing to live my life, even when I can't control reality, is my only option*, then continue forward.

WHY: Immediately jumping to conclusions or assuming the worst about a situation only ensures panic. That's how much your thoughts affect your emotions and behaviors. It's no wonder everyone from the Stoics, seminal philosophers in the early third century, to Zen masters to contemporary pioneers in cognitive therapy prescribe working on thinking to improve coping. As much as our circumstances can feel depleting, negative thinking can make life even harder. The point isn't to delude yourself but to think more realistically and effectively. A client recently told me that every step he takes, whether professionally or romantically, leads to hitting a brick wall. I suggested that he swap "wall" with "speed bump," which improved his ability to continue trying even when disappointing news arrived.

No. **12** Look at your assumptions.

WHEN: You're angry with someone else or feeling harshly criticized yourself, and you're clinging to those negative feelings. While snap judgments ideally help us quickly and accurately assess a situation or person, that's not the case when we make a *fundamental attribution error*, or blame someone's behavior on their character (e.g., *what a jerk*) rather than considering the full picture (e.g., *he's doing his job by enforcing the parking laws*). By labeling or making assumptions about someone (including a loved one or ourselves) rather than taking a step back and seeing what might be going on in a broader way, we're at risk not only of misperceiving but of creating undue resentment.

HOW: By realizing the immense role that context plays in every single interaction you have, you can open the door to healthier interpretations. Start by reflecting on instances where you've assumed the worst about someone but there was more to the story. An example that stands out is one that Stanford University professor Geoffrey Cohen shared in his book, *Belonging: The Science of Creating Connection and Bridging Divides*. He described a teacher punishing a student for wearing sunglasses in class, assuming that the boy was being rude, but he was actually hiding a black eye. Merely remembering this distortion can help you begin to replace frustration with curiosity.

To reduce the likelihood of falling into a fundamental attribution error, Dr. Cohen recommended "navigating social traffic with eyes wide open" and practicing "mental calisthenics" by stretching your automatic assumptions. Bring to mind current situations that are leaving you irritated and consider a wider range of explanations. That starts with giving people the benefit of the doubt and, when it's appropriate, asking for more information so you can gain understanding instead of speculating or stewing.

I was elated when a former client who came to see me to work on social anxiety asked, "Are you annoyed with me?" I wasn't annoyed, but I *was* pregnant and happened to be experiencing major morning sickness. My client was highly perceptive, so he could tell that I wasn't my usual self. But he also tended to be anxious, often thinking others didn't like him, so he made a fundamental attribution error, assuming that he'd done something to disturb me. I quickly apologized for looking less than sanguine, told him the reason, and let him know how delighted I was that he brought it up. His courage in asking led us to feel closer and also highlighted how snap judgments can be worth checking, especially in an ongoing relationship when there are facts to support your concerns (in my case, I'm sure I looked a bit queasy).

WHY: Considering other vantage points improves how we feel about others and ourselves in profound ways. In a study led by psychologist Eli Finkel, a professor at Northwestern University, sixty married couples were invited to write for roughly twenty minutes about a recent marital argument from the perspective of a neutral third party who wants the best for all involved. The couples were also encouraged to remember this technique and its potential benefits during conflicts. Compared to the group who didn't do this exercise, the couples who did reported feeling happier about their relationships over the next year. Coming up with a more generous interpretation of an event takes a bit of initial effort yet creates more peace, both within you and in your interactions with others.

No. 13 Think of emotions as coming in waves.

WHEN: You're feeling an intense emotion and are convinced that things will never get better. This reset will also make a huge impact if you typically suppress your emotions, which is not only stressful but can actually lead to emotions intensifying. You can also try this if you have a history of avoiding situations that feel hard because you worry that certain emotions, like sadness or fear, will be too much for you to bear.

HOW: Step back and observe your emotions without trying to block them or judging yourself, pinpointing where you feel them in your body. Now imagine that you are on a surfboard or a boat, staying balanced as the waves rise and fall. Remind yourself that emotions are like waves, coming and going. Practice staying with what is currently happening rather than predicting what you might feel in the future or reminding yourself of what you've felt in the past.

WHY: People are notoriously bad at *affective forecasting*, or predicting how they'll feel in the future. That means that worrying about how you'll feel in the future (i.e., *I'll never move past this!*) only adds hopelessness to whatever else you're carrying. "Surfing the waves" of your emotions instead of judging them will help you see that you don't need to run from your feelings or even take action. Once you sit with them, you'll also find that they typically don't last very long. I like to think of this exercise as a mental Chinese finger trap, a fidget toy that constricts when you try to pull your fingers out, but frees you when you let your fingers relax inward. In the same way, allowing your emotions to run their course is the only way to free yourself. Accepting your current emotions can also help you enjoy positive experiences (a relaxing weekend away with friends) without worrying about those experiences ending or thinking about what's coming next (a stressful work week).

No.14 Turn your nightmares into dreams.

WHEN: You are experiencing nightmares that are interfering with your sleep and functioning, as do many of my clients who have experienced trauma.

HOW: Take a minute to brainstorm a couple of ways to relax (e.g., find a photo of a serene spot or queue up a calming song). Spend a moment seeing if what you've selected actually helps you relax. Use these if you need to recharge at any point during this exercise.

Next, choose a recurring nightmare. If you have several nightmares to choose from, begin with one that feels less intense. Write down your nightmare in as much detail as possible, but change the ending to something positive—the more absurd and memorable, the better. One example: If your nightmare entails feeling panicked while standing on a high diving board with spectators staring, predicting that you're not only about to embarrass but also gravely injure yourself, you can change the ending so that you soon lock eyes with Olympic diver Tom Daley, who gives you a thumbs-up as you bravely and gracefully submerge into the pool. Then, before you go to bed, spend a few minutes mentally rehearsing your new dream.

Going forward, if you wake up in the morning recalling that you had a nightmare, repeat this process while the bad dream is fresh in your mind.

WHY: While nightmares are clearly not your fault, they can become mental habits after a distressing life experience. But *imagery rehearsal*— the technical term for the process I described above—can help you gain control over your nightmares and improve sleep quality. Plus, thoughtfully approaching your recurrent nightmares when you're awake will prove more preventative than worrying about them reoccurring.

No. 15 Open yourself up to finding meaning.

WHEN: Things aren't going as you hoped and you want to inspire yourself to persevere.

HOW: First, know that your feelings are understandable. Honor them. Rushing from feeling upset to finding purpose in your pain without normalizing the legitimacy of your struggle can feel dismissive.

Next, without trying to push away your negative emotions in the process, consider if there is an opportunity for growth in whatever is causing you distress. Some of my clients try to frame their own struggles as opportunities to support others facing similar experiences—say, helping someone through an illness you've had yourself.

Another way to find meaning is to gain perspective. Imagine that "future you" goes back in time to visit "present you." What wisdom might future you offer to help you right now? Alternatively, what might your ultimate supporter highlight to encourage you? You can also try imagining that your setback is somehow part of a master plan that you can't yet understand.

Whatever strategy you try, the goal is to learn how to simultaneously hold distress and meaning. Dr. Marsha Linehan's own struggles with self-harm contributed to her development of DBT, which has saved the lives of countless individuals dealing with intense emotions and circumstances. When teaching therapists how to help their clients make lemonade out of lemons, she said it's about "finding the silver lining without denying that the cloud is indeed black."

WHY: The research is powerful and clear—a sense of purpose mitigates stress, so much so that people who experience a strong sense of purpose are less likely to experience negative emotions and physical symptoms in the face of stressors. When you find meaning, you bridge the gap between difficulty and growth. For example, maybe you're exhausted and running to help an ill family member and you just missed your train. Pausing to normalize your frustration and consider that this is your chance to slow down, practice patience, and finally listen to your mindfulness app for twenty minutes may ease the sting, as opposed to dwelling on the situation and replaying all of the unlucky things that have happened to you lately.

No. 16 Cool down—literally.

WHEN: You're feeling stuck or panic ridden or are struggling to think clearly because you're emotionally overwhelmed or depleted. This reset is especially effective if you're considering giving in to unhealthy escapes that will end up hurting you more than they help.

HOW:

1. Fill a large bowl with ice water. Don't skimp on the cubes— you want the water quite cold, though no less than 50°F. (Note: While the most powerful way to do this is with ice water, you can also try this sans water with an ice pack or a bag of frozen vegetables.)

2. Set a timer for thirty to sixty seconds. (If you're using ice water, start with thirty seconds; if you're using an ice pack, it may help to do this for a full minute.)

3. Take a deep breath to prepare, then hold your breath as you dip your face in the water up to your temples and aim to remain in that position until the timer goes off. (You can also discontinue once you're feeling reset or if you need to breathe.[1])

   If you're on the go or want to try something more mild to center yourself, try sucking on an ice cube or using an ice roller on your face, fully attending to the sensation of coolness as you do so.

---

1 Dipping your face in ice water is taught in DBT as a crisis survival skill. While this exercise works wonders on its own, you can supercharge your coping by combining it with #17, #18, and #21. In DBT, this combination of exercises is referred to with the acronym TIPP—temperature, intense exercise, progressive muscle relaxation, and paced breathing—because it's meant to tip, or overturn, your body's chemistry.

WHY: When your face is immersed in cold water without oxygen, the vagus nerve—the main component of the parasympathetic nervous system—is activated, slowing your heart rate and redistributing blood flow to your brain. That naturally dampens your physiological and emotional intensity. Similarly, if you've ever jumped into a cold body of water, you may notice that the jolt of cold disrupts thinking and leaves you feeling refreshed. By doing something difficult (like the ice plunge) with the goal of learning to cope more strategically, you'll stretch your comfort zone, find relief, and appreciate your innate resilience.

No.17 Move your body in short, quick bursts.

WHEN: You're feeling keyed up, frustrated, exhausted, or anxious, or you're overthinking.

HOW:

▶ *Pick an activity that you think will hold your attention—for instance, a combination of three push-ups, three squats, and three crunches. Set a timer for the amount of time you can realistically commit to, whether that's three minutes or twenty minutes, and do as many reps as you can.*

▶ *Do a round each of high knees, squat jumps, scissor jacks (like jumping jacks but with your legs going forward and backward rather than sideways), jumping lunges, and modified burpees (no push-up required).*

Feel free to modify to accommodate your needs. You can put on some music to make the session more fun. If you have a fitness app you like or enough time to do a longer workout, fantastic. Alternatively, you can try more gentle forms of movement if rigorous exercise won't work for you. If your mind wanders to whatever you're stressed about, bring yourself back to the activity as often as you need to without judging yourself.

WHY: When your body is full of anxious energy, a quick cardio session can help dispel it. Plus, we know that regular exercise significantly decreases stress, depression, and anxiety, not to mention that it's good for your body and heart. In one study, twelve minutes of intense exercise created widespread improvements related to cardiovascular health and stress.

The specific body weight exercises suggested in this reset were found to provide similar physiological effects to those you get when running on the treadmill. Even twenty minutes of aerobic exercise can cause brain changes that correlate with improved cognitive functioning and mood as well as reduced stress. My clients have told me that if their heart rate is elevated  due to the stress of an urgent deadline, they may feel too anxious and riled up to focus. But by bringing their full attention to doing a few minutes of burpees, they find that the panic lessens, their mind quiets, and they can more easily get back to what they need to do. It feels better to attribute palpitations to exercise rather than feeling unable to manage. The same holds true when it comes to experiencing tension due to anger: If you can channel it into focusing on enjoying upbeat music as you attempt to reach your push-up limit, you'll likely find that your rage will abate. Getting your mind and body engaged in exercise, even for a short period, serves as a stress relief valve.

No. 18 Tense to let go
(progressive muscle relaxation).

WHEN: You're struggling to fall asleep or feeling physical signs of stress (think tension headaches or knots in your shoulders). Sitting at the computer for long periods of time can also lead us to tighten our muscles or clench our teeth, often without our noticing.

HOW: Introduced in the 1920s by Dr. Edmund Jacobson, a physician passionate about natural ways to treat anxiety, progressive muscle relaxation (PMR) has been repeatedly shown to improve stress and sleep (even for those facing uncomfortable medical conditions) as well as alleviate symptoms of anxiety and depression in people diagnosed with heart disease. As you move through the muscle groups listed below, tense each body part for five seconds and then release for ten seconds. After you release, bring your full focus to your breath and notice the difference between tensing and releasing.

1. Start by sitting in a comfortable chair or lying down (especially if you're doing this before bed). Begin at the top of your body by scrunching your eyebrows together and then slowly releasing, noticing the difference in your forehead.

2. Tense your lips by pursing them together like you're applying lip balm, then release, separating your upper and lower lips.

3. Bring your teeth together and push your tongue toward the roof of your mouth, then release, creating space between your upper and lower teeth and allowing your tongue to settle.

4. Bring your chin to your chest until you feel tension in your neck, then release and observe the relaxed feeling from your brows to your neck.

5. Shrug your shoulders to meet your ears. Drop them, then notice the difference between tension and rest from your face to your shoulders.

6. Arch your back by bringing your shoulders together, then release, allowing your shoulders to drop and separate. Breathe in and out, letting go of any tension.

7. Tense your belly by sucking in your stomach, then let your belly distend. Notice the difference, continuing to breathe and letting go of tension from your face to your abdomen.

8. Clench your fingers into a fist, then release, separating your fingers.

9. Tense both of your forearms and biceps by making a muscle and holding your arms at a 90-degree angle, then drop your arms, noticing the difference between tension and rest in your hands and your lower and upper arms. Bring your awareness to inhaling and exhaling.

10. Clench your butt, then release, letting go of any tension.

11. Push your thighs together so that they're touching. Notice the tension, then let your legs separate.

12. Finish by flexing and tensing your toes and calves.

13. Scan your body from head to toe while breathing in and out, noticing how your body relaxes.

WHY: Many of us store stress in our body, which can make us feel uneasy as well as physically uncomfortable. The nice news is that releasing stress in the body can create an ambience that allows our thoughts to settle down. (You might even find that simply reading these instructions quiets your mind.)

Often, stress and physical complaints go hand in hand. But even chronic conditions like recurrent headaches and certain gastrointestinal problems can improve when you learn to deliberately relax your body by becoming more mindful of your posture throughout the day. Unlike getting a massage, which is passive, you are acting as the masseuse in this reset, which means your mind can't drift off as easily as it would if you were on the massage table. Learning to let go of tension is also a nice way to reconnect with your body and practice self-compassion (think of the exercise as someone who cares about you warmly placing their hands on your tense, hunched shoulders). I also love the message implicit in progressive muscle relaxation: Through mindful attention, you can systematically improve how you feel.

No. **19** Scan your body.

WHEN: You're having a hard time settling down before bed or you find yourself up in the middle of the night, tossing and turning and worrying about what an awful day you'll have tomorrow if you don't fall asleep this instant. You can also try this whenever you want to expand your attention from pain or other concerns, like negative feelings about your weight/shape. That's because this reset helps cultivate a broader sense of appreciation for your body.

One caveat: If you're craving more energy, this exercise can make you so calm that you'll get sleepy, so I don't recommend this for times when you need to get up and go.

HOW:

1. Lie down on your back and bring attention to your breath and the sensations in your body. Take a moment to notice the places where your body is touching the bed or the floor, allowing yourself to sink deeper with each exhale. Keep in mind that your goal is being aware, not falling asleep. You're not striving to achieve anything beyond staying present.

2. Focus on the feeling of breathing, allowing your belly to rise and fall with each breath. Notice the changes in your abdomen as you breathe—how it rises as you inhale and descends as you exhale.

3. Move your attention to your left foot all the way down to your toes. Focus on each toe, paying attention to the sensations in each of your toes without judgment. As you breathe, imagine your breath reaching your toes on your left foot.

4. Move your attention to the bottom of your left foot—your sole and your heel. Notice any sensations, especially wherever your heel is touching a surface. Continue being aware of your breath as you focus on your foot.

5. Slowly do the same as you move up your body from your feet, spending a little time at each part (e.g., left ankle, left shin, left knee, left thigh, right toes, right foot and ankle, right shin, right knee, right thigh, pelvic area, hips, lower back, abdomen, upper back, chest, shoulders). Then move to your hands (you can do both at the same time), starting with your fingers and moving to your thumbs, palms, backs of your hands, wrists, lower arms and elbows, upper arms, shoulders again, armpits, neck, face (jaw, mouth, lips, nose, cheeks, ears, eyes, forehead), and the back of your head. If your mind wanders (and it will), notice that and guide your focus back without judging.

WHY: The body scan, which is similar to progressive muscle relaxation but a nice alternative if you don't want to incorporate tensing, helps you bring kind attention to your whole body. Doing so makes it easier to appreciate your health while allowing you to move past unrealistic goals (e.g., falling asleep in seconds). This exercise is a central component in both mindfulness-based stress reduction (MBSR) and mindfulness-based cognitive therapy (MBCT), two gold-standard approaches to improving quality of life and preventing relapse into depression. It will also train you to shift your focus away from stress, with an end result of warmth and tranquility. Dr. Jon Kabat-Zinn, the founder of MBSR, explained that while we still don't know why the body scan helps on a molecular level, many professionals working in palliative care and treating people in incredible pain have observed this practice bringing moments of peace to the mind and body.

No.20 Sigh it out.

WHEN: You're in a tough situation and need a subtle way to improve how you feel.

HOW: Gently close your lips and inhale through your nose, then take another inhale through your nose, so you're taking in two breaths back to back. Then take an extended exhale through your mouth. This is called the *physiological sigh*; repeating it is known as *cyclic sighing*. Feel free to try this two to three times in a row. You can also add in short breath holds: Inhale, then hold your breath for three to four seconds, then inhale again, briefly hold, and take a relaxed, extended exhale.

WHY: Sighing is a reflex that helps you maintain homeostasis and regulates your breathing. We naturally take a deep breath and an extended sigh roughly every five minutes, and doing so is crucial for lung health, Dr. Jack Feldman, a neurobiology professor at the University of California, Los Angeles, told me. During deep sleep, we also automatically sigh.

By intentionally sighing, you can quickly access the benefits of this reflex, because expanding your lungs allows you to release more carbon dioxide (high levels of carbon dioxide are associated with anxiety). "As far as we know, 'physiological sighing,' which is a special type of sigh, is the fastest way to deliberately calm down," said Dr. Andrew Huberman, a neuroscientist, associate professor at Stanford University, and host of the *Huberman Lab* podcast who has studied sighing and its effects on mood, anxiety, and sleep.

Heaving a physiological sigh is one way to recalibrate from breathing too much or holding our breath, as we tend to do when we're anxious. "This isn't a placebo or magic, it's basic biology," said James Nestor, science journalist and author of *Breath: The New Science of a Lost Art*. Mr. Nestor prefers combining a sigh with breath holds, a practice introduced to him by a neuroscientist. In a recent study led by researchers at Stanford University, including Dr. Huberman, practicing cyclic sighing for five minutes contributed to positive emotions and decreased respiratory rate during sleep, especially when practiced daily over the course of a month. Dr. Huberman told me he takes two to three sighs when he feels "too alert" or to promote relaxation before bed. This isn't to say that you should be sighing all day long. Excessive sighing offloads too much carbon dioxide, which can lead to symptoms of hyperventilation and is associated with panic and other anxiety disorders.

Beyond the psychological benefits of sighing, there's a larger, hopeful message: Regardless of what's challenging in the moment, we are wired to reset and can count on our marvelous physiology to keep us both relaxed and grounded.

No. 21 Inhale for five, exhale for five.

WHEN: Your mind is racing and you want to feel more at ease, both physiologically and mentally.

HOW: This reset, known as coherent or paced breathing, is another subtle breathing-related exercise that can improve your resilience. (When people tell me that it feels challenging to breathe in a certain way when they're panicked, I encourage them to start with alternative soothing activities, like listening to music or doing a quick burst of exercise, and work their way up to paced breathing.) To try it, follow these steps:

1. Sit with your back straight and your shoulders relaxed, either with your eyes closed or gazing at a fixed point. Softly close your lips and breathe through your nose. Remember to breathe gently (when we feel stressed, we tend to exert force, which activates the sympathetic rather than the parasympathetic nervous system).

2. Inhale for five seconds, expanding your belly as you breathe in. If it helps, count to yourself: *One . . . two . . . three . . . four . . . five.*

3. Exhale, ideally through your nose, for five seconds as your belly contracts.

4. Repeat this cycle for several minutes.

You can also try doing this exercise with a guided recording—I especially love ones that include metronomes or chimes. I recommend Joachim Nohl's Breathe app.

If you want to boost your ability to cope beyond the moment, work up to practicing fifteen to twenty minutes of coherent breathing a day. Then you can also try stretching your inhales and exhales to 5.5 or six counts.

WHY: A healing practice throughout history and a cornerstone of meditation practice, bringing attention to your breath and maintaining a slow and deep pace of breathing can help anyone manage better, even without any formal mindfulness training. Specifically, slowing your breath to five to six inhalations a minute increases the activity of your vagus nerve, reducing your blood pressure and triggering a host of other physiological benefits, including increased tranquility and resilience. No matter what else is going on, "as long as you are breathing, there is more right with you than wrong with you," as meditation master and researcher Dr. Jon Kabat-Zinn likes to say.

Psychiatrists Richard Brown and Patricia Gerbarg, coauthors of *The Healing Power of the Breath: Simple Techniques to Reduce Stress and Anxiety, Enhance Concentration, and Balance Your Emotions*, have devoted their careers to prescribing breathing practices to people coping with traumatic experiences. "Breathing makes you better in every system in your mind and body," said Dr. Brown, who has taught therapeutic breathing to refugees for decades. "Our culture has made it seem like there's a pill for anything that's uncomfortable, but you have the tools to change the energy in your system," Dr. Brown told me. "Breathing connects us to ourselves and improves how we relate to others."

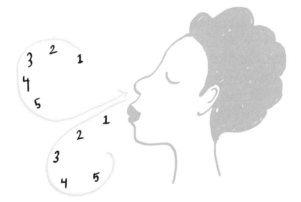

No. **22** Try box breathing.

WHEN: You're looking for a way to focus and find more tranquility in tough circumstances.

HOW: Somewhat similar to paced breathing but with breath holds between inhales and exhales, box breathing is a technique used by Navy SEALs to quickly come down from fight-or-flight mode. Breathe in through your nose while counting to four, savoring the air filling your lungs. Then hold your breath for four seconds, without compressing your mouth or nose. Slowly exhale for four seconds, then hold your breath for four seconds. Repeat the cycle for several rounds, eventually working up to five, six, or seven seconds. Keep practicing until you can do this for five minutes at a time, once a day. (For extra help, try Joachim Nohl's Breathe app.)

WHY: As I've mentioned before, slowing your breath down has a positive impact on your autonomic nervous system, which is responsible for regulating functions such as your heart rate, blood pressure, and digestion. It also calms your central nervous system—your body's processing center, responsible for your ability to think and sense—as well as your emotional state. I love the way science journalist James Nestor described the link between breathing and emotions: "We are anxious because we over-breathe, we over-breathe because we're anxious." Breathing techniques that reduce the number of breaths per minute have been shown to increase activity in areas of the brain responsible for impulse control while also reducing emotions like sadness and anger. Practically, there's something nice about putting down whatever is anxiety-provoking and actively absorbing yourself in this fluctuating pattern of counting and holding.

No. 23 Adopt a half smile.

WHEN: You want to immediately improve your ability to accept what *is* rather than raging against it.

HOW: Start by relaxing your face, neck, and shoulders. Imagine softening the space around your eyes, as if you're erasing tension between your eyebrows. Ever so slightly raise the upper corners of your lips into a half smile (which may look more like a quarter of a smile). This will release tension in your forehead and jaw. Your face should feel tranquil—not like you're posing in front of a camera and saying "cheese!" Feel free to look in the mirror to check your expression; you should look as if you're peacefully smiling with your eyes. Practice your half smile during an activity where you may feel on edge, such as sitting in traffic or walking into a party by yourself.

WHY: Half smiling is something a lot of DBT therapists I know try to practice most of the time (myself included). This reset is grounded in the *facial feedback hypothesis*, the theory that our face influences our emotional states. Noticing your expression and turning up the corners of your mouth ever so slightly offer a nice inroad to beginning to improve how you feel. In a study with 3,800 participants in nineteen countries led by Dr. Nicholas Coles at Stanford University, people who altered their facial expressions to appear happier felt more frequent and stronger positive emotions as a result.

Keep in mind that half smiling isn't about faking it. It's for *you*, not a way to acquiesce to others. Still, relaxing your face from a sulk to a half smile will also put others at ease. A client in her eighties who struggled with loneliness told me that she was surprised by how quickly the impact of half smiling enhanced her life. After several decades spent living in the same New York City apartment building, she was able to create connections with neighbors she'd been seeing for years but had never spoken with.

No. 24 Rest your legs up against the wall.

WHEN: You need to physically or mentally take a load off for a few minutes.

HOW: Lie on your back with or without a pillow under your head and inch your butt toward a wall so that your legs are resting against the wall as close to vertical as possible. Your body should be close to an L shape, without locking your knees. You can put your arms anywhere, whether that's with one hand on your heart and another on top of your belly or letting your arms naturally fall into a T shape. Once you've found a restorative position, hold it for several minutes (you can also play music if it helps you relax). Slowly return to a seated position by rolling to one side and sit comfortably for a minute before getting back to your to-dos. For an even calmer experience, you can slow your breathing (see "Inhale for five, exhale for five" on page 96).

WHY: Standing or sitting all day can affect your circulation. But studies suggest that positioning your legs above your head reduces heart rate and improves blood flow (if you have uncontrolled high blood pressure, consult with your doctor before trying this). Many people who practice yoga find that inversions—postures that bring your legs above your upper body—ease low back pain. The posture is also conducive to slowing your breathing, which not only contributes to feeling more restored but has also been found to help you make better decisions. I love that the practice forces you to do less, not more, as well as adopt an upward viewpoint. Another perk is that it allows you to relax without tempting you to take a nap.

No. 25 Expand your gaze.

WHEN: You're trying to convince yourself to "stop worrying" and it isn't working. (It never does.) You can also use this in challenging settings where you feel trapped—say, if you're at a family dinner where people are expressing political views you find upsetting.

HOW: Simply zoom your gaze out to shift into a more relaxed panoramic view of the space you're inhabiting. You don't even have to move your head to do this one. You can also experiment with expanding your attention by noticing three sights, three sounds, and three sensations. Focus on each item, sound, or sensation you see, hear, and feel, one at a time, without judgment. Note: This isn't a creativity test. It's okay if you're in a quiet space and the only noise you notice is your breathing. Don't rush or hunt down sensations. Instead, allow them to arrive.

WHY: When we feel stressed and overwhelmed, our pupils dilate and our field of vision narrows (part of the fight-or-flight response), leading us to feel stuck. By changing the way you focus your eyes (literally adopting a wider view) and retraining your attention, it's possible to mitigate your stress response. Additional perks: Focusing on one thing in the distance helps counter stress-inducing multitasking, plus learning to shift your attention outside of your struggles and adopt a broader view, especially one that is pleasant, is a nice way to free yourself from a negative self-focus. So many of us try to force ourselves to be grateful during tough times, but my clients notice that by allowing their senses to take the lead, they're more open to a genuine sense of wonder and appreciation.

No. 26 Comfort yourself with touch.

WHEN: You just need a hug.

HOW: Start by taking a couple of deep breaths and concentrating on the warm air you are breathing and the pressure of your hands resting on your lap. Then place your right hand on the left side of your chest, above your heart, and your left hand on your belly, for twenty seconds.

WHY: Skin-to-skin contact is a profound source of comfort to us from the moment we're born. Frequent hugging reduces blood pressure, heart rate, and cortisol levels, even improving immunity. If someone is around to give you a hug, you can shamelessly ask for one (it can feel nicer than receiving unwanted advice). But if no one is around, you can still benefit from the power of gentle touch. In one study, participants were exposed to stressful tasks, including being asked to give a short speech and counting backward from 2,043 in increments of 17. Next, each person was assigned to either receive a hug from a research assistant, practice the hand-on-heart technique, or build a paper airplane. Both the hug and the hand on the heart—a risk-free and always available act of self-compassion—were found to rapidly reduce cortisol levels.

No.27 Just . . . STOP.

WHEN: It feels as though emotions are driving your behaviors and your life.

HOW: Rather than letting go of your better judgment and sliding into patterns that will keep you stressed, you can use the STOP acronym to pause and pivot. Gently remind yourself to *stop* and follow these instructions:

Slow down.
Take a step back.
Observe.
Proceed mindfully.

Feel free to write STOP on a sticky note you'll see regularly, or even get a stop sign charm or cute sticker to help you short-circuit self-destructive, impulsive behavior, like saying something hostile or procrastinating for hours.

WHY: When you're going the equivalent of one hundred miles an hour in your brain and body, there's no room to do any damage control. That's when you need to (nicely) encourage yourself to STOP so you don't make things worse by acting on your emotion-driven impulses.

A lot of people tell me that they simply *can't* stop, and that's a great thought to notice rather than believe. The truth is, most people find that with practice, stopping *is* possible. And there's a bonus: The more you do it, the more you'll strengthen your ability to manage better and develop healthier habits. Amazingly, exercising self-control in one area of your life can spill over to other areas of your life.

If thinking STOP only inspires you to rebel, you can replace it with something more appealing to you, like RESPECT—even spelling out that word to the tune of the Aretha Franklin song is a way to help you remember that self-respect will ultimately free you.

No. 28 Surf your urges.

WHEN: You're looking to free yourself from all-consuming, unhealthy temptations.

HOW: When we're stressed, it can sometimes feel like not acting on an urge will make that urge go on forever, draining your willpower. But whatever is nagging at you, whether it's going way out of your way to pick up a pint of ice cream (again) when you're hoping to improve your blood sugar, checking social media (again), or wanting to blurt out something that you'll later feel guilty about, surfing those urges will help you struggle less. This technique is also used to prevent people who have grappled with substance use from relapsing. Here's how to do it:

▷ *Observe and describe the details of your urge, such as when it came up, your thoughts, physical sensations, and the intensity of your urge.*

▷ *Most people notice that if they aren't hyper-focused on whatever is tempting them and they can turn their attention to something else, their urges are more like waves (see A below), cresting and receding, than a rising slope (B).*

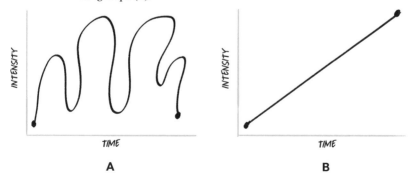

A

B

▶ *Remind yourself that giving in to an urge isn't a must—urges come and go. You can "surf" your urges by accepting them and seeing them from a distance rather than automatically engaging with them or judging them (e.g.,* It's getting worse—I can't stand this . . .*).*

▶ *If you realize that boredom is fueling your craving or you continue to be hyper-focused on your temptation, turn to a healthier activity you enjoy, like watching an episode of a favorite new series or delving into an absorbing book or going for a walk.*

WHY: Initially developed by Dr. Alan Marlatt, a psychologist who specialized in harm reduction and addiction, *urge surfing* is a way to lower the discomfort of cravings. Similar to accepting thoughts, physical sensations, and emotions as fleeting, bringing mindful awareness to temptations—and realizing that they are also fleeting—improves our ability to cope. In one study led by psychologist Sarah Bowen, an associate professor at Pacific University, smokers who engaged in a host of triggering cues, including placing a cigarette in their mouth, while also paying close attention to their thoughts, feelings, and urges (without judging or trying to change them) smoked significantly fewer cigarettes the next week than the control group, despite experiencing a similar number of urges. This was after only 11 minutes of urge-surfing training. By practicing this reset over time, you'll not only conserve your resources but also discover that you *can* choose how to respond to your cravings.

No.29 Take a walk outside.

WHEN: You're lost in rumination or feel stuck.

HOW: Mentally prepare by deciding you're leaving what's stressing you out at home. The goal is to participate in your walk, focusing your full attention on the experience. Leave your phone at home, if that's a safe option, and aim to walk briskly for at least ten minutes. If you can get a glimpse of nature, even better.

WHY: As you likely know from your own experience, walking, spending time in nature, and being mentally present all improve your bandwidth. Combine the three and you're making a fantastic investment in your well-being. In one fMRI brain mapping study, people who walked in nature for sixty minutes showed reduced activity in the amygdala, the brain region associated with emotional responses. But walking for just ten minutes works, too, as long as you put some energy into it. Being in nature is also associated with positive emotions and reduced rumination. It's easy to think *I just don't have time to take a break right now*, but focused attention and a change in scenery can help you get unstuck and, as research shows, walking can enable you to think more clearly and creatively. If you allow yourself to truly relish your surroundings, you'll be reminded that there is so much more to life than whatever is consuming you at the moment, if only you take a few minutes to enjoy what's around you. Walking can also reduce your risk of cancer and heart disease. In looking at more than 196 studies, researchers found that walking briskly for a minimum of eleven minutes a day was found to significantly reduce risk of mortality.

No. 30 Be your own DJ and get "weightless."

WHEN: You're feeling anxious, experiencing pain, or want to improve your mood.

HOW: Begin by naming your emotions and their intensity. Then queue up the ambient song "Weightless" by Marconi Union, a piece crafted specifically to bring on calm feelings. (You'll find it on all music streaming services and on YouTube, where it's set to visuals of a tranquil landscape.) Set a timer for five minutes and bring your full attention to the music for that period of time. If you start judging whether or not you like it or if the reset is working, shift into listening more wholeheartedly, knowing that you can evaluate your experience when your time is up. After listening, reassess your emotions and their intensity.

Finally, create playlists of your own, choosing songs to suit your mood, like a relaxing lineup for when you're stressed or a more energizing list for when you're having a hard time getting out of bed. One of my clients loves listening to Lizzo when she's heading out to a social event and finds herself feeling insecure about her appearance. Update your playlists regularly so they don't get stale; choosing favorite songs is a pleasant activity in and of itself.

WHY: Music has been proven to dramatically impact our mood. In one study at the University of Pennsylvania, preoperative patients receiving peripheral nerve blocks either listened to Marconi Union's "Weightless" or were administered a benzodiazepine to calm them. Remarkably, the serene music proved nearly as effective in easing patients' jitters as the medication, with no side effects. "'Weightless' is believed to be the most relaxing song ever made," Dr. Veena Graff told me. Dr. Graff, who spearheaded the study, explained that Marconi Union collaborated with sound therapists to optimize the song's impact. They tested it on volunteers and noted that their blood pressure and heart rate decreased while listening.[1]

Not all music is beneficial in all situations, however. If you're feeling down and listen to a song that matches your state of mind (say, an anguished breakup ballad), your state of mind may not shift as much as it might if you listened to an upbeat song. In a study looking at inducing emotions through music, listening to three minutes of sad music (slower in tempo with minor tonality) or happy music (think fast tempo and major tonality) seemed to generate those respective emotions. In another study, people who identified with the self-description of "needy and self-critical" felt better about themselves after listening to upbeat music.

Music has also been found to improve both physical and emotional symptoms of stress. Neurologist and writer Oliver Sacks put it best: "Music can lift us out of depression or move us to tears—it is a remedy, a tonic, orange juice for the ear."

1 "Weightless" is deemed so relaxing that experts advise against listening to this song while driving!

No. **31** Build a hope kit.

WHEN: You find yourself focusing on the negative, questioning your ability to manage, or feeling hopeless about your life or the state of the world.

HOW: Think about what you might include if you were going to collect things that fill you with hope and joy, whether those are uplifting photos, inspiring quotes,[1] playlists of moving music, or mementos like thoughtful cards or messages. Then start collecting! You can also make a list of activities that fuel feelings of hope or a change in perspective, like taking a class, training for a 5K, gazing at the night sky, working on a puzzle, or watching your favorite funny video clips.

Keep a physical collection of these objects, photos, and other mementos plus your activity list somewhere handy. When you need some hope, spend time with your collection or try something on your list. If you notice yourself thinking negative thoughts (*What's the point of this, anyway?*), let them go. Feel free to continue to add items and ideas to your collection. Bonus: Keeping an eye out for things that nourish hopeful feelings can, in itself, nourish hope.

You can also create a portable hope kit with, say, a slideshow of your favorite photos, a bookmarked video clip, or a note on your phone full of inspiring reminders. If you enjoy using apps, download the empirically supported Virtual Hope Box, which includes customizable tools proven by research to facilitate coping, relaxing, and distraction.

---

1 One I've recently revisited: "I can't speak, can't walk, can't raise my arm but I can still fight for good. I call that proof that nothing is impossible" —tweet by Brian Wallach, an ALS advocate.

WHY: Think of a hope kit as first aid for hopelessness. A study run by Dr. Wendy Duggleby, a professor and researcher at the University of Alberta in Canada who focuses on nursing and quality of life, found that creating a hope kit significantly increased optimism in individuals with terminal cancer. In research led by Dr. Nigel Bush, a psychologist and researcher at the US Department of Defense, veterans receiving mental health treatment for depression and suicidal feelings reported significantly improved ability to cope with unpleasant emotions and thoughts when using the Virtual Hope Box app, compared with controls.

If you struggle with hopelessness, it's easy to think in all-or-nothing terms, like imagining you'll *never* reach your goals, when in fact there's a good chance you will, but maybe not on your exact timeline. You might also assume someone *always* disappoints you when actually their ability to show up for you may ebb and flow. Reminding yourself of people and experiences that matter can help you see that there is so much more to your situation than whatever you're grappling with at any given moment. Personally, I keep photos of my late, cherished grandparents holding me as a baby and toddler in small frames on my desk to remind me that I don't need to be perfect or achieve anything to be loved. I also keep my marathon medal by my computer to remind myself that by taking small steps, I can reach what matters to me, even when it feels impossible.

No. 32 Cultivate a willing attitude.

WHEN: You're muttering (or screaming) expletives; feeling frustrated or inflexible; or dragging your feet or doing the opposite—overdoing it or being controlling in pursuit of perfection.

HOW: Harness your willingness—the ability to bring together your mind and body to do what's needed in the moment, especially when you don't feel like it. Then imagine you work at a grocery store and a customer drops a jar of pasta sauce, which splatters everywhere. That's bad enough, but they then summon you over to clean it up (without a tinge of remorse). How would you handle that if you were aligning your actions with your goals? I'm guessing that if you behaved as though you were happy to help clean up the mess, if only to spare someone else from slipping and falling, you'd manage better than if you spent the rest of the afternoon fuming.

Bring to mind the times you've felt willful (inflexible and ineffective) and times you've felt willing (ready to act or respond). What do you notice about the differences between these instances? If you're anything like me or my clients, I'm betting that regardless of how natural willfulness feels, choosing willingness (when that aligns with your values) will make you proud.

As you go about your life, notice when you're being willful. Acknowledge it, then choose to let go and embody openness in the moment. Step back and look at the situation you're in and ask yourself what you would do if you felt willing—then do that. If you feel as though being open and capable is miles away from where you're currently at, you can start by mentally rehearsing it and build from there.

WHY: We all face situations where we have to deal with metaphorical or literal messes. But we get to choose whether we'll go with the flow of events (like a palm tree) or resist and snap, losing our chance of getting the outcome we truly desire. Acting flexibly isn't suppressing your feelings—it's realizing what actions will promote your peace of mind and help you reach your goals. If you're thinking you're just not that kind of person, know that willingness is a skill that can be learned—it's taught in DBT to foster distress tolerance—and you can use it to cope with hard times.

No. 33 Take a break from your incoming messages.

WHEN: You can't focus, you feel driven to multitask, and your stress is spilling into interactions with people who matter to you—or when you're relaxing on your own.

HOW: Determine a specific time when you want to take a break from your messaging platforms and be more present in the moment, like when you don't need to respond right away to personal texts or work emails (e.g., after the workday ends and you're winding down or when you want to do deep work without distractions). During this time, keep your phone (and other devices) somewhere out of sight and reach and log out of your email. If you're anxious about not being immediately reachable, take a moment to pinpoint your fears: Do you worry you'll fall behind and have to face a pileup in your inbox or that you'll feel out of the loop in your personal life? Hold those worries, then check in after your break to gauge what actually happened.

If you want to go big and maximize your results, consider checking your messages at set times. Studies have found that checking email at prescheduled moments is less stressful than unrestrained peeking. You can also brainstorm ways to minimize unnecessary communication, like replacing a lot of back-and-forth emails with a quick call.

If you fear you may be judged for not quickly replying, thoughtfully share your plan with others so they know when to expect your responses. Another idea is to let friends know you'd love to catch up in real time rather than engaging in a flurry of piecemeal updates throughout the day. Be sure to revisit and fine-tune your goals as your needs evolve.

WHY: Even if you assume that clutching your devices, staying in the know, and immediately replying helps you get things done, being "on" all the time will burn you out and take a toll on your relationships. I find it heartbreaking that it's now considered normal to respond to random messages while in the presence of others, which only perpetuates the feelings of loneliness and disconnectedness so many of us experience. Research suggests that simply keeping your phone on the table during dinner (even if you're not using it) results in less joy and more distracted interactions. Just as bad, keeping your smartphone anywhere in sight causes "brain drain," hindering your cognitive abilities and focus.

Acting as if you're on call 24/7 makes you feel like you are. Not only will that create anxiety, but it can make you ineffective, because quickly responding to a tsunami of incoming messages is bound to derail you from your most essential tasks. I've come to realize that rather than decluttering your inbox, responding to messages instantly only keeps them coming.

As most of us have experienced, *email overload*, or feeling like your inbox is out of control and overwhelming, contributes to perceived stress. Studies estimate that people glance at their email seventy-four times a day and switch tasks every ten minutes, creating "time confetti," a term coined by writer Brigid Schulte that means shredding what could be meaningful moments of our lives into useless pieces. In my own life, I often find text messages to be as derailing as emails, so I aim to check my texts only during what I now think of as scheduled catch-up sessions.

At the end of the day, we all want to feel seen and reassured that we matter—so why not offer others that gift? This seems so obvious, yet resisting distraction is hard for many of us. Our social ties are stress buffers and our devices are stress generators, so it seems like a double win to take a break and be fully present with others. If you doubt that changing your habits is worth the effort, consider this: Researchers who asked college students to either abstain from or reduce smartphone use for a week found that the students *were* actually able to cut back. As a result, both groups experienced higher levels of life satisfaction and physical activity compared to a control group that didn't change their habits. They also enjoyed reduced symptoms of anxiety and depression, with the benefits persisting months later.

No.34 Try a social media hiatus.

WHEN: You find yourself overwhelmed and in need of more time in the day. You can also try this to improve your mood if you're experiencing sadness, loneliness, or envy.

HOW: Start by being your own behavioral scientist and tracking your thoughts and emotions before you start scrolling on social media. Are you bored? Jittery? Tired? After a scrolling session, note what you find yourself thinking and feeling. Drained? Irritable? Insecure? Jealous?

Next, reflect more broadly on some of the upsides and downsides of your social media habit. If you notice clear perks (e.g., a greater sense of connection with old friends) and consequences (e.g., losing ten hours a week and experiencing FOMO), there may be better ways to attain your goals, like reaching out to three people every week by phone, text, or email.

Set a practical abstinence goal: That could mean taking a day or a week off all your platforms to see how you feel. You can also choose to set time limits for using social media (e.g., thirty minutes a day after work). Experiment with a couple of options to see what feels best.

If your goal is to take a break, consider removing apps from your portable devices to reduce temptation. You can try using Freedom, a program that blocks you from browsing on your phone and computer, or consider purchasing kSafe, a time-lock container for stowing your device so you can truly engage with loved ones at dinner or get work done. Even though it might seem silly to go that far, the most productive people I know lean on these aids to reclaim their focus.

Finally, gather some ideas of activities you can do when you need a quick break that may feel more rewarding, like reading a book or calling a friend.

WHY: Periodically examining your habits to see how they are serving you is enriching—and that's doubly true when the habit involves escaping your life to follow someone else's. It can feel absolutely masochistic to look at images that make it seem as if everyone else has the perfect life. So many people notice that social media prompts stressful comparisons, making us tempted to buy more or do more to perfect ourselves—the opposite of the contentment we deserve to experience when we're unwinding. It makes sense, then, that researchers have found that a weeklong social media break reduces feelings of depression and anxiety and improves well-being. Plus, think of the hours you'll save: On average, people spend 147 minutes a day on social media, which amounts to 17.25 hours a week and close to 70 hours a month! (Don't blame yourself—the algorithms are designed to break your willpower and rope you in.) Wouldn't it make sense to spend more of that time investing in your joy?

BEHAVIOR
RESET

No. **35** Give yourself
a set bedtime.

WHEN: You're delaying going to bed. This can happen for a variety of reasons, including feeling stressed and trying to get more done; taking time for yourself because the rest of your day was packed (known as revenge bedtime procrastination); scrolling on your phone; catching up on your favorite shows; or even because you're worried that you won't be able to fall asleep.

HOW: Spend a few minutes thinking about things you do that might be impacting your sleep quality (e.g., keeping your phone in or next to the bed; watching late-night TV; imbibing caffeine too late in the day; having wine at dinner). Then identify steps you can take to reduce those behaviors (e.g., leaving your phone in your closet; planning to watch only one episode before nine p.m.). Also think about what time you'd need to be in bed and turn off the light to get an optimal amount of sleep (generally seven to nine hours for most people). Figure out how long it takes you to get ready for bed and wind down, then add that in. You might want to set an alarm to give yourself ample time for your pre-bedtime rituals. If you tend to struggle with sticking to your plans, create a pros and cons list (page 72) and practice willingness (page 111).

WHY: Stress and lack of sleep are a bad combination. Think of going to the market when you're famished or trying to resist having another drink when you're already tipsy. Similarly, at the end of the day, you're not thinking as sharply, so it can be tough to stick to a reasonable bedtime. "It's a problem to be awake when reason sleeps," as Dr. Michael Perlis, the director of the Behavioral Sleep Medicine Program at the University of Pennsylvania, likes to say. That's why it's helpful to mentally prep and commit to trying this in advance, just like it helps to lay out gym clothes if you want to make sure you do your workout in the morning.

Another motivator to try this reset: If you're sleeping less than six hours a night, you're compromising your ability to think clearly during the day. Studies suggest that sleep deprivation also amplifies your cortisol levels, affecting your immunity, blood pressure, and metabolism.[1] Many of my clients notice that despite seeming "fun," staying up late only makes them feel worse, heightening their risk of slipping into unhelpful behaviors.

Not sleeping enough can also contribute to a pervasive bad mood. Conversely, getting more sleep improves depression and can set you up to better navigate life stressors, because feeling well rested empowers the mind and body. And you don't need to compensate for a bad night's sleep by sleeping in the next morning, napping, or going to bed early on subsequent nights—those strategies can backfire. What's key is maintaining regular sleeping and waking times (more on that in the next reset).

If your sleep problems persist for more than a week despite improving your habits, I highly recommend six to eight sessions of cognitive behavioral therapy for insomnia (CBT-I), which we'll touch on in Part Three (see page 161). It works wonders, without medication.

---

1 If you're using a smartwatch or another device to help you optimize sleep and it's helping, fantastic. But you don't need to get fancy technology involved in your plan—keeping a simple log, similar to the one on page 161, is sufficient. According to Dr. Perlis, "Wearables can be very informative. They can also be misleading."

No. 36 Get up at the same time every day.

WHEN: You have a hard time falling asleep at night, are tempted to compensate for a bad night's sleep by sleeping in, or find yourself starting the day already feeling pressed for time.

HOW: Think about how many hours of sleep you need (generally around seven to nine hours for most of us). Set a wake-up time that feels realistic and that you can commit to. (You can add an hour on weekends.) Take a moment to think about what usually helps you get out of bed on time (e.g., going to bed on time, using a simple alarm clock with no snooze, stowing your phone in another room, turning your lights on, leaving your window shades open, booking an early appointment). Then think about what typically derails you (e.g., going to bed late, repeatedly snoozing for *just five more minutes*, mindlessly scrolling in bed, falling back asleep, not having any real consequences outside yourself).

Before you go to sleep, mentally rehearse getting up on time and commit to doing so even if you've slept poorly. If this seems impossible,

think about designating an accountability buddy, rewarding yourself with a fancy coffee, or even setting up a consequence, like having to give five dollars to a cause that makes you cringe, which many find to be a helpful motivator (the stickK app helps enforce anti-charity commitments).

On a day that you've gotten up on time, pause midmorning to consider how your optimal wake-up impacted your feelings of capability.

WHY: When you feel exhausted, the best insurance policy for getting good sleep is getting up at a set time, counterintuitive as it may seem. Opting to hit snooze sets you up to perpetuate behaviors that cause insomnia. Establishing a schedule, on the other hand, allows your biological clock to kick in, making it easier to maintain balanced sleep habits, almost like the way you'd overcome jet lag.

It helps to frame getting up on time as your chance to cement the realization that you can count on yourself to show up for yourself and others, even when it's difficult. And if you have a hectic day ahead of you, it can seem much easier to get going knowing you won't have to rush, play catch-up, or craft excuses for being late.

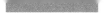

No. 37 Take one step forward.

WHEN: You're procrastinating because everything feels overwhelming or you're multitasking instead of meeting your goals.

HOW: Move what's circling around in your mind onto paper so you can more easily see and approach your list. Determine what's making you most anxious and what's most pressing. If nothing is urgent, consider beginning with a task that would feel good to complete but isn't excessively difficult, to boost your confidence.

Once you've picked a to-do to take on, break it into a SMART goal. SMART is an acronym that stands for **S**pecific, **M**easurable, **A**chievable, **R**ealistic, and **T**ime-sensitive. How it works: Rather than telling yourself you'll write a memo that wows your boss, which is both vague and daunting, go for a concrete and reasonable goal, like setting a timer for twenty minutes to quickly summarize the information you found. Be sure to set yourself up for success by removing distractions, including putting your phone in a drawer and closing all the tabs on your desktop. Doing one thing at a time is the only way to get tough things done.

When your derailing thoughts, urges to procrastinate, or uncomfortable emotions arise, notice them and continue to persist with your task, perhaps by reframing the goal as self-management instead of perfection. Once you're finished, you may discover that you feel energized enough to choose another task. Go for it! You can also schedule your tasks into specific time slots so you move from a pileup to a workable plan.

WHY: If you can swap avoidance with good problem-solving skills, you'll free yourself from to-do lists that get longer and longer and become endlessly stressful. Sort of like using a credit card on a shopping spree, procrastinating may be freeing in the moment, but you'll end up paying a premium later. Learning to problem solve improves stress and boosts our sense of competence.

So many of us spend more time thinking about what we have to do than actually doing it. For that reason, I sometimes have clients with this issue start a dreaded assignment during our session, say, by jotting down a rough outline. Instead of ending up in a panic, as they predict, they often feel a sense of pride once they get going. While it's natural to avoid discomfort and pursue pleasure, knowing that you can take steps toward your goals—and doing so—is the best way to free yourself from those *I can't* thoughts.

Tackling your to-dos systematically can also lift your mood. Specifically, an approach called Problem Solving Therapy, which teaches people to define goals and break them into workable components, has been found to alleviate symptoms of depression. Officer John Moynihan, a detective in the Boston Police Department, was shot in the face while on the job and had a long recovery ahead of him. After seven surgeries, he still struggled to walk and maintain his balance, because having a bullet removed from his ear had affected his vestibular system. What helped, he told me, was setting a single goal. For him, it was doing the seven-mile run he completed every summer on Cape Cod. Every day, he took steps to rehabilitate and strengthen himself to prepare for that run. "If there's a person who focuses on one thing, and there's someone else focusing on five things, I'll guarantee you that the person who focused on one thing is going to get more done," said Officer Moynihan, who teaches a training course on resilience for police officers.

No. **38** Do good deeds.

WHEN: You're feeling like you have no say in your life. This reset counteracts that by creating a sense of agency. It's also a useful way to hold yourself accountable rather than letting yourself off the hook for less-than-considerate behavior by telling yourself (and others) that you just can't do any better given how stressed you feel.

HOW: Here are some easy ideas to improve the lives of those around you:

▷ *Donate to causes that matter to you.*

▷ *Think of someone who may not feel noticed or appreciated and make contact with them (e.g., call an isolated family member or purposefully say hello to someone who looks tired).*

▷ *Go out of your way to buy something you need from a local store (you can even do this online!).*

▷ *Be extra pleasant with coworkers or family members you may otherwise dump your stress on.*

▷ *Message someone who has helped you in the past, such as a former teacher who wrote you a letter of recommendation or a faraway friend who got you through a tough time, to express your ongoing gratefulness.*

▷ *Quietly do a favor for someone who needs it.*

▷ *Pick out or make a few beautiful greeting cards to mail to people you care about and add short handwritten notes, simply because you're thinking of them.*

▷ *Send a voice note or text to someone who needs a lift.*

▷ *Research volunteer opportunities that take just one morning or afternoon (volunteermatch.org is a great resource).*

WHY: We know that receiving support when we're struggling is helpful, but so is providing support to others. A University at Buffalo study that focused on eight hundred older adults who had experienced a major stressor found that those who engaged in helpful activities, like assisting family members with errands or providing childcare, had a lower chance of dying from stress-related causes.

In the short term, helping others can break us out of a cycle of ruminating, overfocusing on our problems, or seeing all the ways others seem to have it easier. Contributing to the well-being of others also boosts mood and feelings of self-respect, making life feel more meaningful. A client of mine who felt frustrated by a pileup of medical bills and endless calls to her insurance company found that taking a break to pick out cute greeting cards to mail to friends not only helped in the moment but also brought her bursts of joy during the week as she imagined her friends opening them. And research led by Dr. Elizabeth Dunn at the University of British Columbia in Canada suggests that spending a little money on someone else—known as *prosocial spending*—promotes well-being. In studies tracking people all over the world, those who contributed money to charity were happier than those who didn't, nearly to the same degree that doubling one's income would increase happiness. To make donating especially beneficial, be sure to take a moment to think about the impact you are making and how all of humanity is connected.

No.

39 Appreciate and lean on the people who want to help.

WHEN: You're craving connection, perspective, or validation, or feeling as if you're on your own and struggling to get unstuck.

HOW: Before you try this reset, take a moment to rate the intensity of your emotions on a scale of 0 to 5 (5 being most intense). If you're at a 5, you may want to wait before trying this particular reset, because it can be challenging to talk or listen when emotions are at peak intensity.

Consider who would be a helpful person to reach out to now, whether that's a friend or a wise and warm relative. (If no one comes to mind, consider trying Warmlines—warmline.org—where volunteers offer emotional support via phone in forty states in the US.) Then think about the best way to connect, whether by phone if you're up for talking or email or text if that's what you have the energy for. Some of my clients find that merely sending me an email sharing what's happening, describing their emotions, and addressing their coping plan helps them feel both connected and accountable, even before I get back to them. Before you reach out, think about what you need. Is it someone to hear you out? Help you problem solve? A bit of both? No one can read your mind, so be prepared to get specific about what might comfort you. The last thing you deserve in a tough moment is for a misunderstanding to make you feel worse.

When you do connect, briefly share what's happening and stick to the basic facts rather than ruminating or placing your stress on someone else, which negates the benefits of social support. Avoid describing a worst-case scenario, too, because that can make catastrophe feel more real to you and create a dynamic where you need to rely on others for reassurance (e.g., *My doctor said I need to come in for a follow-up* versus *I may have cancer*). Instead of trying to solve the issue in one conversation, which is probably unrealistic, make your goal limited and practical, whether that's creating a coping plan for today or feeling understood.

Even if things still seem hard after you connect, express some gratitude. Looking at the good will give you a boost. Plus, it makes sense to appreciate those who support you so they will be there next time you reach out.

WHY: Even if you're an introvert, we're all social beings, which is why having another person listen and help you move forward is such a gift. If you can bring awareness to how you communicate in times of stress, others can remind you that you matter and things will get easier. In brain studies, getting support from others has been shown to positively impact our neural responses to threats, enhancing our ability to manage. Similar to our relationship with stress, much of our experience of social support is about perception—so much so that *perceived social support*, or believing that people are there for us, can matter more than actually getting support, meaning it's imperative to not minimize or forget about the people who care about us.

Beyond seeking help, take the time to notice when you're feeling cared for and find ways to remember the people who are cheering you on, even when they are physically absent. A friend told me that he jotted down a list of all the people he knew who stood behind him when he was preparing to make a tough decision. Afterward, he described feeling like they were present with him, even though they were just names scribbled on a piece of paper.

No. 40 Feign energy.

WHEN: You're feeling lethargic, acting apathetic, or pushing things off (unless it's your bedtime or you're sick—save this reset for another time in those cases).

HOW: Think about how you'd behave if you were feeling enthusiastic and like the best version of you, then do just that. Keep in mind that your goal isn't to feel energized but to manufacture motivation so you can face what matters to you and live better. Given your fatigue, remember that you're not aiming for perfection or completion but to do the best you can do right now. If this feels overwhelming, start small with something like lifting your head and shoulders and acting more engaged in the task at hand. If you start to drag, boost yourself up with encouraging self-talk (e.g., *I can do hard things*) and keep trying.

WHY: Behaving the way you feel when you're drained is, in itself, exhausting. Here's what I mean: If you're a sleep-deprived college student attending a lecture, parking yourself in the back and dozing off—as tempting as it sounds—will likely make you feel *more* stressed down the line than sitting in front, taking notes, and asking questions. Not only will acting interested earn you participation points and shave the time it'll take to prepare for an upcoming exam, it'll boost your energy and feelings of accomplishment. (The same goes for participating in a meeting at work.) Plus, there's something refreshing about realizing that you can choose your behavior, even if it doesn't feel natural.

Another example: Many of my clients who describe themselves as too overwhelmed to regularly tidy up feel that much worse when they find themselves out of clean socks and with loads of dirty laundry piled up. But pepping yourself up to put forth your best effort is a path forward, and it's not as much work as it may seem: A study found that when participants behaved in a more outgoing way, even if they weren't feeling outgoing, they experienced more positive emotions. Interestingly, experts who revisited several studies on the upsides of acting extroverted discovered that the mood benefits associated with seeming outgoing don't come from being social—they arise from behaving more energetically.

No. 41 Stay humble.

WHEN: You're taking risks that you'd typically avoid if you weren't feeling stressed or you have already started doing something you'll inevitably regret.

HOW: Remember that stress heightens the chance you'll take risks, so proceed with extra caution, knowing that your decision-making may be impaired. Notice yourself entertaining permissive thoughts (*I had a long day; I deserve it. It's no big deal . . .*), then see those as Sirens to distance yourself from rather than move toward. It can help to remove temptations (e.g., toss the pack of cigarettes you just bought, delete the number of that bad-for-you ex, close the tabs of online shopping websites). And if you've already engaged in a behavior that's problematic for you, notice the steps you can take to move forward right now rather than beating yourself up for being human or giving yourself permission to continue indulging because it's "too late."

WHY: Similar to how it's tempting to buy lottery tickets when you're financially pressed or push the speed limit when you're running late, so many of the ideas we have when we're struggling are unrealistic or arrogant or put us at risk. Over the years, I've noticed a trend: When I ask someone who has struggled with substance use about cravings, a response that's too cocky (e.g., "That's the last thing on my mind—I'm not at risk!") can predict relapse. But appreciating that the rules apply to you and that you need to be aware of your vulnerabilities can spare you from facing big setbacks. In fact, research suggests that humility can buffer the toll that stress takes on your well-being. Here's why: Humility, or accurately seeing yourself as you are and what you're vulnerable to, can inspire you to be cautious, lean on others, notice your slipups, accept your imperfections, and look beyond yourself.

PART THREE

Stress Buffers for Building Resilience

MENTAL HEALTH, FOR MANY OF US, is linked to our behaviors. That's why, in this section, you'll find thirty-four buffers—ways to supercharge your resilience and help you reset in the long term. Unlike the stress resets, which are meant to help you cope during moments of intense stress, these strategies are designed for you to use on a regular basis to build a life that feels more nourishing. In other words, if the resets are the emotional version of urgent care, buffers are your preventative medicine. By developing good habits and continuously facing your life in a way that feels courageous, you'll build an emotional cushion, making it easier to reset and persevere during trying times.

Some of these buffers focus on self-care, because doing something as straightforward as establishing a daily routine that includes opportunities for pleasure and accomplishment can be as effective as medication at warding off severe depression. Add a dose of mindfulness and some regular exercise, and, as clinical trials repeatedly demonstrate, you'll boost your emotional immune system. By infusing your days with healthier habits and implementing a structure that recharges you, they will feel less reactive—no more playing Whac-A-Mole with every problem—and more carefree. You'll also feel more confident in your ability to manage when challenges do pop up.

Rather than waiting for a special occasion, like New Year's or a big birthday, you can preemptively try a few of these buffers and view them as vital ingredients for better mental health. To maintain motivation, make yourself accountable to a partner or friends so you can inspire each other. Relaying your favorite takeaways to others is a great way to embrace these tools while empowering the people who matter to you. In fact, stress experts have found that the combination of inviting people to process new information and having them share those ideas with others engenders lasting change.

As you integrate some of these strategies into your life, you can track your progress by copying the chart on page 58 in a notebook or using a habit-tracking app, like Habit Tracker or Streaks. Personally, I love my Action Day paper planner, which has space for to-do lists, goals, and notes; I like to make a heart on days when I follow my own healthy routine, which includes a formal slow-breathing mindfulness practice, validating others, putting my phone out of sight for most of the day, and going to bed by eleven p.m., all of which allow me to stay efficient, focused, and connected. Feel free to experiment with your own way of monitoring your wins (bonus points if it inspires you to keep your streak alive!).

Just like the stress resets, some of these practices might feel rewarding immediately; others may not feel as comfortable but will provide real benefits over time. Maintain an open mind and give them a few tries, and I'm confident they will set you up to manage better now and in the future.

No. 1 Untangle yourself from your negative core beliefs.

WHEN: You have a hard time separating old, outdated, negative core beliefs—often instilled by your upbringing or negative experiences—from your current reality. As a result, you may find yourself disqualifying positive experiences or interactions (like brushing off compliments as insincere or misguided) or feeling heightened distress when you're in situations that activate those beliefs. For example, if you were endlessly criticized as a child and came to see yourself as fundamentally "not good enough," you may struggle with letting go of a mistake you made because, to you, it symbolizes something much bigger than a one-off slip.

HOW: Noticing your *core beliefs*, a term described by psychiatrist Aaron Beck, the founder of cognitive therapy, will improve your ability to be more objective about yourself and your life. Often, core beliefs feel so much a part of us that we are not even fully aware of their grip, much less feel able to change them. But by identifying unhelpful or painful core beliefs (e.g., *I'm unlovable* or *People can't be trusted*) and acting counter to them, you can free yourself from unnecessary emotional pain.

The first step is to notice when you feel especially vulnerable. Ask yourself what happened and what set you off. Is it an ongoing sensitivity or a hot-button issue from your past? To be more aware of what is likely to provoke you, think about how you generally see yourself, others, and the world. Are there certain experiences in your life that shaped your self-perception in a negative way? Are there more positive circumstances you are overlooking because your core beliefs are dictating your perceptions?

You can also unearth your core beliefs by trying the "downward arrow" technique, where you dig deeper into what's upsetting you by listing your thought and what it means or represents to you. For example:

Situation: *She didn't respond to my message.*

↓

Automatic thought: *I can't count on her.*

↓

Core belief: *I can't trust anyone.*

A quick way to gain perspective, according to Dr. Martin Seligman, a professor and the director of the Positive Psychology Center at the University of Pennsylvania, is by observing if you're falling into the three Ps after facing a setback—making things pervasive, permanent, and personal. For example, you weren't invited to a friend's event and you assume: *I'm always overlooked* (pervasive) *and that's always going to be the case* (permanent) *because no one seems to actually like me* (personal). This narrative hurts so much more than *I'm disappointed that I wasn't invited to Caroline's holiday party.*

Rather than judging your core beliefs and vulnerabilities or believing them outright, you can notice them without being hard on yourself or feeling demoralized. Compassionately remind yourself that you're not being hypersensitive or overreacting—you're responding to a core belief that has been activated.

To untangle yourself from these negative beliefs, implement behaviors that can help you transcend them. Consider how you would behave if you deliberately defied your core belief rather than letting it control you. For example, despite having a core belief of *I don't fit in*, you can make plans with someone you'd like to know better, even if it stirs up anxiety. One more: When one of my clients witnessed a loved one endure a serious injury when he was a child, he came to believe "the world is a dangerous place" and coped by taking abundant caution. But his approach to life, as he came to see, was almost like saving money for something fun but then using the funds to upgrade his home alarm system that worked just fine.

Only by taking reasonable risks, like making spontaneous plans without doing excessive research, was he able to chip away at his core belief that was perpetuated by remaining guarded.

WHY: It's stressful to feel as though no matter what you do, you can't shake the negative or outdated way you see yourself or the world (e.g., as an awkward adolescent at risk of being bullied). Unfortunately, experiences that seem to support our core beliefs tend to "stick like Velcro," according to Dr. Cory Newman, a professor in psychiatry and the director of the Center for Cognitive Therapy at the University of Pennsylvania. "We often feel bad when we compare ourselves to others because we're judging our private knowledge of ourselves with other people's public displays. That's not a level playing field. You can't fairly compare your private self with someone else's public self," Dr. Newman explained, sharing how our core beliefs can set us up for feeling "less than."

Many years ago at a professional conference for psychologists, I participated in an exercise where we all wrote our core beliefs on our name tags. Mine was *I'm an imposter.* My colleagues' beliefs were equally unflattering—several people who I'd long been inspired by had written *I'm a bad person* in large letters on their labels—which was both eye-opening and reassuring. Rather than running from our unhelpful views of ourselves and the world (which is almost like trying to run from your own shadow), you can "make peace with the shadow," as Dr. Newman put it. At the same time, you can take a closer look at the parts of yourself and your life that contradict your core beliefs, allowing you to better understand and be fair to yourself.

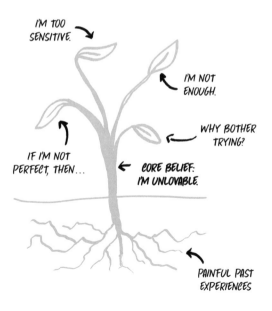

No. 2 Cope ahead.

WHEN: You're approaching something that matters to you and you're looking for an alternative to dreading, obsessing, or avoiding.

HOW: Choose a situation that's bringing up strong emotions, whether you're feeling worried or excited (e.g., you're leading a big meeting at work). Strategize how you can best problem solve and navigate whatever you're facing in detail, so you're swapping unproductive worrying with creating a more productive plan. For instance, you could schedule several test runs; if you struggle with perfectionism, set a time constraint on how long you are allowed to prepare beforehand; choose what you'll wear; plan to start your day with a workout; give yourself extra time to get to the office and listen to an upbeat playlist during your commute; or pack a midmorning snack. Imagine yourself in the situation and mentally rehearse your optimal performance. That might mean feeling a little shaky in the conference room before the presentation, yet planting your feet, looking at a friendly coworker, and remembering to pause between sentences.

WHY: When something matters to us, it's all too easy to spend a lot of mental energy procrastinating and predicting we'll struggle. That only increases the likelihood we'll slip up, because too much anxiety hinders performance. Some people think *too* optimistically—*I work best under pressure!*—which also doesn't set the stage for managing well. The alternative is to strategically map out your game plan, also known as *coping ahead*, a skill taught in DBT. Doing this helps ward off *planning fallacy*, which means underestimating the logistics and time involved in working through a task. By slowing down to cope ahead, including evaluating the steps involved and potential issues that may arise, you can head off potential obstacles and avoid undue stress that comes from not being prepared. In my own life, I've realized that so much of the stress I experience around traveling would be eased if I was more realistic about the time it takes to get a ride, how much traffic there will be (because I live in LA), and TSA lines.

Mentally running through your performance beforehand activates the brain regions you'll use when executing the task. Mental rehearsal and preparing ahead are also a huge part of sports psychology, bolstering athletes before they compete to improve their actual performance. When I asked Keeley Abram, a firefighter with the Los Angeles Fire Department, how she navigates her stressful job, she told me her training included sitting in 450°F heat for five minutes. Knowing that she could tolerate scorching temperatures with her equipment was instrumental in performing in actual fires. Ms. Abram also regularly works on her physical endurance, practices mindfulness in the evenings before bed, and mentally rehearses some of the more challenging parts of her role. Once a call comes in, "I envision exactly what my job will be once I get there. That's really helpful—reassuring myself that I know exactly what I am going to do so I can slow down a bit once I get there," she told me.

The trick is to mentally rehearse how you'll succeed, focusing on both the logistics and how you'll effectively navigate the emotions that will likely come up. What you don't want to do: Envision a disaster or casually assume everything will be fine. Believe it or not, I actually used this coping technique to write *this paragraph*. Beyond scheduling time for writing and making sure to exercise before sitting for a prolonged period (otherwise I'll have a hard time sitting still and focusing), I recognize that when I sit down to write, my mind convinces me that I need to check and respond to unessential emails, unearth too many research papers, or scour online sales. So before writing, I rehearse focusing with my full attention for a set period of time, seeing my urges to procrastinate as impulses to avoid rather than indulge in.

No. 3 Carve out time to stress or worry.

WHEN: You find yourself worrying about things outside your immediate control for more than a few minutes over the course of a day, especially if worries frequently run in the background of your mind like a news ticker.

HOW: Make an appointment to worry, which will help you focus on what's in front of you for the rest of your day. Pick a "worry time" that will work well for you (e.g., not right before bed or first thing in the morning if you already wake up with a sense of dread). Set a timer for twenty to thirty minutes or plan two fifteen-minute sessions to simply . . . worry. And feel free to wrap up earlier, if you're feeling bored by worrying.

During your worry period, you can list your concerns on a piece of paper or begin to problem solve ones that lend themselves to solutions. If you have a wide range of worries, consider breaking them into chunks (e.g., on Monday, health worries for ten minutes and climate change for ten minutes, then on Tuesday, family worries). That way, you can actually process what's on your mind rather than quickly zipping across different topics.

Outside of your worry appointment, focus on the moment you're in. If you catch yourself worrying, you can note and postpone worries that don't inspire immediate solutions until your next worry session. If you forget your worry appointment, no problem—you can reschedule it or wait until your next set time.

WHY: Our mind likes to keep problems afloat, especially when we can't solve them right away. It's also easy to assume that our worrying is somehow helping us because it feels as if we're doing *something* rather than nothing to fix the issue. But in reality, worrying doesn't get us anywhere except more tired and stressed.

By planning exactly when to worry and for how long, you can cut hours of intrusive worrying from your day. Worry appointments are also beneficial because they encourage what psychologists refer to as *self-monitoring*, or observing when and where your mind wanders rather than mindlessly losing hours to stressful thinking. By setting aside a time for worrying, you'll also be less likely to associate worry with a wide variety of activities, a concept known as *stimulus control*. Finally, worrying for a certain period of time is a form of exposure therapy: Sitting with your fears instead of weaving in and out of them allows you to realize that thoughts and feelings come and go and that you don't need to worry all day to manage your life. The best part of worry time is that it allows you to better compartmentalize so the rest of your moments can be worry-free, making your life more pleasurable.

No. 4 Try expressive writing.

WHEN: You want to make sense of your stress, emotions, and experiences in a way that's cathartic instead of draining.

HOW: There's something about writing down your challenges on paper that can help release whatever is weighing on you and create a sense of distance and perspective. Grab a pen and paper and pick a time and a place where you can quietly focus and you won't be interrupted. Then set a timer for fifteen minutes and write about one of the following:

▶ *What you're thinking or worrying about*

▶ *Something you're dreaming about*

▶ *An issue that's impacting your life in an unhealthy way*

▶ *Something you've been avoiding*

Don't worry about spelling or grammar. What's important is that you express your deepest thoughts and feelings on whatever topic you've chosen. You might also reflect on how you can grow from or find meaning in whatever it is you're enduring. If you're writing about something that happened in the past, be sure to recount it in detail and in the past tense. Repeat the exercise three or four days in a row so you can truly face and work through what's on your mind, knowing that you don't have to write about the same thing every time. And if you find yourself feeling extremely upset when you're writing, feel free to stop or switch topics. It's also okay to feel emotional; notice how your feelings change over time.

WHY: *Expressive writing*, a technique pioneered by Dr. James Pennebaker, is a research-backed way of journaling. Instead of scribbling about whatever is on your mind, focusing on your significant concerns and allowing yourself to go deeper will help you tap into your emotions. This is important because painful, unprocessed events can hold us back and manifest in other problems.

If you worry about feeling depleted from writing about something distressing, try tweaking your focus to find meaning or hope in the event—say, by imagining the steps you'd take to achieve a different, happier ending. For instance, if you're writing about your fears about and dissatisfaction with your marriage, you might follow that by writing about what you can do today that will have a positive effect on your relationship five years from now, advised Dr. Joshua Smyth, a leading stress expert, professor in biobehavioral health at Penn State, and one of Dr. Pennebaker's long-term collaborators.

If you have faced a life-threatening event and find yourself repeatedly haunted by it, you might have PTSD, which affects how you experience daily stress. While some trauma treatments may seem complicated or time-consuming, expressive writing has been shown to help people with PTSD move forward after a trauma in only a handful of sessions. Dr. Denise Sloan, an associate director at the National Center for PTSD, gave a group of people five thirty-minute writing exercises with instructions and prompts (*Describe exactly what you remember; how did this event shape your life?*). People who had experienced trauma and did the exercises in the presence of a trained professional (please don't try this on your own) showed significant reduction in their PTSD symptoms, comparable to the improvement of people who went through twenty sessions of another research-based trauma therapy.

In my own practice, I've witnessed clients who have endured horrific experiences feel dramatic relief after five writing sessions completed during our appointments. Why? Given the intensity of a life-threatening event, traumatic memories tend to be stored in a splintered way to protect us from reliving the full impact of the trauma. But by organizing your experience—giving it a beginning, a middle, and an end—and then repeatedly recounting it, you'll be able to systematically correct how your memory is stored in a way that allows for closure. You'll also come to see that you can separate yourself from the memory rather than letting it control you.

When dealing with daily upsets *and* life's most painful events, expressive writing can help you map out and process what feels messy.

No. 5 Look for the good.

WHEN: You want to enjoy daily life and feel more content.

HOW: Here are a few options to try:

▶ *For a few minutes every day, list three to five (small or large) things that you feel thankful for. (You can write them in a journal or use a gratitude app.)*

▶ *Consider people you are grateful for and reach out to them to express your thanks.*

▶ *Pick one activity that usually annoys you, whether that's exercising, doing laundry, going to the grocery store, or calling a family member, and shift your perspective by dropping gratitude into that specific activity (e.g., I get to bring groceries to my apartment). You can swap your focus each day or week. You might even rename your to-do list as your "get-to-do list."*

▶ *Using pen and paper, write about one of the following scenarios in two or three paragraphs, being sure to give your description a beginning, a middle, and an end:*

  - *Something that went well and why*
  - *Something you're thankful for*
  - *Strengths you've used recently*
  - *Progress you've made toward your goals*
  - *Something nice that someone did for you, big or small*

WHY: According to the *negativity bias*, humans are programmed so that our upsets inevitably tend to overshadow positive experiences. From an evolutionary perspective, it's to our advantage to be especially attuned to threats. But to counter the tendency to veer negative, whether about your life or yourself, make a habit of purposefully looking for the good. Gratitude helps you do that. Studies show that spending five to fifteen minutes a day writing about what you're grateful for by using prompts like the ones on the opposite page—known as *positive affect journaling*—reduces stress and sadness, even for people who are experiencing medical problems. Practice it regularly and you'll improve your mood, outlook, and relationships and even feel more altruistic and humble. Researchers have noticed that people who are grateful also feel as if they have more social support, which buffers stress and wards off the risk of depression.

Making a habit of finding the good benefits your physical health as well: Research has linked gratitude to improved blood pressure and sleep quality. Interestingly, gratitude isn't only helpful for the person practicing it. Experts notice that expressing gratitude to someone you're collaborating with lowers their physical markers of stress.

No. 6 Revisit your beliefs about your emotions.

WHEN: You want to remind yourself that having a stressful moment doesn't necessarily translate into having a terrible day.

HOW: If you typically overestimate the longevity of your emotions and cope by avoiding them or inadvertently intensifying them, you'll find that experimenting with inducing different moods by watching brief video clips can help you be more present and less judgmental of your emotions. Here is a list of clips that can help you experience different emotions (you don't have to watch for longer than two minutes):

▶ *The final scene from the movie* The Champ

▶ *Sarah McLachlan's music video for "Angel"*

▶ *The "I'll give you Szell" scene from the movie* Marathon Man

▶ *The documentary* College Conspiracy

▶ *Pharrell Williams's music video for "Happy"*

Minimize distractions by closing other browsers and paying attention to what's in front of you. Try to stay focused on the clip itself rather than creating parallels between what you're seeing and your own life. When it's over, take a moment to reflect and jot down any larger observations you want to remember going forward. Use this format to track your experience:

What did you notice? Write down your thoughts, feelings, and behaviors (e.g., looking away).	How effective were you at being nonjudgmental? (Use a 0 to 10 scale, with 0 being not at all and 10 being extremely.)	How well were you able to stay present while watching? (Use a 0 to 10 scale, with 0 being not at all and 10 being extremely.)

WHY: One of the most liberating experiences is realizing that emotions come and go, especially if you allow them to just be and can stay present in the moment. Over the years, I've worked through this list of clips with hundreds of clients who tell me they feel their emotions intensely, and I continuously see people tear up *and* experience happiness during the span of ten minutes, with each emotion peaking and lasting less than two minutes.

Learning to stay present while watching video clips correlates with managing the emotions that arise in your life. Why? Studies show that watching video clips *does* create real emotions. That said, your own emotional experiences will understandably affect you more than watching less personal material. The point is to practice building up your ability to be mindful of your current emotions. In doing so, you'll come to realize that you don't need to make emotions go away, especially by engaging in behaviors that won't serve you. Once you fully enter the moment, you'll find that those emotions will dissipate on their own.

Many years ago, I heard Dr. John Gottman, a leading expert in couples therapy, describe in a professional training that a good predictor of a couple's resilience is if they're able to laugh shortly after a conflict. And the same holds true for us as individuals: The more we stay present and allow ourselves to open up to what's happening now rather than staying stuck in what's happened, the healthier we'll feel.

No. **7** Pursue your life purpose.

WHEN: If you want to continuously build a life that you're proud of, do this monthly or yearly.

HOW: Pick a day that feels meaningful, whether it's the first of every month, quarterly, or ahead of your birthday, and set aside twenty minutes to an hour or more to identify a few key values that matter most to you. Consider the main virtues and actions you want to focus on to improve your own quality of life (e.g., being more patient with yourself) and to make a difference in the lives of others (e.g., acting more generously toward the people around you).

Next, come up with a practical plan to connect with those values. For instance, if you value being part of a community, rather than assuming it's too hard to find one that feels right, list a few group activities you can try to see if any feel like a good fit. Think about how you can regularly implement actions that express your values. For instance, if one of your values is caring for the environment, you might decide to eat vegetarian most of the week. Even if it seems like there's much more to be done, give yourself credit for taking steps in a positive direction.

WHY: Defining what matters to you and committing to focusing on it more often can help you see the bigger picture and offer a sense of autonomy. In Japan, there's a concept known as *ikigai*, which roughly translates to "a reason to wake up in the morning." Experts have noticed that individuals who practice ikigai by aligning what they love, what they're good at, and what they can be paid for to fulfill a need in the world enjoy increased longevity. That's why I am enthusiastic about psychotherapies like ACT and DBT, which help people clarify their values and pinpoint steps to move closer to them. Counterintuitive as it may sound, many of my clients notice that volunteer commitments that link to their value of making the world a better and more equitable place seem to reduce their stress rather than feeling like another task on their to-do list. And studies show that people who feel there is meaning in their life report less distress and repetitive thinking. The bottom line: Mapping out ways to turn your values into actions and taking a moment to acknowledge how your current actions already sync with your values will give you a sense of power and fulfillment.

No. **8** Take a break from being judgmental.

WHEN: You're feeling critical of a situation, yourself, or those around you.

HOW: Start by noticing when you're judging, whether or not you're saying anything out loud. You can even count how many judgmental thoughts you have within one hour, which is an eye-opening and concrete way to bring awareness to this habit. Clues that you're judging: your face or body is tensing or you're talking in a harsh tone.

Try replacing your judgments (e.g., "I can never count on you") with the facts and your feelings (e.g., "When you cancel at the last minute, I can't easily make other plans, and I feel disappointed . . ."). Doing so will feel both easier for you to sit with and more palatable for someone else to hear, because giving feedback in a critical tone can increase the likelihood that whoever you're speaking to will respond defensively rather than empathetically. Because we judge so often, it can help to pick specific situations or people (like a partner) to practice on, then work up to withholding judgment in other areas of your life. If you need extra motivation to reduce judgments, consider whether you want to be right or maintain relationships.

WHY: By paying attention to when and what you're judging, you can let those judgments—and that negativity—go, which will improve how you feel and boost your ability to problem solve. As natural and automatic as judgmental thoughts may seem, tormenting yourself with thoughts like *I'm the worst* can hinder coping. Stress has so much to do with how we perceive and assess situations, ourselves, and others. Making judgments not only contributes to stress but also breeds painful feelings such as anger, anxiety, and hopelessness.

No. 9 Practice different types of empathy.

WHEN: You're absorbing the pain of others in ways that drain you or impede your ability to actually help.

HOW: Try observing what another person is going through without blurring the line between what they're experiencing and what you are experiencing. Take a few breaths, then shift into a more cognitive form of empathy rather than emotional. For example, if you see a person rummaging through the trash, consider that they must be hungry and offer them a hand, rather than feeling overwhelmed with despair around food insecurity, which hinders your ability to lend a smile and provide a meal.

WHY: Whether you work in a helping profession, volunteer, serve as a resource to friends struggling, or get caught up in tragic news, it's easy to lose yourself in the pain and injustice around us. And yet, if you're not actually going through a crisis, imagining how you'd feel if you were gets in the way of your ability to offer support. In one study, physicians who acknowledged their own emotions rather than overly identifying with their patients' emotions experienced less burnout. When I asked Dr. George Everly Jr., a professor at Johns Hopkins School of Public Health who specializes in crisis intervention and humanitarian aid, about how he trains people to help in disasters, he said, "We are taught that the way to help others is through empathy, but that can be a trap." He suggested trying to understand the world from another's point of view rather than taking on their feelings; the latter will hurt you and won't effectively diminish their distress. Remember, you don't need to fully feel something in order to help—it's nearly impossible to offer assistance while feeling overcome with suffering.

No. 10 Enjoy sympathetic joy.

WHEN: It feels like everyone has it easier or better than you. You can also try this if you often feel lukewarm about other people's achievements and you want to celebrate them more wholeheartedly. As the Dalai Lama has been known to say, "It only makes sense to cultivate happiness for the happiness of others because then you increase your own chances of happiness six billion to one."

HOW: If you can't rejoice in the well-being of others, it's tough to feel content in your own life. To feel happier for those around you, begin by asking yourself if you are holding on to any underlying negative assumptions—for instance, that another person's success means your good fortune will dwindle. (Happiness is not a limited commodity.) It can also help to notice if you're creating stories in your head, like imagining that the person you're envious of has had it easy. Try these exercises:

▷ *Take a moment to truly feel or act celebratory when a friend gets nice news. Instead of giving them a thumbs-up on LinkedIn, send them a personal text or a card. Start by doing this with your closest friends, then expand to your outer circles.*

▷ *If someone shares good news with you in real time, rather than responding politely with a lukewarm, "Congrats!" try revving up your energy and enthusiasm, in both your words and your body language. That might look like: "I am SO thrilled for you and can't think of anyone more deserving of this win!"*

▷ *After you complete your loving-kindness practice (see page 74 for more on this), hold a vivid picture of that person in your mind as you repeat, "May your happiness increase." If your attention wanders, bring it back to the image. Practice with the same person for a few days, then switch to someone else.*

WHY: Similar to the biblical commandment "Love thy neighbor as thyself," *sympathetic joy*, which Buddhists describe as genuinely delighting in the good fortune of others, can help you move past the stressful assumption that life is a competition. Given how often we're exposed to other people's heavily curated and perfect-seeming lives on social media, learning to override feeling unlucky and instead experiencing happiness for others can reduce envy and loneliness. "The underlying truth is that we're all connected," explained Sharon Salzberg, a mindfulness teacher and author who has taught the practice of sympathetic joy for decades. Instead of obsessing over who deserves what and stewing in feelings of resentment, she said it makes more sense to consider how you want to use your time. Because Ms. Salzberg was raised by her immigrant grandparents, she initially felt disconnected from most of her peers, who were raised by their parents. "Sympathetic joy made me aware of the vulnerability we all share—no one's life is perfect, and certainly not perfect forever," she said.

No. **11** Commit to
three minutes
of mindfulness.

WHEN: You want to more easily notice your thoughts, feelings, and behaviors so you don't get stuck in unhelpful loops.

HOW: Start by sitting in an upright position with your feet flat on the floor or in a comfortable cross-legged position with your spine straight. If you're open to it, close your eyes or focus your gaze on a set point.

Minute 1: Notice where your body is coming into contact with the chair or the floor. Then consider: *What is my experience now? What thoughts are going through my mind? What bodily sensations am I feeling?* Do your best to acknowledge thoughts and physical sensations without trying to change them in any way.

Minute 2: See if you can let go of what's on your mind and bring your focus to the physical sensations of your breath in your belly: the way your stomach extends as you inhale and contracts as you exhale. Follow your breath all the way in and out as a way to center your attention.

Minute 3: Expand your awareness by moving your attention from your breath to your body as a whole, from the crown of your head to the bottom of your feet, then widening your attention to the space you're in. When you're ready, open your eyes.

Try scheduling two or three specific times to do this every day for a week. Practicing at set times can help you make it a habit so it's easier to tap into the skill when you need it, almost like muscle building. After a week, think about how often you could benefit from doing this going forward—ideally, once a day at a set time. If you prefer to listen to a guided recording, you can find a video of this practice, titled "Three-Minute Breathing Space," on YouTube, led by Dr. Zindel Segal, one of the developers of mindfulness-based cognitive therapy (MBCT) and a professor at the University of Toronto in Canada.

WHY: Because your breath is always with you, it's a readily accessible tool that can help you become more present in the moment. The three-minute breathing space primes you to notice your thoughts, feelings, and sensations so you're not just on autopilot. The more you do it, the more you'll be able to observe yourself in other situations, which makes it easier to bring your attention back to the present. While brief, "this choreography of awareness" underscores shifting your attention, checking in, and moving on, as Dr. Segal described it. Those are just the mental superpowers we need when it comes to getting unstuck.

Remarkably, studies have shown that completing an eight-week course in MBCT and subsequently repeating this three-minute mindfulness practice every day is as effective at preventing relapses into major depression as medication, Dr. Segal told me.

No. 12

Give yourself a panic attack to feel less afraid of them.

WHEN: Your stress typically causes uncomfortable bodily symptoms or you suffer from panic attacks and feel on edge about them reoccurring.

HOW: Because physical sensations like shortness of breath can hijack your attention during challenging moments, you can practice robbing your body's stress responses of their power by repeatedly re-creating your specific physical symptoms and embracing them for a minute in a safe environment. While this will require you to stretch your comfort zone, *interoceptive exposure*, or facing physical symptoms you typically avoid, will free you from feeling derailed by physical sensations of anxiety.

Consider which physical sensations arise in your body when you're panicked, whether it's rapid heart rate, shortness of breath, muscle tension, feeling hot and sweaty, claustrophobia, dizziness, disorientation, or shakiness. When you experience these sensations, notice whether you tend to judge your body's response to them. One clue: You have thoughts like *I can't breathe!* or *It's getting worse!* If so, know you can learn to remember that these sensations are transient rather than judging them as "bad" or "dangerous." Re-creating these symptoms during otherwise calm moments can help you do that.

Try all the exercises[1] from the list below, which aim to induce a variety of panic- or stress-related sensations (these may seem less than appealing, but they won't take more than five minutes in total). The goal is to mimic the distress you feel when these physical symptoms show up in your life spontaneously. Use a chart like this one to keep track of which ones work best for you:

EXERCISE	SENSATIONS	SIMILARITY TO REAL-LIFE DISTRESS

Then tweak the exercises to make them more intense if necessary. If you usually feel claustrophobic, hot, and as if your heart is racing when you're nervous or stressed, you might work up to doing some of these exercises in a small closet after downing an espresso while wearing a winter jacket.

▶ *Hyperventilate (for up to sixty seconds): Take rapid deep breaths, using a lot of force. This exercise can create dizziness.*

▶ *Breathe through a thin plastic straw, pinching it to narrow its diameter by about half while simultaneously pinching your nose closed. Continue for up to sixty seconds. (It should feel as if you're barely getting enough air.)*

▶ *Spin in circles for sixty seconds, either sitting in a swivel chair or standing. Try to do one full rotation every three seconds.*

▶ *Run in place vigorously for sixty seconds, trying to touch your knees to your nose, to get your heart rate up and make you sweaty.*

▶ *Hold a plank position for sixty seconds or until you feel shaky all over.*

---

1 If you have asthma, vertigo, or other physical conditions that may contraindicate doing these exercises, consult with your physician before trying them.

Repeat the exercises that most closely match your stress symptoms until those sensations feel familiar and nonthreatening. That could mean doing them a few times in a row and several times a week for a couple of weeks, then revisiting them before a real-life stressful situation during which you might experience the same symptoms. This will leave you warmed up and ready to welcome them if they appear.

WHY: I often wish I could do a public service announcement about how interoceptive exposure is the fastest and most proven way to treat panic attacks. That's because purposefully bringing on symptoms of panic and facing what you dread uncouples stress and anxiety symptoms from escalating interpretations, like *I'm in danger!* The more you practice approaching sensations of anxiety nonjudgmentally, the more likely it is that you'll come to see them as temporary rather than terrifying. Learning that these physical symptoms won't harm you makes you less likely to avoid situations that bring them on, taking away their power. Research has shown that experiencing and accepting your bodily sensations, even if they're unpleasant, improves functioning in an overwhelming number of people with anxiety disorders. It's incredible to see my clients who have shrunk their lives to avoid panic now brainstorming ways to welcome stressful sensations, then enlarging their lives in ways they never could have predicted.

No.13 Swap your screen for morning sun.

WHEN: You want to start the day with a healthier perspective, especially if you struggle with your sleep and focus.

HOW: Instead of using your smartphone as an alarm clock, put a real alarm clock by your bed and stick your phone in another room to ward off the temptation to mindlessly scroll in bed, whether at night or when you first wake up. Invest the time you're saving by not scrolling in taking a quick two- to ten-minute walk or sitting outside to absorb early-morning sun within an hour of waking up (you don't have to look directly at the sun, just in its general direction). If it's cloudy, try to spend closer to twenty minutes outdoors.[1]

WHY: When you view morning sunlight (sans sunglasses) within an hour of waking up, you'll help regulate your body clock, increasing your energy, sharpening your focus, and improving your sleep. That's because the body's ability to regulate sleep-wake cycles is dependent on our getting natural light. Another benefit: The vitamin D we get through the sun is also known to improve mood.

Holistically, I love the reminder that there's so much more to life than our tiny screens. Think about it: Our grandparents never woke up like this. Losing ourselves in email, skimming the news, peeking at random people's stories, or pondering your to-do list (that you won't get to work on for an hour) feels like a missed opportunity to begin your morning by celebrating your life.

---

1 If it's impossible to get morning sun exposure where you live, you might talk to your doctor about trying a light box, especially if your mood dips during winter months.

No. **14** Seal your lips.

WHEN: You habitually breathe through your mouth or snore.

HOW: Gently place a postage stamp–size piece of nonallergic surgical tape over the center of your lips for ten or twenty minutes to get into the habit of breathing through your nose. (Don't try this while eating or speaking, of course!) If you suspect you breathe through your mouth or snore while sleeping—if you wake up with a dry mouth, odds are you're mouth breathing—you can experiment with taping your lips overnight.[1]

WHY: Nasal breathing lowers your blood pressure, improves sleep quality, and has even been found to reduce snoring in people with mild sleep apnea. When you breathe through your nose, you filter and humidify the air entering your body more efficiently than when you breathe through your mouth. In addition, nasal breathing allows the lungs to extract oxygen more efficiently so you can take deeper breaths. It also raises levels of nitric oxide, a molecule that affects circulation and delivers oxygen to our cells, improving vital functions as well as boosting mood and immunity. Nasal breathing enthusiasts even do it during vigorous exercise to improve athletic performance.

Personally, I've found that sticking a little taut tape on my lips for ten minutes at a time primes me to gently close my mouth more often throughout the day, and tape is easy enough for me to wear overnight. If you want to learn more about nasal breathing, science journalist James Nestor delved into lots of detail in his book *Breath: The New Science of a Lost Art*.

---

1 If you're experiencing congestion or obstructive sleep apnea, consult with your physician before trying this.

No. 15 Eat mindfully.[1]

WHEN: You're multitasking when you eat or you're noticing that you eat too little or too much in a sitting. You can also practice this if you're looking for more ways to find gratitude throughout your day.

HOW: Hold a strawberry or any other small piece of fruit and bring your full focus to noticing what it looks like, what it feels like between your fingers, and what it smells like. Put it in your mouth without biting down, bringing your attention to that sensation. Then take a bite, noticing where the strawberry touches your teeth and tongue, how it changes shape and texture in your mouth, what flavors emerge . . . If it helps, you can close your eyes as you chew to bring all of your attention to your sense of taste. Continue to slowly savor your strawberry. No need to judge the food as good or bad. If you want to further heighten your awareness, you can also consider all the people who were involved in the strawberry making its way from the ground to your table, including those who work in the field, drive trucks, and stock the produce section at the grocery store. Afterward, note anything interesting

---

1 Also remember to stay hydrated! Forgetting to drink water throughout the day can lead to sensations that are similar to stress. However, drinking five glasses of water over the course of the day is associated with decreased risk of depression and anxiety. Other research suggests that closer to ten glasses of water per day is optimal and that the benefits include improved longevity, cognition, mood, and sleep. If you need a gentle nudge, some of my clients like water bottles with time markers designed to help you stay on track.

you experienced and think about how this practice differs from the way you normally eat. Start small with a few mindful bites and sips, then progress to using this technique during an entire meal, perhaps once a day to start.

It's also important to bring awareness to your hunger—eating when you're moderately hungry and stopping when you're moderately full, knowing that it can take twenty minutes to experience fullness. Other guidelines to eating more mindfully include plating your food; eating only while sitting with no other distractions; and eating more slowly so you can pay attention to your satiety.

If you're worried you just don't have time to eat mindfully, see how long it takes you to eat your meal in an enjoyable, non-rushed way without multitasking. Ten minutes? Then carve out the time to do that going forward, knowing that it won't take as long as you previously assumed and is much more satisfying.

WHY: It's common for acute stress to lead to reduced eating, which can hinder your ability to think clearly and manage your emotions, while chronic stress can prompt emotional eating or overeating, which can worsen your mood. Whether you lose your appetite or find yourself eating too much when you're stressed, you'll create more bandwidth by fueling yourself with reasonable amounts of healthy foods. Eating more mindfully can also help prevent you from swinging from starving to stuffed, improving your endurance, digestion, and sense of well-being. (If you have a history of struggling with eating too little or too much, experts recommend aiming for three meals and two snacks.)

Eating in a way that feels out of control can negatively impact self-worth, making you feel like you can't count on yourself. Many of my clients notice that whatever is stressing them out becomes even more stressful if they feel like they're abandoning their healthy habits. Mindful eating is an opportunity to cultivate self-compassion by giving yourself permission to enjoy food.

No.**16** Spend less time in bed to improve your sleep.

WHEN: You're having a hard time sleeping and there's a notable discrepancy between the amount of time you're in bed and how many hours you're actually sleeping.[1]

HOW: It's hard to feel well—mentally or physically—if you're not experiencing good quality sleep. If you're part of the 30 percent of people who struggle with untreated insomnia, *sleep restriction*, the technical name for this exercise, can help. Start by tracking the following to get a clear sense of your sleep patterns:

1. The time you go to bed

2. The approximate time it takes you to fall asleep

3. The time you spend awake in the middle of the night (if any)

4. The time you wake up

5. The time you get out of bed

Calculate the difference between your time in bed and the number of hours you actually spent sleeping. Keep this log every day for a week to get a clear picture of the average number of hours you're sleeping.

Next, select the ideal time you'd like to wake up every day. Keep this time the same every day, but go to bed *later*, so you're setting yourself up to be in your bed only for the amount of time you've typically been sleeping (e.g., if it's taking you an hour to fall asleep and you're up for twenty minutes in the middle of the night, go to bed an hour and

1 If you have a medical condition that is worsened by limiting your sleep, such as migraines, bipolar disorder, or epilepsy, don't try this without consulting with your physician first.

twenty minutes later than usual). Make sure to give yourself a minimum of 5.5 hours in bed. If you find yourself awake in your bed for more than fifteen minutes, get out of bed and do something boring, such as sitting in a chair and reading a book that doesn't particularly interest you or listening to a podcast designed to facilitate sleep, until you feel tired.

Take note of any barriers that may be keeping you awake, such as going to bed while watching TV, using substances before bed (e.g., alcohol or cannabis), allowing pets in your bed, or reading your phone in bed. Start by removing one barrier at a time, so you don't feel too overwhelmed. Keep in mind that you may sleep less in the beginning, but once your time in bed closely matches the time you're sleeping, you can add to your sleeping time every five days by going to bed twenty minutes earlier.

WHY: Limiting your time in bed is an effective, drug-free approach to treating insomnia that outperforms medication. Sleeping poorly creates the urge to linger in bed, which is the opposite of what sleep experts advise. In contrast, reducing your time in bed whets your appetite for sleep and sets you up to do it more efficiently and restfully, often in a matter of weeks. If you feel you need more help than these instructions offer, there are many apps available, including a free one I like called CBT-i Coach, as well as web-based programs like Cleveland Clinic's Go! to Sleep, Sleepio, and Somryst that can help you practice sleep restriction. You may also decide to consult a professional who specializes in CBT-i and can support you as you relearn how to sleep restfully.

No.17 Prioritize an exercise routine.

WHEN: Your physical and mental health matter to you but you haven't been regularly exercising.

HOW: Take a moment to think about your health goals. If you were feeling incredibly motivated, what sort of physical activity would you be doing? How often would you be doing it? If you had a routine that worked well for you in the past, what did it entail?

Because it can feel hard to start a new behavior, brainstorm a SMART (specific, measurable, attainable, realistic, and time-sensitive) goal, whether that's doing a certain number of steps and/or burpees per day; using an app like Couch to 5K, which can help you get into running; finding an online workout you like and committing to doing it three times a week; trying a few group fitness classes until you find one that you want to regularly participate in; or enrolling in a sports league. Once you find an activity you can do and enjoy, pencil in the workout and the number of times you can commit to it this week, being sure to reschedule any missed sessions. Not sure how often you should exercise? Studies pinpoint that doing moderate or high-intensity exercise for an hour three times a week for six weeks improves sadness in people diagnosed with moderate depression. Researchers who studied more than 116,000 adults found that participating in a combination of moderate and vigorous physical activities for an average of 7.5 hours a week significantly increased longevity.

Before you start, ask yourself how likely it is that you will meet your goal on a scale of 0 to 10 (0 being highly unlikely, 10 being very likely). Then think about whether there is anything you can do that might increase that number, like putting your sneakers and workout outfit next to your bed the night before; getting a good playlist ready; or having an accountability buddy. Some of my clients put aside five dollars every time they finish a workout, then eventually reward themselves with a long-coveted workout-related item, like a cool pair of leggings or a new pair of sneakers. Alternatively, some people respond better to the threat of punishment. For example, I like to book workout classes that charge the full fee if I don't cancel twelve hours before—the threat of losing something, technically known as *loss aversion*, motivates me to show up.

After a week, evaluate how you're feeling and revisit your SMART goals to see if you want to tweak anything, like the activity or the number of days you're exercising.

WHY: The research is persuasive: Regular exercise is rich with benefits, such as improved symptoms of depression, anxiety, and stress; more focus and sleep; and reduced cognitive decline and risk of dying. Studies looking at more than 120,000 people have actually shown exercise to be more powerful than antidepressants. Exercise also improves feelings of competence and strengthens one's sense of purpose in life. Many people I work with notice that exercise can kick off a positive chain of events, such as committing to a bedtime, eating better, and even fostering a sense of community. One of my clients who was coping with a brother and a parent who were seriously ill decided that the only thing in his power to do to get unstuck was to increase the number of steps he was walking each day. So he set a goal of walking 8,000 steps a day. Watching himself reach that goal on a daily basis transformed his "stuck" mindset, allowing him to see that there were possibilities in his life and that he didn't have to remain stagnant.

My friends like to joke that group fitness classes are my happy place, and it's true. I go to the same classes[1] at the same times each week, buying discounted class packs and scheduling in advance so I don't have to think much about it. And unlike other parts of my day or life, I maintain the attitude that showing up is what counts; it doesn't matter how I perform as long as I am present and put in effort. That means exercise also helps me move past the urge to be a perfectionist.

---

1 A big thank-you to Brian Evans, Justin Jairam, and Donald Pennington, whose classes I've taken religiously while writing this book. You bring profound joy (and good pain) to my days.

No. 18 Routinely slow your breathing.

WHEN: You want to overhaul your nervous system to reduce chronic stress.

HOW: It's ideal to get in the habit of pacing your breathing for at least twenty minutes once or twice a day. Start by finding a time that works well for you. Then set a timer for twenty minutes and, either sitting up or lying down, gently close your lips. If it's helpful, you can rest your hands on your belly and notice how it rises and falls as you breathe. Gradually slow your breath so that you are inhaling and exhaling every five to six seconds. To maintain this cadence, you can count, use an app, or synchronize to the second hand of a watch. After practicing daily for three months, you can try dropping short periods of paced breathing into your life whenever and wherever you need them (though not when you're driving!).

WHY: By slowing and deepening your breathing, you'll reap multiple benefits, including lowering your resting heart rate; improving your peace of mind; and increasing feelings of relaxation, contentment, alertness, and energy. Inhaling and exhaling for five-second intervals reduces your breathing rate by more than a third (the average person takes eighteen breaths per minute) and has also been shown to lower blood pressure (high blood pressure is associated with irritability and the tendency to be reactive).

For "deeper transformation of how the nervous system and stress response systems function, aim to do this for twenty minutes, ideally twice a day," explained Dr. Patricia Gerbarg, who has taught and researched paced breathing for decades. By formally practicing, it's easier to access this calming pattern of respiration when you're stressed, she explained.

If you're reluctant to set aside that much time, know that investing in a couple of minutes of healthy breathing isn't enough, according to James Nestor, science journalist and author of *Breath: The New Science of a Lost Art*, who likened isolated breathwork practice to eating a salad, then filling yourself with junk food the rest of the day.

No.19 Log your substance use.

WHEN: You regularly consume alcohol or use other substances and wonder if they are affecting your well-being.

HOW: Start by tracking your substance intake to get a clearer picture of your habits over the course of a week or month (you can use an app or pen and paper). Also think about the potential benefits of reducing your use, like sleeping better and making healthier decisions.

Once you have some data on your substance use, get specific about when you want to consume and an amount that would feel ideal. Daily? On weekends? How many drinks total over the course of a week? How do these metrics sync with your life goals?

After you've come up with a concrete target, rather than relying on your memory, start logging (in real time if you can) when you use and how much. I recommend the app Reframe, which focuses on drinking habits, to help clients stay accountable. To track vaping, you can try Quit Vaping or Puff Count. There are lots of options to track cannabis use, including Grounded and QuitNow. You can also use the I Am Sober app for any addiction. Or you can create your own way to track, using a format like this:

Situation	Urge to use (on a scale of 0 to 5)	Emotions and thoughts I noticed prior to using	Was substance used? If so, describe amount.	Short-term impact	Long-term impact

As you make a habit of tracking, give yourself credit not just for reducing your amount but also for simply logging each time you use. It takes effort and vulnerability to log, especially if you're not yet making significant changes. By persisting with careful self-monitoring (the first step to changing a habit), you'll set yourself up to make progress, even if that's cutting a drink a week.

WHY: If you've struggled with your energy, focus, or mood, it may be worth watching your substance intake. Tracking in real time can be an enlightening first step if you want to get a better sense of your habits and tweak them. My patients often notice that there's a sizable discrepancy between their recall of how much they've used and what they log in real time. Knowing you'll be recording every time you ingest sets you up to be more intentional about your use—it forces you to truly notice how much you're using and allows you to observe patterns around when and why you choose to use substances.

Experts notice that initially, the drive to use is primarily for pleasure, but it often evolves into an ingrained habit or a way to manage negative emotions and ward off cravings. Drinking just one to two servings of alcohol within four hours of going to bed can diminish sleep quality by 24 percent, and using cannabis reduces the amount of REM sleep in your sleep cycle. A study looking at more than 36,000 people showed that having one to two alcoholic drinks per day was associated with reductions in brain volume; scarily, consuming more than three to four drinks on a regular basis can lead to brain atrophy. Finally, leaning on substances seems like a missed opportunity to practice skills that can boost your confidence in your ability to cope and be present in your life, whether alone or with loved ones. Knowing you can set a goal and stick to it is a tremendous win in itself.

No. 20 Laugh more!

WHEN: You want to lighten and brighten your life and make those around you feel happier, too.

HOW: According to Stanford University professor Dr. Jennifer Aaker and lecturer Naomi Bagdonas, who teach a course on humor in business, "Our brains are wired to find what we set out to look for." That means it's possible to cultivate a mindset of levity, even if you don't think of yourself as funny. Here are some ways to open your mind and eyes to joy:

▷ *Look for and then list three things that made you smile each day.*

▷ *Notice quirky or entertaining incidents or sights.*

▷ *Catch people smiling or laughing around you and join in.*

▷ *Think about who makes you laugh and spend time with them.*

▷ *Revisit humorous content.*

▷ *Think of behaviors you can implement to take yourself less seriously.*

▷ *Keep a mental list of your favorite funny stories to share with others and try delivering them like you're onstage (think pausing and amping up your animation).*

▷ *Stretch your comedy skills and comfort zone by taking an improv class.*

WHY: Humor boosts resilience, connection, and joy; daily laughter even correlates with longevity. Laughter also lowers blood pressure, heart rate, and stress hormones such as adrenaline and cortisol—that's part of why laughing can feel like such a relief (it's also contagious—if you're skeptical, check out videos on laughter yoga). In one study, caregivers who participated in an improv course designed specifically for their experience saw significant decreases in symptoms of depression and stress. Other studies have found that brief improv training can reduce perfectionism, depression, and anxiety.

Psychologically, laughter can feel like an opportunity to experience lighthearted self-reflection. "When comedians make us laugh, they're often expressing uncomfortable truths we may not easily articulate, creating an experience of catharsis," according to my friend Dr. Peter Shore, a psychologist at the VA Medical Center who also serves as the CEO of The Comedy Store in Los Angeles. Unlike some traits that may feel out of reach, "anybody has the capacity to be funny if they allow themselves to be vulnerable," explained Dr. Shore, who happens to be hilarious and grew up entrenched in comedy (his mother, Mitzi Shore, cofounded the celebrated comedy club and helped launch the careers of many beloved comedians). "It starts with looking at yourself and laughing at your own shortcomings," he said. I can't think of a better tactic to improve your relationship with yourself, others, and your stress than training yourself to notice and create opportunities to giggle.

Comedian Neal Brennan, who has cowritten comedy shows and headlined his own Netflix specials, told me that comedy is also a carthartic way to rebel and spread happiness. "Humor gave me a way to respond to the world," Mr. Brennan told me, explaining how it helped him navigate trauma and depression. "It's an incredible gift." And if your life feels too irritating to find the funny, that's all the more reason to humor me (and yourself!) by trying these strategies.

No. 21 Use a script to make conflict less stressful.

WHEN: You're overthinking asking for what you want or expressing your needs—and don't end up feeling heard or getting what matters to you.

HOW: Think of a current situation where you want to ask for something, resolve an issue, or say no, whether it's in your personal life or at work. Take a moment to get clear on your specific hope for the interaction. You might consider how you want to feel about yourself during and after the exchange and how you want the other person to perceive you.

Next, plug your request into a DBT framework known as DEAR MAN, which helps you make a request or say no without overthinking the issue. It goes like this:

Describe the facts.

Express how you feel.

Ask for what you want.

Reinforce/reward what's in it for the other person.

(Be) **M**indful.

Act confident.

Negotiate as needed.

Being mindful is one way to prevent you from getting lost in past pains or asking for too much. By focusing on your current request in the here and now, you'll be less likely to feel overwhelmed or overwhelm the person you're speaking to. Acting confident is more than just an act; it can help you *feel* confident rather than over-apologizing for expressing your needs. And by showing willingness to negotiate, you can potentially improve a circumstance, even if you don't get your entire request met.

Also reflect on the tone that's appropriate for the situation, whether that's asking gently or being insistent. You can envision a scale of 0 to 10, where 0 is saying nothing, 7 is asking confidently, and 10 is not taking no for an answer. If you're not sure how strongly to ask, consider these questions:

▶ *Can the person you're speaking to actually give you what you want?*

▶ *Do facts support your request (e.g., if you want a raise, consider whether you have researched compensation for similar roles)?*

▶ *Does your ask feel appropriate in the context (e.g., if you're asking a friend for a favor, consider whether you have been a generous friend, too)?*

▶ *Is it a good time to ask?*

Now try out your script in real time. Knowing you have a structure to rely on can make asserting yourself feel less stressful.

WHY: I often think the term "elephant in the room" is a misnomer—there's actually an elephant on our shoulders when we stew over something or put off making a request that matters to us. While it's inevitable that you'll have conflicts in relationships, knowing you can speak up can prevent stress from hanging around. Being able to share your wants and needs in a way that fosters self-respect and increases the odds that you'll be heard is freeing. While the DEAR MAN technique may seem a bit formulaic at first, the more you practice, the more personal and natural it will feel. It will also help you avoid being passive or becoming judgmental, which would likely elicit a negative response.

Finally, using DEAR MAN can allow you to grow closer to the people in your life. Admitting your needs isn't only relieving for you—your feedback can be a gift for others, such as a colleague who inadvertently offended you or a friend who has recently seemed distant.

No. 22 Drop negative gossip.

WHEN: You fill silence or try to improve how you feel about yourself by talking about others.

HOW: To understand what provokes you, think about when you feel most compelled to gossip in a way that isn't driven by a clear intention, like trying to protect someone from being hurt. If you're snarky about others when you're feeling anxious or self-conscious, notice what situations cause those emotions (e.g., dinner with a friend you haven't seen in a while), then remind yourself to be more intentional with your words rather than letting your feelings drive you to blurt out something you'll later regret. It can be hard to break the gossip habit, but there's no reason to compromise your values (like treating others as you'd want to be treated) by spreading details about people that you wouldn't mention in their presence. If certain friends seem to relish gossip, brainstorm an authentic line that warmly encourages them to rethink their urge, like, "Ugh, I know it's so tempting to talk about their drama, but I want to hear about *you*!"

WHY: It's hard to feel connected to others if you speak in alienating ways—and isolation breeds stress. While it's easy to think that sharing juicy tidbits gives you something to bond over and makes *you* seem entertaining, broadcasting your disloyalty is likely to make people cautious about being vulnerable with you. Of course, we all get the temptation to chat about others, especially when we're feeling awkward. Recently, when I met up with a friend, the conversation stalled and I blurted out that a mutual friend of ours was getting divorced. Despite rationalizing my sharing as a way for us to both be supportive

of her, I walked away from what would have otherwise been a joyful meetup worrying that I had said too much and feeling regretful. I found myself thinking that I wouldn't want people talking about intimate, painful details of my life during a casual catch-up.

Rather than believing you're missing out by not gossiping, allow yourself to feel inspired by your ability to be with others in a way that shows you are present and intentional. "Mindless speech only keeps us small and apart from others. Mindful speech comes out of a deep reverence for life," said Dr. Tara Brach, a renowned mindfulness teacher and psychologist. If you're not sure where to start, Dr. Brach cited the Buddha's advice to speak what is true (without exaggerating) and what is helpful. Socializing can be so uplifting—there's no reason to contaminate conversations and your sense of self with chatter that feels negative and takes you away from opening up and focusing on the present.

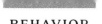

No. 23 Cultivate casual connections.

WHEN: You want to reduce your loneliness and make others feel like they matter.

HOW: Smile at and create genuine interactions with people you come across in your daily life. If this sounds like a reach, begin by choosing one person each day who you encounter in a casual way and making that person feel seen. Start to notice people you regularly cross paths with and interact thoughtfully with them, whether that's offering a warm expression or getting their name and remembering it. These small gestures are the building blocks of community.

WHY: Loneliness and stress are intertwined. That's because feeling isolated elicits a stress response in your body. With more than half of adults in the US reporting that they feel disconnected, it's worthwhile to rethink how you approach your interactions. That starts with realizing that efficiency (say, keeping your head down or peeking at your messages instead of making small talk) can be overrated. In one study, a group of volunteers was instructed to go to a Starbucks and avoid unnecessary conversation and interaction with others. A second group was encouraged to be social by smiling and striking up quick conversations. Results showed that merely taking a few minutes to act gregarious increased positive emotions in participants and improved their sense of connectedness.

I asked my friend Dr. Jonathan Fader, a sports psychologist who seems able to talk to just about anyone, from elite athletes to corporate executives, why casual conversation comes so easily to him. He said he makes bonding a perpetual mission. "I've learned how to say maybe ten words in seventy languages," he told me, describing how trying to instantly establish rapport with people of different backgrounds by greeting them in their primary language is fun—and touching to the receiver. And if you're rushing, Dr. Fader recommended thinking of it as an opportunity: "I'm going to be here anyway— let me be playful with people. In a brief second, that's an act of kindness."

BEHAVIOR
BUFFER

No. **24** Give the gift of curiosity.

WHEN: You quickly dismiss people or you worry about what to say in social situations.

HOW: Rather than prematurely writing people off and missing opportunities to expand your mind and establish new relationships, try leading with curiosity. Pick someone, then approach a conversation eager and open to learning something new (consider doing this with one person a day). Keep your questions open-ended and as short as possible. "Resist that impulse to say, 'Oh yeah, something similar happened to me.' Don't equate your experience with those of others; that really cuts down on your ability to learn something new," advised Celeste Headlee, an award-winning journalist, author of *We Need to Talk: How to Have Conversations That Matter*, and creator of the popular TEDx talk "10 Ways to Have a Better Conversation."

During the conversation, listen well and ask follow-up questions that reflect genuine interest. If you're worried about toeing the line between interested and nosy, Ms. Headlee suggested asking yourself if you'd pose the same question if you were in front of an audience. When the opportunity arises, drop in words of validation, showing understanding and empathy for the person's experiences. If your mind gets pulled into self-focused thoughts, such as what you're going to say next, think of the DBT acronym GIVE (**G**entle, **I**nterested, **V**alidating, and **E**asy manner), which describes how to build and strengthen relationships.

WHY: With Google always at our fingertips, many assume they're experts on everything, Ms. Headlee told me. Yet there is wisdom to be learned from the people we come across, if only we seize these opportunities to engage. "The more you listen to other people's perspectives and stories, the more empathetic you become, the more compassionate you become, the less racist you become," she said. "The upsides are almost limitless."

Curiosity can also broaden your community. Experts who study ways to reduce loneliness pinpoint that it isn't about a lack of social opportunities—it stems from *maladaptive social cognitions*, or thoughts that fuel loneliness, such as mentally critiquing the people around you (*We have nothing in common!*) or negatively judging yourself (*I'm not cool enough, so there's no point in inserting myself*). This kind of thinking perpetuates cynicism and makes it tough to connect.

Research also suggests that paying attention to others without judging them or yourself reduces social worries. If you experience social anxiety, you know that it's easy to hyperfocus on yourself during interactions with others. Repeatedly worrying about what others think isn't only stressful; it can create a self-fulfilling prophecy, because most people don't enjoy interacting with someone who seems distracted. But when you let yourself be fully present by shifting the spotlight from yourself to the other person, you will radiate charisma. "We actually enjoy conversations more the less we talk," Ms. Headlee explained.

Remember that you don't have to be brilliant or hilarious, you merely have to GIVE, which will keep you focused on listening. Letting someone know that you're attentively listening is the ultimate gift, because, at the end of the day, we all want to feel truly seen and heard.

No. 25 Make your bed.

WHEN: You want to start your day feeling accomplished.

HOW: Carve out two minutes to make your bed nicely every morning.

WHY: "If you want to change the world, start off by making your bed," said Admiral William McRaven, a professor at the University of Texas, Austin, in a commencement speech that went viral and evolved into the *New York Times* bestselling book *Make Your Bed: Little Things That Can Change Your Life . . . And Maybe the World.* As a Navy SEAL in training, Admiral McRaven's first task of the day was to ensure his bed was pristine and ready for inspection, with the corners square, his blanket tucked neatly, and his pillow centered in the middle of his headboard. This small chore seemed ridiculous to him at the time, given his long days of strenuous activity, sleep deprivation, and being uncomfortably cold and wet. But he came to appreciate the deeper meaning of this simple task and took pride in completing it.

While I'd recommend finding a middle ground between perfectionism and carelessness, I love the concept of beginning your day in a way that fosters self-respect and accomplishment. A survey of 68,000 people organized by Hunch.com found that 71 percent of bed makers report being happy, while 62 percent of non–bed makers acknowledge being unhappy. Another poll, led by the National Sleep Foundation, found that people who make their beds are 19 percent more likely to have a better night's sleep. While making your bed isn't the sole cause of happiness or good sleep, engaging in positive behaviors *can* spark feelings of competence.

"Making your bed will also reinforce the fact that the little things in life matter. If you can't do the little things right, you will never do the big things right," Admiral McRaven said. "And if by chance you have a miserable day, you will come home to a bed that is made—that you made—and a made bed gives you encouragement that tomorrow will be better."

No. **26** Stick to your plan, not your mood.

WHEN: You haven't been doing much because you're feeling down or unmotivated.

HOW: Realizing that the way you spend your time doesn't have to depend on how you feel at a given moment will help you live a bigger life. Reflect on how your mood impacts your behavior and how your behavior affects your mood. While it's natural to want to push off tasks or cancel plans when you're down or to wait until you're feeling confident to begin working toward a goal, those instincts contribute to a painful cycle, perpetuating your sadness.

Schedule a few activities that will make you feel accomplished or appreciated, even if you're feeling down and sluggish. Start small with something like setting a time to get out the door or rereading the instructions you've been given for an assignment at nine a.m. at your desk, then working on a rough outline for the next thirty minutes. It can help to brainstorm ways to stick to your plans, such as allowing yourself to peruse social media for fifteen minutes only

6:30 A.M.	WAKE UP, MORNING SUN, COHERENT BREATHING
7:00 A.M.	EXERCISE
9:00 A.M.	DEEP WORK
11:30 A.M.	CHECK EMAIL
12:00 P.M.	MINDFUL LUNCH
6:00 P.M.	WALK WITH A FRIEND
10:30 P.M.	BODY SCAN BEFORE BED

after you've spent two hours on your job search or asking a friend if they want to join you on a walk so it's harder to skip it on a whim. Once you complete an activity, take a moment to track how sticking to your plan made you feel (e.g., ticking it off in your planner and pausing to give yourself credit rather than rushing to cross off another item on your list). This will help reinforce your efforts. And if you miss an activity, simply reschedule it. Remember that your goal is to create an antidepressant life, not wait for motivation to carry you forward.

WHY: *Behavioral activation*, or doing more activities that align with your goals and hopes for your life, is an evidence-based approach used to treat depression; when practiced regularly, it has been shown to be as effective as antidepressant medications. How you feel is interconnected with what you do, so letting sadness and/or anxiety dictate your activities only maintains and exacerbates your negative feelings. Experts also encourage behavioral activation for people who experience grief that doesn't seem to lessen over time, as we all need to make space for our sadness while finding ways to move forward.

It's tempting to fall into *procrastivity*, or engaging in lower priority (and lower reward) tasks—say, meticulously organizing your desk or clearing your inbox—instead of doing the most important things, like getting started on a pressing assignment. This only maintains stress, explained Dr. J. Russell Ramsay, a professor at the University of Pennsylvania who runs the Adult ADHD Treatment and Research Program. So beyond acknowledging what you have to do and creating a tentative plan, it's key to understand exactly how and where you may be getting in your own way (e.g., making tasks too big or vague; letting thoughts and emotions drive your behavior). This will help you regularly pivot and "touch" (rather than push off) the tasks that matter to you, Dr. Ramsay told me.

If you're concerned about staying organized, lean on a paper planner or the Structured app. If you want to focus on seeing the connection between accomplishing more and feeling differently, the Daylio Journal app can help.

No. 27 Plot your joy.

WHEN: You're so bogged down by your to-do list that you're postponing having some fun.

HOW: To add doses of happiness to your day, you can:

▶ *Practice loving-kindness (page 74).*

▶ *Pursue your life purpose (page 146).*

▶ *Notice three things you're grateful for.*

▶ *Find a good deed to do.*

▶ *Reminisce about a positive memory.*

▶ *Just as you make appointments, schedule a slate of pleasurable events to look forward to, whether that's taking some time to watch the sunset, hanging out with a friend, trying a new restaurant, exploring a new neighborhood, enrolling in a recreational class, doing a craft project, watching comedy, or fostering a puppy. Pursue a mix of positive experiences, including ones that will boost your joy now (e.g., listening to live music or visiting a museum) and others that will feel meaningful long-term (e.g., strengthening your friendships).*

▶ *Do an activity that's outside your comfort zone. It can be big or small, and you can do it alone or with others—say, taking a dance class or reaching out to someone you respect but are intimidated by.*

Whatever you choose to do, stay present. Nothing spoils a favorite TV show like checking work emails.

WHY: Having enjoyable experiences broadens your mind and behaviors, serving as a protective shield against loneliness and overthinking; these experiences also help connect us to others and to the moment. Merely looking forward to nice plans can fuel anticipatory joy, which has been found to lower stress. Purposefully pursuing positive emotions can even undo the harmful cardiovascular aftereffects of negative emotions. Studies have shown that participants who gave a stressful speech and then watched uplifting video clips recovered faster than participants who watched sad or neutral content. Additionally, researchers have found that moving out of one's comfort zone boosts happiness, perhaps because doing so offers a sense of accomplishment and improves self-perception.

The bottom line: Creating opportunities for happiness shouldn't be an afterthought, because feeling joyful improves your immunity, increases your financial earning power (the happier you are, the more likely you are to pursue opportunities), and strengthens your relationships. We often forget that we can allow ourselves to live more joyfully *now* instead of waiting until we have a wide-open calendar and a mountain of confidence; if we waited until then, we'd be postponing fun for ages.

No. **28** Do one thing at a time.

WHEN: You tend to multitask and often feel distracted or forgetful.

HOW: Given how easy it is to multitask when we have multiple windows and messages popping up, it's crucial to brainstorm how to limit the lure of jumping around on your screens, which drains your ability to monotask. "It's like someone is pouring itching powder on you, then telling you to meditate," Johann Hari, author of *Stolen Focus: Why You Can't Pay Attention—And How to Think Deeply Again*, told me.

Reflect on instances where you're juggling more than one task at a time and how that's working for you (e.g., texting during weekly Zoom meetings leading to poor participation; talking on the phone while you're running an errand resulting in forgetting a key item on your list). If you need extra motivation, jot down the pros and cons of being fully present as opposed to multitasking in various contexts. Then pick a task, personal or professional, where you might experience more enjoyment or productivity by giving it your full focus and commit to doing so (reading a book is a great practice, so you're already off to a nice start).

WHY: Multitasking may be pervasive (and for some of us, a point of pride), but it's virtually impossible to do more than one thing at a time and do them well. "Multitasking is almost always a misnomer, as the human mind and brain lack the architecture to perform two or more tasks simultaneously," according to Drs. Kevin Madore and Anthony Wagner, researchers at Stanford University. Not only is multitasking inefficient, hindering recall and performance, it's stressful: Frequently cited research led by Dr. Gloria Mark, a professor in informatics at the University of California, Irvine, calculated that on average, people spend about three minutes on a task before being interrupted or switching tasks—and it took participants roughly twenty-three minutes to return to the original task!

Whenever logistically possible, getting into the habit of slowing down and exercising your full attention can make a dent in your to-dos *and* mood. Doing one thing at a time is also a key tenet of mindfulness, empowering you to stay centered rather than get sidelined by unhelpful thoughts and impulses. Finding flow—where you're so absorbed in what you're doing that you lose sense of time—starts with fully participating in whatever you're doing. "Being able to focus isn't the biggest issue in the world. There are bigger issues," Mr. Hari told me. But "if we don't get this right, we won't get anything right. Because the person who can't pay attention is drastically less effective at everything they're trying to achieve."

No.29 Sit with uncertainty.

WHEN: You have a hard time accepting the things you can't control and cope by worrying, excessively researching, and painstakingly preparing in ways that don't improve your relationship with anxiety.

HOW: Make a list of the various ways you try to avoid sitting with uncertainty. CBT experts call these subtle forms of avoidance *safety behaviors* (e.g., spending too much time researching before making small and big decisions; asking too many people for their opinion). Think about the specific worries that drive you to do this (e.g., *If I don't make it perfect, people won't respect me* or *If I don't ask people what I should do, I'll make a massive mistake*). Design and try an experiment to test whether your worry is actually accurate. For example, if you'd usually ask a friend to look at a draft of an important email before sending it, send it without getting their opinion first. Track what actually happens, both logistically and emotionally, when you allow for uncertainty. Use those insights to create new opportunities to take small risks (e.g., setting a reasonable time limit for a work assignment rather than endlessly trying to perfect it). Initially, you may experience more anxiety as you let go of your habitual ways of coping, but the more you practice, the more self-confident you'll feel.

WHY: Some people are more prone to what experts refer to as *intolerance of uncertainty*. For these individuals, the combination of facing stress and the difficulty of sitting with not knowing increases the likelihood of ongoing struggles with anxiety. While there are multitudes of ways you can attempt to ward off uncertainty, life ultimately remains uncertain, whether we like it or not. If you're asking friends to interpret ambiguous messages from a dating app, consulting a flight attendant about whether you should expect turbulence, or carrying emergency items everywhere you go in case you need a first aid kit, you know that coping by overpreparing is depleting.

One of my clients endlessly worries about her longevity, wondering how and when she'll die. This is tragic—she's losing time while her unanswerable questions remain unanswerable. So now, instead of running to the doctor every time a health complaint comes up, she is learning to accept minor ailments without a physician's reassurance, which reduces the stress of rushing to last-minute appointments and allows her to appreciate her health.

Throughout writing this, I've felt tempted to ask those around me if they think this book is as good as my last book, or if they think this book will help people and earn good reviews. But how can anyone possibly know what prospective readers will think? So I continually practice noticing when I want assurance, sitting with not knowing, and then self-validating (see page 70), focusing on what I *can* control. Unpacking how you avoid risk is a powerful first step toward facing your fears. By testing your predictions and experimenting with acting differently, you can improve your ability to view the unknown with more acceptance.

BEHAVIOR
BUFFER

No. **30** Approach what you want to avoid.

WHEN: You're procrastinating or trying to escape what's making you anxious, and that behavior is holding you back.

HOW: Notice what you're dodging and how your avoidance is interfering with moving toward what you really want. For instance, maybe you're dreading a long-overdue difficult conversation with your partner, so instead, you busy yourself by doing unnecessary decluttering. To break the pattern, make a list of what you're putting off, from least distressing task to most difficult, then start with what feels easiest (even if that's opening up a blank Word document to start a report). As you approach the task, swap derailing thoughts with more motivating ones (e.g., *It's too much!* → *I can set a timer for ten minutes and just start*). To maintain your motivation, track your experience. You can use a chart like this one:

Task I've been avoiding	Unhealthy assumption	More encouraging thought	Step(s) I took	Takeaway(s)

It's also helpful to track what happens as you inch toward your goals, because it's often easier to remember our fears than what actually transpired. Recording your experiences can also be a nice reminder that overcoming the initial hurdles is worth it.

WHY: Repeatedly facing what you irrationally want to avoid, also known as *exposure therapy*, is the gold standard for treating anxiety. Ultimately, it's the only way to transform your beliefs about your ability to cope and change your relationship with what stresses you out. Over the years, I've worked with many clients who avoid driving due to negative past experiences, yet they find depending on unreliable rideshare apps to be incredibly stressful. By taking small steps—say, signing up for a driving lesson, then driving in a residential area, then driving on a busy road during off-peak hours—people can experience the priceless feeling of capability, even if they feel anxious at times. In fact, the goal of approaching what you want to avoid isn't to extinguish fear—it's to expand your mind and create a life that feels more free. It's normal to experience a surge of fear after seeing a car accident, but instead of trying to make it go away by immediately exiting the freeway, you can keep going, learning that it's possible to feel terrified *and* drive safely. I see so many clients who even avoid uplifting opportunities, such as applying for a new job, due to worries about not being able to tolerate rejection. But avoiding isn't dodging discomfort—it's discounting what you're capable of and what's possible in your life.

No. 31 Rebel, but do it well.

WHEN: You have an urge to express your autonomy and find yourself experiencing impulses that you may later regret if you act on them.

HOW: Try *alternate rebellion*, a DBT strategy that can help you live more authentically without doing any damage. Brainstorm little rebellions, or ways to express your uniqueness, that will give you a taste of freedom, such as breaking all the decorating rules in your living room, performing random anonymous acts of kindness, going to an amusement park in playful garb, trying a new temporary hair color, or dancing to a song in your car. When you get the urge to rebel in a way that won't help you down the line, try an activity from your list. To keep this practice novel, continue to add ideas to your list.

WHY: Feeling as though you have no way to express your individuality is stressful; it's also limiting to assume that the only way to feel free is by doing something drastic. Some people crave expressing their autonomy and find acting rebelliously particularly thrilling. If that resonates with you, find a middle path that honors your urge to rebel without hurting yourself or others. One friend of mine felt very closed in while taking an intense course load in college and decided to wear Adidas sandals with an array of woolly socks year-round rather than conforming to seasonally appropriate trends. My mother channels her rebellious streak and sense of humor by setting up silly pranks, like hiding plastic cockroaches if she hears you're afraid of them. While I don't feel especially rebellious, I love wearing glitter sneakers in professional settings and sending most of my emails in all lowercase letters. The key is channeling your desire to not play by the rules without doing something that leads to self-sabotage.

No. 32 Get a physical (and a therapist) when you need one.

WHEN: You've missed annual medical appointments, especially if you're not feeling your best or you have an injury you've been trying to ignore.

HOW: Check to see if you're overdue for a health-related appointment—it could be physical or emotional (maybe it's time to check in with a former therapist or make an initial appointment with someone new[1]). If you're concerned about fees, find an in-network provider, or if you don't have health insurance, explore low-cost clinics in your community. The No Surprises Act protects you from unexpected bills and requires treatment providers to give you a good faith estimate for the cost of your care up front.

WHY: Improving your relationship to stress can help ease nagging physical issues like headaches and gastrointestinal complaints. But it's also important to take preventative health measures and make sure that you're not missing any underlying medical problems, because untreated health issues can take a toll on our mind, body, and mood. I can't tell you the number of times my clients have discovered that undiagnosed problems such as Lyme disease, sleep disorders, thyroid conditions, autoimmune issues, and vitamin deficiencies explained mental health symptoms that weren't responding to therapy. Skipping routine dental appointments can leave you with a pricey and painful root canal—and also lead to cardiovascular problems. So rather than wait until things are absolutely terrible, make sure that you pursue routine appointments for your physical and emotional health.

---

1 Mental Health America offers free screening questionnaires to help you determine if you meet the criteria for a mental health condition; you can check them out at screening.mhanational.org /screening-tools. ABCT.org is a great resource for finding a behavioral therapist. If you're looking for lower-fee options, calling 211 in the US can help you find local resources.

BEHAVIOR
BUFFER

No. **33** Face your finances.

WHEN: You're worrying about money, whether you're overwhelmed by debt, living paycheck to paycheck, or irrationally anxious about your finances, perhaps due to your upbringing.

HOW: If you've been avoiding looking at your financial statements, credit card bills, or bank account, set a window of time to:

▶ *Look at whether your fixed costs are sustainable.*

▶ *Automate paying your bills, if that's feasible in your situation.*

▶ *Tally up your debt and research payment plan options.*

▶ *Draft a realistic spending plan and plan a recurring time to review your finances.*

▶ *Get a clear sense of your spending patterns with a financial planning app such as You Need a Budget (YNAB).*

If you have some wiggle room, it can be empowering to create what Ramit Sethi, author of *I Will Teach You to Be Rich*, calls a conscious spending plan by dividing your money into four categories: fixed costs, savings, investing, and guilt-free spending. Ideally, your fixed expenses (e.g., your car and rent) amount to less than 60 percent of your post-tax earnings. If not, consider trying to reduce these costs or increase your income. If you overspend on your fixed costs, everything else is going to be tight, said Mr. Sethi, who is contagiously enthusiastic about approaching money more rationally and joyfully. Once you cover recurring expenses, the goal, according to Mr. Sethi, is to save 5–10 percent and invest 5–10 percent of your income in your 401(k) and Roth IRA. After you've accounted for those costs, allow yourself to spend what makes sense in your situation on treating yourself.

If your finances feel too daunting to navigate on your own, know that there are free financial counseling services available, whether through credit agencies or the Foundation for Financial Planning (ffpprobono.org), which offers pro bono services for those who qualify.

WHY: According to a recent study on stress spearheaded by the American Psychological Association, 72 percent of adults worry about money. That's understandable, especially given income inequality and the increasing cost of living. But I was also struck by the simple fact that, according to Mr. Sethi, "Most people don't know the basics of their numbers. For example, 90 percent of the people I talk to who have debt don't know how much money they owe." By making space to sit with the anxiety that arises when taking a closer look at expenses, many people find that they can initiate changes that create more peace of mind. Remarkably, one study showed that pairing low-income parents with a financial coach not only led to increased income and savings but also improved attendance at pediatrician visits.

I don't want to minimize the painful reality that many can't afford to live comfortably despite working constantly. But if you do have flexibility, looking at your income and costs and creating a plan (without excessively checking your accounts due to irrational worries) can make your relationship with your money feel less like an impossible mystery.

No. **34** Examine your mistakes to spark lasting change.

WHEN: You tend to beat yourself up after a setback, blame others for the mistake, or give up, assuming that progress is beyond reach.

HOW: Choose a recent setback you want to focus on (e.g., showing up late to an important event and missing your friend's speech). Rewind the tape of what happened to take a closer look using *chain analysis*, a technique used in DBT to target behaviors you'd like to change. On the left side of a piece of paper, write down exactly what happened, step by step. You might consider what made you more *vulnerable* to being late (poor sleep the night before, not having your coffee ready), the specific *prompting event* (not having a set time to leave your house), *links* that contributed to your mistake (feelings, behaviors, and thoughts, such as *I can do one more thing before I go*), and finally, the *consequences* (feeling stressed the entire way there, not enjoying the night because of your guilt, snapping at your partner when you got home). You can use a format like this:

	WHAT HAPPENED	WHAT I CAN DO DIFFERENTLY
Vulnerabilities		
Prompting event		
Links (including details on your thoughts, feelings, and behaviors)		
Consequences		

Once you have a clear analysis of the key details that contributed to your mistake (despite what you may tell yourself, you're not an idiot who can never get things right), generate solutions at each juncture that can prevent a repeat performance. That way, if you get into a similar situation, you can go about it differently. Continuously approach behaviors you want to change using this technique.

WHY: While it's easy to fall into the *abstinence violation effect*, where you slip up, decide you don't have what it takes to change, and give up, it's key to remember that change is rarely a linear process. That's why, when you face a setback, it's crucial to react flexibly and strategically and continue to grow. Being able to look at and understand why something went awry can help you learn how to do better next time, especially because the same factors repeatedly show up in our lives, leading to similar mistakes. By analyzing and addressing a comprehensive list of the behaviors that factor into holding you back, you can create meaningful and lasting change.

A Final Note: Stress Is Also an Opportunity

OVER THE YEARS, I'VE OFTEN found myself thinking about the first client I had the privilege of meeting with. When we met, I was nervous—I was only a senior in college, majoring in psychology and social work and participating in a clinical internship. Deon was in his forties and living in a men's shelter affiliated with New York City's Bellevue Hospital, where he was receiving treatment for substance abuse and schizoaffective disorder (a condition that impacts mood and can cause psychosis). During our first session, I asked him about his background and his goals. Deon told me about his trauma history and his dependence on crack, which started before he was ten years old to try to escape his emotional pain. I desperately wanted to help, but given my lack of experience and the complexity of his situation, I doubted that anything I could offer would ease his anguish. But I continued asking him questions: "Was there ever a time, in your three decades of substance use, when you had a period of sobriety?" He politely answered, "Barnes & Noble." When I looked at him quizzically, trying to connect how the bookstore chain related to him staying sober, he continued, "I went there every day like it was my job, opening to closing, and spent the time reading books." He went on to explain that this routine helped him achieve his longest period of sobriety—six months—even though he wasn't in a structured program. He did it by setting a realistic goal—showing up every day—which kept him away from temptations and allowed him to experience pleasure and growth in the presence of others.

No one should ever have to experience the hardships Deon endured, yet too many of us face horrific stressors that can lead anyone into crisis. But while we're hoping and advocating for systemic changes to address the societal underpinnings of stress, Deon's experience proves that leaning on accessible lifelines *can* make a difference. Of course he also needed professional help to address his traumas as well as medications to help treat his illness, but his words left a lasting impression on me about the power inside each of us to affect our own mental health by making changes that are within reach.

When you find yourself on the cusp of a vicious cycle—wanting to avoid, escape, or act out due to stress, which will likely cause more stress—remember that you can choose to reset in small or big ways instead. When you do, you'll initiate a virtuous cycle, where you increasingly choose to cope with strategies that reduce stress and amplify your self-worth. Remember, the intention behind resetting isn't for you to do even more but to struggle less and allow your values to light up your life.

I'm repeatedly inspired by witnessing how my clients come to approach frustrating life experiences and injustices with a skillfulness they never imagined possible. Even if implementing the strategies in this book feels overwhelming or out of character at times, improving your relationship with your thoughts, emotions, and physical sensations as well as trying new behaviors won't always feel like a massive reach. Considering how we want to live, harnessing our attention, connecting to people, and slowing our breath and behavior all lack instant allure yet allow us to experience more ease. Almost like stringing together beads on a necklace, stacking these resets and buffers to build long-lasting habits will help you create a life that's full of possibility.

As for me, it's been enlightening to dip into these strategies when I felt depleted myself or was tempted to do something impulsive I'd later regret. On days when I have been up in the middle of the night consoling my toddler after a nightmare, hear disappointing news, and see clients in crisis back to back, I feel grateful for these tools, because we, and the people around us, deserve the best versions of ourselves. Because I'd never prescribe anything to my clients that I'm not personally committed to, I'm glad to say that over the years these skills have helped me get through difficult moments, serving as catalysts for further positive change and bringing more meaning to my life. I feel lucky to have spent decades studying best practices for living, and I want the tools that have changed my days to transform yours as well. Indeed, these resets and buffers can orchestrate a cascade of real changes in every one of us, transforming our physiology and our personal narrative.

Because the goal of self-help isn't only to better ourselves but also to touch others, consider that your efforts, no matter how small, can make a real difference to the people around you. As psychiatrist Jerome Motto famously discovered in a study that followed more than 800 individuals, doing something as simple as sending brief caring letters to someone who experienced a psychiatric crisis significantly reduced the risk of that person dying by suicide. This says so much about the impact of telling others that they matter and you care, whether in good times or more challenging ones.

I hope you never underestimate the power of taking deliberate actions to change the course of your life—and to create a positive ripple effect in the lives of others. What could be more liberating than starting now?

Resources

For links and additional resources, visit drjennytaitz.com/stressresets.

If you need crisis support (for those in the US):

- *Crisis Text Line (crisistextline.org; text HOME to 741741): Trained volunteers can help you cope by text when you are most in need.*

- *The Trevor Project (thetrevorproject.org; text START to 678-678): Offers 24/7 crisis support services to young people in the LGBTQIA+ community.*

- *It Gets Better (itgetsbetter.org): Provides resources and information to LGBTQIA+ youth around the world.*

- *988 Suicide and Prevention Lifeline (988lifeline.org; dial 988): Provides 24/7 free and confidential support to people in distress.*

- *211 (211.org; dial 211): Offers referrals for services ranging from housing to health resources.*

- *Now Matters Now (nowmattersnow.org): Provides DBT skills and support to those coping with suicidal thoughts.*

If you need emotional support but aren't in crisis:

- *Warmlines (warmline.org; available in 40 states in the US): A phone line run by peers who are trained to listen.*

- *Mental Health America (screening.mhanational.org): Offers confidential mental health screenings and resources.*

If you want to find a therapist:

▶ *For experts trained in CBT, DBT, and ACT, visit abct.org.*

▶ *For more information on ACT, visit contextualscience.org.*

▶ *For more details on DBT experts, visit behavioraltech.org or dbt-lbc.org.*

▶ *For low-fee counseling for those without insurance coverage or mental health benefits, visit openpathcollective.org.*

If you need assistance with substance use:

▶ *Substance Abuse and Mental Health Services Administration (samhsa.gov): US Department of Health and Human Services agency that offers information and referrals.*

▶ *Marijuana Anonymous (marijuana-anonymous.org): A peer-led community that offers in-person and virtual support groups to help people improve abstinence from cannabis.*

▶ *Alcoholics Anonymous (aa.org): A peer-led community that offers in-person and virtual support groups to help people eliminate dependence on alcohol.*

▶ *Overeaters Anonymous (oa.org): A community of people who support each other in order to recover from compulsive eating and food behaviors.*

Apps and other resources referenced:

▶ *Songify (page 65): Allows you to plug in your thoughts to create a silly anthem.*

▶ *Joachim Nohl's Breathe (page 98): Guides you through coherent breathing and box breathing.*

▶ *Virtual Hope Box (page 109): Includes customizable tools proven by research to facilitate coping, relaxing, and distraction.*

- *Freedom (page 115): Blocks you from browsing on your phone and computer so you can reclaim focus and productivity (freedom.to).*

- *kSafe (page 115): A time-lock container for stowing devices (thekitchensafe.com).*

- *stickK (page 119): Helps you set goals, track habits, and stick to your commitments by setting up consequences.*

- *Volunteer Match (page 123): Find volunteer opportunities near you (volunteermatch.org).*

- *Habit Tracker; Streaks (page 132): Help you build good habits and motivate you to reach your goals.*

- *Action Day (page 132): My preferred paper planner (actionday.com).*

- *CBT-i Coach, Cleveland Clinic's Go! to Sleep (shop.clevelandclinic wellness.com/products/go-to-sleep-online), sleepio.com, somryst.com (page 162): Help you practice sleep restriction and implement strategies from CBT for insomnia.*

- *Couch to 5K, also known as C25K (page 163): A step-by-step program designed for inexperienced runners.*

- *Reframe (page 166): For tracking alcohol use and drinking habits.*

- *Quit Vaping and Puff Count (page 166): For monitoring vape use.*

- *Grounded and QuitNow (page 166): For monitoring cannabis use.*

- *I Am Sober (page 166): For tracking sobriety.*

- *Daylio Journal; Structured Day Planner (page 179): For tracking your mood and activities.*

- *You Need a Budget (page 190): Helps you get a clear sense of your spending patterns (ynab.com).*

- *Foundation for Financial Planning (page 191): Offers free resources and financial counseling to underserved individuals (ffpprobono.org).*

Therapy Attribution List

To give proper credit and in case you want to learn more, here is a list linking each strategy and concept to the therapy from which it's derived (note there is considerable overlap, as they all share underpinnings in mindfulness and behavioral therapy).

Dialectical Behavior Therapy (DBT)

- distress tolerance
- primary vs. secondary emotions
- beliefs about emotions
- opposite action
- states of mind
- wise mind
- radical acceptance
- self-validation
- list the pros and cons
- mindfulness of emotions
- find meaning
- dip your face in ice water
- intense bursts of exercise
- progressive muscle relaxation
- coherent or paced breathing
- half smile
- STOP
- willingness
- cope ahead
- nonjudgmental stance
- DEAR MAN
- consider how intensely to ask
- GIVE
- plan pleasant events and opportunities to feel accomplished
- do one thing at a time
- alternate rebellion
- chain analysis

Acceptance and Commitment Therapy (ACT)

- *acceptance and willingness*
- *bull's-eye values clarification exercise*
- *matrix exercise*
- *cognitive defusion; sing your thoughts*
- *pursue your life purpose*

The Unified Protocol (UP)—a cognitive behavioral therapy (CBT) program

- *ARC of emotions*
- *think flexibly*
- *staying present during mood induction clips*
- *accept and face physical sensations*
- *approach what you want to avoid*
- *anchoring*
- *core beliefs*
- *beliefs about emotions*
- *subtle forms of avoidance*

Mindfulness-Based Cognitive Therapy (MBCT)

- *the body scan*
- *the three-minute breathing space*

References

INTRODUCTION

American Psychological Association. 2022. More than a quarter of US adults say they're so stressed they can't function. https://www.apa.org/news/press/releases/2022/10/multiple-stressors-no-function

Carlucci, L., Saggino, A., and Balsamo, M. 2021. On the efficacy of the Unified Protocol for transdiagnostic treatment of emotional disorders: A systematic review and meta-analysis. *Clinical Psychology Review, 87*, 10199.

Ettman, C. K., Cohen, G. H., Abdalla, S. M., Sampson, L., Trinquart, L., Castrucci, B. C., Bork, R. H., Clark, M. A., Wilson, I., Vivier, P. M., and Galea, S. 2022. Persistent depressive symptoms during COVID-19: A national, population-representative, longitudinal study of U.S. adults. *Lancet Regional Health, Americas, 5*, 100091.

Kiecolt-Glaser, J. K., and Wilson, S. J. 2017. Lovesick: How couples' relationships influence health. *Annual Review of Clinical Psychology, 13*, 421–443.

Lazarus, R. S., and Folkman S. 1984. *Stress, appraisal, and coping.* Berlin: Springer.

Reid Finlayson, A. J., Macoubrie, J., Huff, C., Foster, D. E., and Martin, P. R. 2022. Experiences with benzodiazepine use, tapering, and discontinuation: An internet survey. *Therapeutic Advances in Psychopharmacology, 12*, 20451253221082386.

Sandi, C. 2013. Stress and cognition. *Wiley Interdisciplinary Reviews: Cognitive Science, 4*, 245–261.

Sarangi, A., McMahon, T., and Gude, J. 2021. Benzodiazepine misuse: An epidemic within a pandemic. *Cureus, 13*, e15816. https://doi.org/10.7759/cureus.15816

Sauer-Zavala, S., Rosellini, A. J., Bentley, K. H., Ametaj, A. A., Boswell, J. F., Cassiello-Robbins, C., Wilner Tirpak, J., Farchione, T. J., and Barlow, D. H. 2021. Skill acquisition during transdiagnostic treatment with the Unified Protocol. *Behavior Therapy, 52*, 1325–1338.

Selye, H. 1974. Stress without distress. In G. Serban (Ed.), *Psychopathology of human adaptation* (pp. 137–146). Boston, MA: Springer.

Twenge, J. M., and Joiner, T. E. 2020. U.S. Census Bureau-assessed prevalence of anxiety and depressive symptoms in 2019 and during the 2020 COVID-19 pandemic. *Depression and Anxiety, 37,* 954–956.

World Health Organization. 2022. COVID-19 pandemic triggers 25% increase in prevalence of depression and anxiety worldwide. https://www.who.int/news /item/02-03-2022-covid-19-pandemic-triggers-25-increase-in-prevalence-of -anxiety-and-depression-worldwide

PART ONE

CHAPTER 1

Baumeister, R. F., Vohs, K. D., Aaker, J. L., and Garbinsky, E. N. 2013. Some key differences between a happy life and a meaningful life. *The Journal of Positive Psychology, 8,* 505–516.

Beck A. T., Epstein, N., Brown, G., and Steer, R. A. 1988. An inventory for measuring clinical anxiety: Psychometric properties. *Journal of Consulting and Clinical Psychology, 56,* 893.

Beltzer, M. L., Nock, M. K., Peters, B. J., and Jamieson, J. P. 2014. Rethinking butterflies: The affective, physiological, and performance effects of reappraising arousal during social evaluation. *Emotion, 14,* 761–768.

Brooks, A. W. 2013. Get excited: Reappraising pre-performance anxiety as excitement. *Journal of Experimental Psychology, 143,* 1144–1158.

Bystritsky, A. and Kronemyer, D. 2014. Stress and anxiety: Counterpart elements of the stress/anxiety complex. *Psychiatric Clinics of North America, 37,* 489–518.

Carver, C. S., and Conner-Smith, J. 2010. Personality and coping. *Annual Review of Psychology, 61,* 679–704.

Cohen S., Janicki-Deverts, D., and Miller, G. E. 2007. Psychological stress and disease. *JAMA, 298,* 1685–1687.

Cohen, S., Kamarck, T., and Mermelstein, R. 1983. A global measure of perceived stress. *Journal of Health and Social Behavior, 24,* 385–396.

Crum, A. J., Jamieson, J. P., and Akinola, M. 2020. Optimizing stress: An integrated intervention for regulating stress responses. *Emotion, 20,* 120–125.

Dweck, C. S. 2007. *Mindset: The new psychology of success*. New York: Ballantine Books.

Jamieson, J. P., Black, A. E., Pelaia, L. E., Gravelding, H., Gordis, J., and Reis, H. T. 2022. Reappraising stress arousal improves affective, neuroendocrine, and academic performance outcomes in community college classrooms. *Journal of Experimental Psychology, 151*, 197–212.

Jamieson, J. P., Mendes, W. B., Blackstock, E., and Schmadar, T. 2010. Turning the knots in your stomach into bows: Reappraising arousal improves performance on the GRE. *Journal of Experimental Social Psychology, 46*, 208–212.

Kassam, K. S., Koslov, K., and Mendes, W. B. 2009. Decisions under distress: Stress profiles influence anchoring and adjustment. *Psychological Science, 20*, 1394–1399.

Keller, A., Litzelman, K., Wisk, L. E., Maddox, T., Cheng, E. R., Creswell, P. D., and Witt, W. P. 2012. Does the perception that stress affects health matter? The association with health and mortality. *Health Psychology, 31*, 677–684.

Kiecolt-Glaser, J. K., Renna, M. E., Shrout, M. R., and Madison, A. A. 2020. Stress reactivity: What pushes us higher, faster and longer—And why it matters. *Current Directions in Psychological Science, 29*, 492–498.

Lazarus, R. S., and Folkman, S. 1984. *Stress, appraisal, and coping*. Berlin: Springer.

Leyro, T. M., Zvolensky, M. J., and Bernstein, A. 2010. Distress tolerance and psychopathological symptoms and disorders: A review of the empirical literature among adults. *Psychological Bulletin, 136*, 576–600.

McEwen, B. 2000. Allostasis and allostatic load: Implications for neuropsychopharmacology. *Neuropsychopharmacology, 22*, 108–124.

Mendes, W. B., Blascovich, J., Hunter, S. B., Lickel, B., and Jost, J. T. 2007. Threatened by the unexpected: Physiological responses during social interactions with expectancy-violating partners. *Journal of Personality and Social Psychology, 92*, 698–716.

Oveis, C., Gu, Y., Ocampo, J. M., Hangen, E. J., and Jamieson, J. P. 2020. Emotion regulation contagion: Stress reappraisal promotes challenge responses in teammates. *Journal of Experimental Psychology, 149*, 2187–2205.

Ritschel, L. A., Lim, N. E., and Stewart, L. M. 2015. Transdiagnostic applications of DBT for adolescents and adults. *The American Journal of Psychotherapy, 69*, 111–128.

Sakiris, N., and Berle, D. 2019. A systematic review and meta-analysis of the Unified Protocol as a transdiagnostic emotion regulation based intervention. *Clinical Psychology Review, 72*, 101751.

Seery, M. D. 2011. Resilience: A silver lining to experiencing adverse life events? *Current Directions in Psychological Science, 20*, 390–394.

Seery, M. D., Leo, R. J., Lupien, S. P., Kondrak, C. L., and Almonte, J. L. 2013. An upside to adversity? Moderate cumulative lifetime adversity is associated with resilient responses in the face of controlled stressors. *Psychological Science, 24*, 1181–1189.

Tomaka, J., Blascovich, J., Kelsey, R. M., and Leitten, C. L. 1993. Subjective, physiological, and behavioral effects of threat and challenge appraisal. *Journal of Personality and Social Psychology, 65*, 248–260.

Yeager, D. S., Bryan, C. J., Gross, J. J., Murray, J., Krettek, D., Santos, P., Graveling, H., Johnson, M., and Jamieson, J. P. 2022. A synergistic mindsets intervention protects adolescents from stress. *Nature, 607*, 512–520.

Yeager, D. S., Walton, G. M., Brady, S. T., Akcinar, E. N., Paunesku, D., Keane, L., Kamentz, D., Ritter, G., Duckworth, A. L., Urstein, R., Gomez, E. M., Markus, H. R., Cohen, G. L., and Dweck, C. S. 2016. Teaching a lay theory before college narrows achievement gaps at scale. *Proceedings of the National Academy of Sciences of the United States of America, 113*, E3341–E3348.

CHAPTER 2

Aldao, A. 2013. The future of emotion regulation research: Capturing context. *Perspectives in Psychological Science, 8*, 155–172.

Barlow, D. H., Farchione, T. J., Bullis, J. R., Gallagher, M. W., Murray-Latin, H., Sauer-Zavala, S., Bentley, K. H., Thompson-Hollands, J., Conklin, L. R., Boswell, J. F., Ametaj, A., Carl, J. R., Boettcher, H. T., and Cassiello-Robbins, C. 2017. The Unified Protocol for transdiagnostic treatment of emotional disorders compared with diagnosis-specific protocols for anxiety disorders: A randomized clinical trial. *JAMA Psychiatry, 74*, 875–884.

Barlow, D. H., Sauer-Zavala, S., Farchione, T. J., Latin, H. M., Ellard, K. K., Bullis, J. R., Bentley, K. H., Boettcher, H. T., and Cassiello-Robbins, C. 2018. *Unified Protocol for transdiagnostic treatment of emotional disorders,* (2nd ed.). New York: Oxford University Press.

Carlucci, L., Saggino, A., and Balsamo, M. 2021. On the efficacy of the Unified Protocol for transdiagnostic treatment of emotional disorders: A systematic review and meta-analysis. *Clinical Psychology Review, 87*, 101999.

Craske, M. G., Treanor, M., Conway, C. C., Zbozinek, T., and Vervliet, B. 2014. Maximizing exposure therapy: An inhibitory learning approach. *Behaviour Research and Therapy, 58*, 10–23.

De Castella, K., Platow, M. J., Tamir, M., and Gross, J. J. 2018. Beliefs about emotion: Implications for avoidance-based emotion regulation and psychological health. *Cognition & Emotion, 32*, 773–795.

Dimidjian, S., Hollon, S. D., Dobson, K. S., Schmaling, K. B., Kohlenberg, R. J., Addis, M. E., Gallop, R., McGlinchey, J. B., Markley, D. K., Gollan, J. K., Atkins, D. C., Dunner, D. L., and Jacobson, N. S. 2006. Randomized trial of behavioral activation, cognitive therapy, and antidepressant medication in the acute treatment of adults with major depression. *Journal of Consulting and Clinical Psychology, 74*, 658–670.

Folkman, S., and Lazarus, R. S. 1988. Coping as a mediator of emotion. *Journal of Personality and Social Psychology, 54*, 466–475.

Ford, B. Q., and Gross, J. J. 2019. Why beliefs about emotion matter: An emotion-regulation perspective. *Current Directions in Psychological Science, 28*, 74–81.

Goldin, P. R., McRae, K., Ramel, W., and Gross, J. J. 2008. The neural bases of emotion regulation: Reappraisal and suppression of negative emotion. *Biological Psychiatry, 63*, 577–586.

Gross, J. J. 2015. The extended process model of emotion regulation: Elaborations, applications, and future directions. *Psychological Inquiry, 26*, 130–137.

Hayes, S. C., Ciarrochi, J., Hoffman, S. G., Chin, F., and Sahdra, B. 2022. Evolving an idionomic approach to processes of change: Towards a unified personalized science of human improvement. *Behaviour Research and Therapy, 156*, 104155.

Lindsay, E. K., Young, S., Smyth, J. M., Brown, K. W., and Creswell, J. D. 2018. Acceptance lowers stress reactivity: Dismantling mindfulness training in a randomized controlled trial. *Psychoneuroendocrinology, 87*, 63–73.

Linehan, M. M. 2015. *DBT skills training manual,* (2nd ed.). New York: Guilford Press.

Moore, S. A., Zoellner, L. A., and Mollenholt, N. 2008. Are expressive suppression and cognitive reappraisal associated with stress-related symptoms? *Behaviour Research and Therapy, 46,* 993–1000.

Roberts, N. A., Levenson, R. W., and Gross, J. J. 2008. Cardiovascular costs of emotion suppression cross ethnic lines. *International Journal of Psychophysiology, 70,* 82–87.

Schleider, J. L., Mullarkey, M. C., Fox, K. R., Dobias, M. L., Shroff, A., Hart, E. A., and Roulston, C. A. 2022. A randomized trial of online single-session interventions for adolescent depression during COVID-19. *Nature Human Behavior, 6,* 258–268.

Tamir, M., and Bigman, Y. E. 2018. Expectations influence how emotions shape behavior. *Emotion, 18,* 15–25.

Tamir, M., John, O. P., Srivastava, S., and Gross, J. J. 2007. Implicit theories of emotion: Affective and social outcomes across a major life transition. *Journal of Personality and Social Psychology, 92,* 731–744.

Tamir, M., Vishkin, A., and Gutentag, T. 2020. Emotion regulation is motivated. *Emotion, 20,* 115–119.

Troy, A. S., Shallcross, A. J., and Mauss, I. B. 2013. A person-by-situation approach to emotion regulation: Cognitive reappraisal can either help or hurt, depending on the context. *Psychological Science, 24,* 2505–2514.

CHAPTER 3

Boren, J. P. 2014. The relationships between co-rumination, social support, stress, and burnout among working adults. *Management Communication Quarterly, 28,* 3–25.

Borkovec, T. D., Robinson, E., Pruzinsky, T., and DePree, J. A. 1983. Preliminary exploration of worry: Some characteristics and processes. *Behaviour Research and Therapy, 21,* 9–16.

Brosschot, J. F. 2017. Ever at the ready for events that never happen. *European Journal of Psychotraumatology, 8,* 1309934.

Brosschot, J. F., Van Dijk, E., and Thayer, J. F. 2007. Daily worry is related to low heart rate variability during waking and the subsequent nocturnal sleep period. *International Journal of Psychophysiology, 63,* 39–47.

Callesen, P., Reeves, D., Heal, C., and Wells, D. 2020. Metacognitive therapy versus cognitive behaviour therapy in adults with major depression: A parallel single-blind randomised trial. *Scientific Reports, 10,* 7878.

Chung, M-S. 2014. Pathways between attachment and marital satisfaction: The mediating roles of rumination, empathy, and forgiveness. *Personality and Individual Differences, 70,* 246–251.

Elhai, J. D., Rozgonjuk, D., Alghraibeh, A. M., Levine, J. C., Alafnan, A. A., Aldraiweesh, A. A., Aljomaa, S. S., and Hall, B. J. 2020. Excessive reassurance seeking mediates relations between rumination and problematic smartphone use. *Bulletin of the Menninger Clinic, 84,* 137–155.

Gerin, W., Davidson, K. W., Christenfeld, N. J. S., Goyal, T., and Schwartz, J. E. 2006. The role of angry rumination and distraction in blood pressure recovery from emotional arousal. *Psychosomatic Medicine, 68,* 64–72.

Gerin, W., Zawadzki, M.J., Brosschot, J. F., Thayer, J. F., Christenfeld, N. J. S., Campbell, T. S., and Smyth, J. M. 2012. Rumination as a mediator of chronic stress effects on hypertension: A causal model. *International Journal of Hypertension, 2012,* 453465.

Gortner, E. M., Rude, S. S., and Pennebaker, J. W. 2006. Benefits of expressive writing in lowering rumination and depressive symptoms. *Behavior Therapy, 37,* 292–303.

Killingsworth, M. A., and Gilbert, D. T. 2010. A wandering mind is an unhappy mind. *Science, 330,* 932.

King, A. P., and Fresco, D. M. 2019. A neurobehavioral account for decentering as the salve for the distressed mind. *Current Opinion in Psychology, 28,* 285–293.

Kross, E., and Ayduk, O. 2017. Self-distancing: Theory, research, and current directions. In J. M. Olson (Ed.), *Advances in experimental social psychology* (pp. 81–136). Cambridge, Massachusetts: Elsevier Academic Press.

la Cour, P., and Petersen, M. 2015. Effects of mindfulness meditation on chronic pain: A randomized controlled trial. *Pain Medicine, 16,* 641–652.

McLaughlin, K.A., and Nolen-Hoeksema, S. 2011. Rumination as a transdiagnostic factor in depression and anxiety. *Behavior Research and Therapy, 49,* 186–193.

Nolen-Hoeksema, S., and Morrow, J. 1991. A prospective study of depression and posttraumatic stress symptoms after a natural disaster: The 1989 Loma Prieta earthquake. *Journal of Personality and Social Psychology, 1,* 115–121.

Nolen-Hoeksema, S., Stice, E., Wade, E., and Bohon, C. 2007. Reciprocal relations between rumination and bulimic, substance abuse, and depressive symptoms in female adolescents. *Journal of Abnormal Psychology, 116*, 198–207.

Nolen-Hoeksema, S., Wisco B. E., and Lyubomirsky, S. 2008. Rethinking rumination. *Perspectives on Psychological Science, 3*, 400–424.

Ottaviani, C., Shapiro, D., and Fitzgerald, L. 2011. Rumination in the laboratory: What happens when you go back to everyday life? *Psychophysiology, 48*, 453–461.

Ottaviani, C., Thayer, J. F., Verkuil, B., Lonigro, A., Medea, B., Couyoumdjian, A., and Brosschot, J. F. 2016. Physiological concomitants of perseverative cognition: A systematic review and meta-analysis. *Psychological Bulletin, 142*, 231–259.

Palmieri, S., Mansueto, G., Scaini, S., Caselli, G., Sapuppo, W., Spada, M. M., Sassaroli, S., et al. 2021. Repetitive negative thinking and eating disorders: A meta-analysis of the role of worry and rumination. *Journal of Clinical Medicine, 10*, 2448.

Pedersen, H., Grønnæss, I., Bendixen, M., Hagen, R., and Kennair, L. E. O. 2022. Metacognitions and brooding predict depressive symptoms in a community adolescent sample. *BMC Psychiatry, 22*, 157.

Pennebaker, J. W. 1997. Writing about emotional experiences as a therapeutic process. *Psychological Science, 8*, 162–166.

Salzberg, S. 2023. *Real life: The journey from isolation to openness and freedom.* New York: Flatiron Books.

Sloan, D. M., Marx, B. P., Epstein, E. M., and Dobbs, J. L. 2008. Expressive writing buffers against maladaptive rumination. *Emotion, 8*, 302–306.

Smyth, J., and Helm, R. 2003. Focused expressive writing as self-help for stress and trauma. *Journal of Clinical Psychology, 59*, 227–235.

Smyth, J., Zawadzki, M., and Gerin, W. 2013. Stress and disease: A structural and functional analysis. *Social and Personality Psychology Compass, 7*, 217–227.

Watkins, E. R. 2016. *Rumination-focused cognitive-behavioral therapy for depression.* New York: Guilford Press.

Wells, A. 2009. *Metagcognitive therapy for anxiety and depression.* New York: Guilford Press.

White, R. E., Kuehn, M. M., Duckworth, A. L., Kross, E., and Ayduk, Ö. 2019. Focusing on the future from afar: Self-distancing from future stressors facilitates adaptive coping. *Emotion, 19,* 903–916.

Zawadzki, M. J., Graham, J. E., and Gerin, W. 2013. Rumination and anxiety mediate the effect of loneliness on depressed mood and sleep quality in college students. *Health Psychology, 32,* 212–222.

CHAPTER 4

Aaker, J., and Bagdonas, N. 2021. *Humor, seriously: Why humor is a secret weapon in business and life.* New York: Currency.

Albrecht, B., Staiger, P. K., Hall, K., Miller, P., Best, D., and Lubman, D. I. 2014. Benzodiazepine use and aggressive behaviour: A systematic review. *The Australian and New Zealand Journal of Psychiatry, 48,* 1096–1114.

Berwid, O. G., and Halperin, J. M. 2012. Emerging support for a role of exercise in attention-deficit/hyperactivity disorder intervention planning. *Current Psychiatry Reports, 14,* 543–551.

Burns, D. D. 1999. *Feeling good: The new mood therapy.* New York: William Morrow.

Carpenter, J. K., Andrews, L. A., Witcraft, S. M., Powers, M. B., Smits, J., and Hofmann, S. G. 2018. Cognitive behavioral therapy for anxiety and related disorders: A meta-analysis of randomized placebo-controlled trials. *Depression and Anxiety, 35,* 502–514.

Craske, M. G., Treanor, M., Conway, C. C., Zbozinek, T., and Vervliet, B. 2014. Maximizing exposure therapy: An inhibitory learning approach. *Behaviour Research and Therapy, 58,* 10–23.

DeRubeis, R. J., Siegle, G. J., and Hollon, S. D. 2008. Cognitive therapy versus medication for depression: Treatment outcomes and neural mechanisms. *Nature Reviews. Neuroscience, 9,* 788–796.

He, Q., Chen, X., Wu, T., Li, L., and Fei, X. 2019. Risk of dementia in long-term benzodiazepine users: Evidence from a meta-analysis of observational studies. *Journal of Clinical Neurology, 15,* 9–19.

Huijbers, M. J., Spinhoven, P., Spijker, J., Ruhé, H. G., van Schaik, D. J., van Oppen, P., Nolen, W. A., Ormel, J., Kuyken, W., van der Wilt, G. J., Blom, M. B., Schene, A. H., Rogier, A., Donders, T., and Speckens, A. E. 2016. Discontinuation of antidepressant medication after mindfulness-based cognitive therapy for recurrent depression: Randomised controlled non-inferiority trial. *The British Journal of Psychiatry, 208*, 366–373.

Jacob, J. A. 2015. Marijuana use has doubled among US adults. *JAMA, 314*, 2607.

Lac, A., and Luk, J. W. 2018. Testing the amotivational syndrome: Marijuana use longitudinally predicts lower self-efficacy even after controlling for demographics, personality, and alcohol and cigarette use. *Prevention Science, 19*, 117–126.

Lann, M. A., and Molina, D. K. 2009. A fatal case of benzodiazepine withdrawal. *The American Journal of Forensic Medicine and Pathology, 30*, 177–179.

Lopez-Quintero, C., Pérez de los Cobos, J., Hasin, D. S., Okuda, M., Wang, S., Grant, B. F., and Blanco, C. 2011. Probability and predictors of transition from first use to dependence on nicotine, alcohol, cannabis, and cocaine: Results of the National Epidemiologic Survey on Alcohol and Related Conditions (NESARC). *Drug and Alcohol Dependence, 115*, 120–130.

Maust, D. T., Lin, L. A., and Blow, F. C. 2019. Benzodiazepine use and misuse among adults in the United States. *Psychiatric Services, 70*, 97–106.

Miller, W. R., and Rollnick, S. 2012. *Motivational interviewing: Preparing people for change.* (3rd ed.). New York: Guilford Press.

Pélissolo, A., Maniere, F., Boutges, B., Allouche, M., Richard-Berthe, C., and Corruble, E. 2007. Anxiety and depressive disorders in 4,425 long term benzodiazepine users in general practice. *L'encephale, 33*, 32–38.

Roshanaei-Moghaddam, B., Pauly, M. C., Atkins, D. C., Baldwin, S. A., Stein, M. B., and Roy-Byrne, P. 2011. Relative effects of CBT and pharmacotherapy in depression versus anxiety: Is medication somewhat better for depression, and CBT somewhat better for anxiety? *Depression and Anxiety, 28*, 560–567.

Santo, L., Rui, P., and Ashman, J. J. 2020. Physician office visits at which benzodiazepines were prescribed: Findings from 2014–2016 National Ambulatory Medical Care Survey. National Health Statistics Reports ; No. 137; DHHS publication; No. 2020–1250.

Sarangi, A., McMahon, T., and Gude, J. 2021. Benzodiazepine misuse: An epidemic within a pandemic. *Cureus, 13*, e15816.

Soyka, M. 2017. Treatment of benzodiazepine dependence. *The New England Journal of Medicine, 376*, 1147–1157.

Volkow, N. D., Wang, G. J., Telang, F., Fowler, J. S., Alexoff, D., Logan, J., Jayne, M., Wong, C., and Tomasi, D. 2014. Decreased dopamine brain reactivity in marijuana abusers is associated with negative emotionality and addiction severity. *Proceedings of the National Academy of Sciences of the United States of America, 111*, E3149–E3156.

Whitaker, R. 2010. *Anatomy of an epidemic: Magic bullets, psychiatric drugs, and the astonishing rise of mental illness in America.* New York: Crown Publishers.

Williams, A. R., and Hill, K. P. 2020. Care of the patient using cannabis. *Annals of Internal Medicine, 173*, ITC65–ITC80.

CHAPTER 5

Cohen, G. L., Garcia, J., Apfel, N., and Master, A. 2006. Reducing the racial achievement gap: A social-psychological intervention. *Science, 313*, 1307–1310.

Cohen, G. L., and Sherman, D. K. 2014. The psychology of change: Self-affirmation and social psychological intervention. *Annual Review of Psychology, 65*, 333–371.

Cohen, S., Doyle, W. J., Skoner, D. P., Rabin, B. S., and Gwaltney, J. M., Jr. 1997. Social ties and susceptibility to the common cold. *JAMA, 277*, 1940–1944.

Cohen, S., Gianaros, P. J., and Manuck, S. B. 2016. A stage model of stress and disease. *Perspectives on Psychological Science, 11*, 456–463.

Cohen, S., and Wills, T. A. 1985. Stress, social support, and the buffering hypothesis. *Psychological Bulletin, 9*, 310–357.

Daly, M., Baumeister, R.F., Delaney, L., and MacLachlan, M. 2014. Self-control and its relation to emotions and psychobiology: Evidence from a day reconstruction method study. *Journal of Behavioral Medicine, 37*, 81–93.

de Shazer, S., Dolan, Y., Korman, H., Trepper, T., McCollum, E., and Berg, I. K. 2007. *More than miracles: The state of the art of solution-focused brief therapy.* New York: Routledge.

Goyer, J. P., Garcia, J., Purdie-Vaughns, V., Binning, K. R., Cook, J. E., Reeves, S. L., Apfel, N., Taborsky-Barba, S., Sherman, D. K., and Cohen, G. L. 2017. Self-affirmation facilitates minority middle schoolers' progress along college trajectories. *Proceedings of the National Academy of Sciences of the United States of America, 114*, 7594–7599.

Hirsh, J. B., Mar, R. A., and Peterson, J. B. 2012. Psychological entropy: A framework for understanding uncertainty-related anxiety. *Psychological Review, 119*, 304–320.

Lundgren, T., Luoma, J. B., Dahl, J., Strosahl, K., and Melin, L. 2012. The bull's-eye values survey: A psychometric evaluation. *Cognitive and Behavioral Practice, 19*, 518–526.

McCracken, L. M., and Vowles, K. E. 2014. Acceptance and commitment therapy and mindfulness for chronic pain: Model, process, and progress. *American Psychologist, 69*, 178–187.

Ostafin, B. D., and Proulx, T. 2020. Meaning in life and resilience to stressors. *Anxiety, Stress, and Coping, 33*, 603–622.

Park, J., and Baumeister, R. F. 2017. Meaning in life and adjustment to daily stressors. *The Journal of Positive Psychology, 12*, 333–341.

Polk, K. L., Schoendorff, B., Webster, M., and Olaz, F. O. 2016. *The essential guide to the ACT matrix.* Oakland, CA: Context Press.

Schaefer, S. M., Morozink Boylan, J., van Reekum, C. M., Lapate, R. C., Norris, C. J., Ryff, C. D., and Davidson, R. J. 2013. Purpose in life predicts better emotional recovery from negative stimuli. *PLoS ONE, 8*, e80329.

Sung, J. Y., Bugatti, M., Vivian, D., and Schleider, J. L. 2023. Evaluating a telehealth single-session consultation service for client on psychotherapy wait-lists. *Practice Innovations, 8*, 141–161.

Tangney, J. P., Baumeister, R. F., and Boone, A. L. 2004. High self-control predicts good adjustment, less pathology, better grades, and interpersonal success. *Journal of Personality, 72*, 271–322.

Tifft, E. D., Underwood, S. B., Roberts, M. Z., and Forsyth, J. P. 2022. Using meditation in a control vs. acceptance context: A preliminary evaluation of relations with anxiety, depression, and indices of well-being. *Journal of Clinical Psychology, 78*, 1407–1421.

Zhang, A., Franklin, C., Currin-McCulloch, J., Park, S., and Kim, J. 2018. The effectiveness of strength-based, solution-focused brief therapy in medical settings: A systematic review and meta-analysis of randomized controlled trials. *Journal of Behavioral Medicine, 41*, 139–151.

Allen, A. B., and Leary, M. R. 2010. Self-compassion, stress, and coping. *Social and Personality Psychology Compass, 4*, 107–118.

Aytur, S. A., Ray, K. L., Meier, S. K., Campbell, J., Gendron, B., Waller, N., and Robin, D. A. 2021. Neural mechanisms of acceptance and commitment therapy for chronic pain: A network-based fMRI approach. *Frontiers in Human Neuroscience, 15*, 587018.

Balban, M. Y., Neri, E., Kogon, M. M., Weed, L., Nouriani, B., Jo, B., Holl, G., Zeitzer, J. M., Spiegel, D., and Huberman, A. D. 2023. Brief structured practices enhance mood and reduce physiological arousal. *Cell Reports Medicine, 4*, 100895.

Barlow, D. H., Sauer-Zavala, S., Farchione, T. J., Latin, H. M., Ellard, K. K., Bullis, J. R., Bentley, K. H., Boettcher, H. T., and Cassiello-Robbins, C. 2018. *Unified Protocol for transdiagnostic treatment of emotional disorders,* (2nd ed.). New York: Oxford University Press.

Basso, J. C., and Suzuki, W. A. 2017. The effects of acute exercise on mood, cognition, neurophysiology, and neurochemical pathways: A review. *Brain Plasticity, 2*, 127–152.

Baumeister, R. F., Bratslavsky, E., Finkenauer, C., and Vohs, K. D. 2001. Bad is stronger than good. *Review of General Psychology, 5*, 323–370.

Baumeister, R. F., Tice, D. M., and Vohs, K. D. 2018. The strength model of self-regulation: Conclusions from the second decade of willpower research. *Perspectives on Psychological Science, 13*, 141–145.

Beames, J. R., Schofield, T. P., and Denson, T. F. 2018. A meta-analysis of improving self-control with practice. In D. de Ridder, M. Adriaanse, and K. Fujita (Eds.), *The Routledge international handbook of self-control in health and well-being* (pp. 405–417). New York: Routledge/Taylor & Francis Group.

Bell, A. C., and D'Zurilla, T. J. 2009. Problem-solving therapy for depression: A meta-analysis. *Clinical Psychology Review, 29*, 348–353.

Bellissimo, G. F., Ducharme, J., Mang, Z., Millender, D., Smith, J., Stork, M. J., Little, J. P., Deyhle, M. R., Gibson, A. L., de Castro Magalhaes, F., and Amorim, F. 2022. The acute physiological and perceptual responses between bodyweight and treadmill running high-intensity interval exercises. *Frontiers in Physiology, 13*, 824154.

Berk, M. S., Henriques, G. R., Warman, D. M., Brown, G. K., and Beck, A. T. 2004. A cognitive therapy intervention for suicide attempters: An overview of the treatment and case examples. *Cognitive and Behavioral Practice, 11,* 265–277.

Boren, J. P. 2013. The relationships between co-rumination, social support, stress, and burnout among working adults. *Management Communication Quarterly, 28,* 3–25.

Bowen, S., Chawla, N., Collins, S. E., Witkiewitz, K., Hsu, S., Grow, J., Clifasefi, S., Garner, M., Douglass, A., Larimer, M. E., and Marlatt, A. 2009. Mindfulness-based relapse prevention for substance use disorders: A pilot efficacy trial. *Substance Abuse, 30,* 295–305.

Brach, T. 2004. *Radical acceptance: Embracing your life with the heart of a Buddha.* New York: Random House.

Brailovskaia, J., Delveaux, J., John, J., Wicker, V., Noveski, A., Kim, S., Schillack, H., and Margraf, J. 2023. Finding the "sweet spot" of smartphone use: Reduction or abstinence to increase well-being and healthy lifestyle?! An experimental intervention study. *Journal of Experimental Psychology, 29,* 149–161.

Bratman, G. N., Hamilton, J. P., Hahn, K. S., Daily, G. C., and Gross, J. J. 2015. Nature experience reduces rumination and subgenual prefrontal cortex activation. *Proceedings of the National Academy of Sciences of the United States of America, 112,* 8567–8572.

Bratman, G. N., Olvera-Alvarez, H. A., and Gross, J. J. 2021. The affective benefits of nature exposure. *Social and Personality Psychology Compass, 15,* e12630.

Bratman, G. N., Young, G., Mehta, A., Lee Babineaux, I., Daily, G. C., and Gross, J. J. 2021. Affective benefits of nature contact: The role of rumination. *Frontiers in Psychology, 12,* 643866.

Breines, J. G., and Chen, S. 2012. Self-compassion increases self-improvement motivation. *Personality and Social Psychology Bulletin, 38,* 1133–1143.

Brown, R. P., and Gerbarg, P. L. 2012. *The healing power of the breath: Simple techniques to reduce stress and anxiety, enhance concentration, and balance your emotions.* Boulder, Colorado: Shambhala Publications.

Brown, S. L., Nesse, R. M., Vinokur, A. D., and Smith, D. M. 2003. Providing social support may be more beneficial than receiving it: Results from a prospective study of mortality. *Psychological Science, 14,* 320–327.

Bush, N. E., Smolenski, D. J., Denneson, L. M., Williams, H. B., Thomas, E. K., and Dobscha, S. K. 2017. A virtual hope box: Randomized controlled trial of a smartphone app for emotional regulation and coping with distress. *Psychiatric Services, 68,* 330–336.

Byun, K., Hyodo, K., Suwabe, K., Ochi, G., Sakairi, Y., Kato, M., Dan, I., and Soya, H. 2014. Positive effect of acute mild exercise on executive function via arousal-related prefrontal activations: An fNIRS study. *NeuroImage, 98,* 336–345.

Campbell-Sills, L., Barlow, D. H., Brown, T. A., and Hofmann, S. G. 2006. Effects of suppression and acceptance on emotional responses of individuals with anxiety and mood disorders. *Behaviour Research and Therapy, 44,* 1251–1263.

Carey, B. 2011. Expert on mental illness reveals her own fight. *New York Times.* https://www.nytimes.com/2011/06/23/health/23lives.html

Casement, M. D., and Swanson, L. M. 2012. A meta-analysis of imagery rehearsal for post-trauma nightmares: Effects on nightmare frequency, sleep quality, and posttraumatic stress. *Clinical Psychology Review, 32,* 566–574.

Ceccato, S., Kudielka, B. M., and Schwieren, C. 2016. Increased risk taking in relation to chronic stress in adults. *Frontiers in Psychology, 6,* 2036.

Chaudhuri, A., Manna, M., Mandal, K., and Pattanayak, K. 2020. Is there any effect of progressive muscle relaxation exercise on anxiety and depression of the patient with coronary artery disease? *International Journal of Pharma Research and Health Sciences, 8,* 3231–3236.

Cohen, G. L. 2022. *Belonging: The science of creating connection and bridging divides.* New York: W. W. Norton.

Cohen, S., Janicki-Deverts, D., Turner, R. B., and Doyle, W. J. 2015. Does hugging provide stress-buffering social support? A study of susceptibility to upper respiratory infection and illness. *Psychological Science, 26,* 135–147.

Cohen, S., and Wills, T. A. 1985. Stress, social support, and the buffering hypothesis. *Psychological Bulletin, 98,* 310–357.

Coles, N. A., March, D. S., Marmolejo-Ramos, F., Larsen, J. T., Arinze, N. C., Ndukaihe, I. L. G., Willis, M. L., Foroni, F., Reggev, N., Mokady, A., et al. 2022. A multi-lab test of the facial feedback hypothesis by the Many Smiles Collaboration. *Nature Human Behavior.* https://doi.org/10.1038/s41562-022 -01458-9

Cunningham, J. E. A., and Shapiro, C. M. 2018. Cognitive behavioural therapy for insomnia (CBT-I) to treat depression: A systematic review. *Journal of Psychosomatic Research, 106,* 1–12.

Dalgin, R. S., Dalgin, M. H., and Metzger, S. J. 2018. A longitudinal analysis of the influence of a peer run warm line phone service on psychiatric recovery. *Community Mental Health Journal, 54,* 376–382.

De Couck, M., Caers, R., Musch, L., Fliegauf, J., Giangreco, A., and Gidron, Y. 2019. How breathing can help you make better decisions: Two studies on the effects of breathing patterns on heart rate variability and decision-making in business cases. *International Journal of Psychophysiology, 139,* 1–9.

de Witte, M., Spruit, A., van Hooren, S., Moonen, X., and Stams, G. J. 2020. Effects of music interventions on stress-related outcomes: A systematic review and two meta-analyses. *Health Psychology Review, 14,* 294–324.

Diel, K., Grelle, S., and Hofmann, W. 2021. A motivational framework of social comparison. *Journal of Personality and Social Psychology, 120,* 1415–1430.

Diener, E., Lucas, R. E., and Scollon, C. N. 2006. Beyond the hedonic treadmill: Revising the adaptation theory of well-being. *The American Psychologist, 61,* 305–314.

Ditzen, B., and Heinrichs, M. 2014. Psychobiology of social support: The social dimension of stress buffering. *Restorative Neurology and Neuroscience, 32,* 149–162.

Dixon, S. 2022. Average daily time spent on social media worldwide 2012–2022. https://www.statista.com/statistics/433871/daily-social-media-usage-worldwide/

Dreisoerner, A., Junker, N. M., Scholtz, W., Heimrich, J., Bloemeke, S., Ditzen, B., and van Dick, R. 2021. Self-soothing touch and being hugged reduce cortisol responses to stress: A randomized controlled trial on stress, physical touch, and social identity. *Comprehensive Psychoneuroendocrinology, 8,* 100091.

Duggleby, W. D., Degner, L., Williams, A., Wright, K., Cooper, D., Popkin, D., and Holtslander, L. 2007. Living with hope: Initial evaluation of a psychosocial hope intervention for older palliative home care patients. *Journal of Pain and Symptom Management, 33,* 247–257.

Dunn, E. W., Aknin, L. B., and Norton, M. I. 2014. Prosocial spending and happiness: Using money to benefit others pays off. *Current Directions in Psychological Science, 23,* 41–47.

Dwyer, R., Kushlev, K., and Dunn, E. W. 2018. Smartphone use undermines the enjoyment of face-to-face interactions. *Journal of Experimental Social Psychology, 78*, 233–239.

Edwards, M. K., and Loprinzi, P. D. 2018. Experimental effects of brief, single bouts of walking and meditation on mood profile in young adults. *Health Promotion Perspectives, 8*, 171–178.

Finkel, E. J., Slotter, E. B., Luchies, L. B., Walton, G. M., and Gross, J. J. 2013. A brief intervention to promote conflict reappraisal preserves marital quality over time. *Psychological Science, 24*, 1595–1601.

Fredrickson, B. L., Cohn, M. A., Coffey, K. A., Pek, J., and Finkel, S. M. 2008. Open hearts build lives: Positive emotions, induced through loving-kindness meditation, build consequential personal resources. *Journal of Personality and Social Psychology, 95*, 1045–1062.

Garcia, L., Pearce, M., Abbas, A., Mok, A., Strain, T., Ali, S., Crippa, A., Dempsey, P. C., Golubic, R., Kelly, P., Laird, Y., McNamara, E., Moore, S., de Sa, T. H., Smith, A. D., Wijndaele, K., Woodcock, J., and Brage, S. 2023. Non-occupational physical activity and risk of cardiovascular disease, cancer and mortality outcomes: A dose-response meta-analysis of large prospective studies. *British Journal of Sports Medicine*, bjsports-2022-105669. https://doi.org/10.1136/bjsports-2022-105669.

Goldin, P. R., McRae, K., Ramel, W., and Gross, J. J. 2008. The neural bases of emotion regulation: Reappraisal and suppression of negative emotion. *Biological Psychiatry, 63*, 577–586.

Gooding, L., Swezey, S., and Zwischenberger, J. B. 2012. Using music interventions in perioperative care. *Southern Medical Journal, 105*, 486–490.

Graff, V., Cai, L., Badiola, I., and Elkassabany, N. M. 2019. Music versus midazolam during preoperative nerve block placements: A prospective randomized controlled study. *Regional Anesthesia and Pain Medicine*, rapm-2018-100251.

Gross, J. J., and John, O. P. 2003. Individual differences in two emotion regulation processes: Implications for affect, relationships, and well-being. *Journal of Personality and Social Psychology, 85*, 348–362.

Haber, M. G., Cohen, J. L., Lucas, T., and Baltes, B. B. 2007. The relationship between self-reported received and perceived social support: A meta-analytic review. *American Journal of Community Psychology, 39*, 133–144.

Hann, K. E. J., and McCracken, L. M. 2014. A systematic review of randomized controlled trials of acceptance and commitment therapy for adults with chronic pain: Outcome domains, design quality, and efficacy. *Journal of Contextual Behavioral Science, 3*, 217–227.

He, Z., Lin, Y., Xia, L., Liu, Z., Zhang, D., and Elliott, R. 2018. Critical role of the right VLPFC in emotional regulation of social exclusion: A tDCS study. *Social Cognitive and Affective Neuroscience, 13*, 357–366.

Hill, P. L., Sin, N. L., Turiano, N. A., Burrow, A. L., and Almeida, D. M. 2018. Sense of purpose moderates the associations between daily stressors and daily well-being. *Annals of Behavioral Medicine, 52*, 724–729.

Jacobson, E. 1938. *Progressive relaxation.* Chicago: University of Chicago Press.

Kabat-Zinn, J. 2013. *Full-catastrophe living: Using the wisdom of your body and mind to face stress, pain, and illness.* New York: Bantam Press.

Kassam, K. S., and Mendes, W. B. 2013. The effects of measuring emotion: Physiological reactions to emotional situations depend on whether someone is asking. *PLoS ONE, 8*, e64959.

Kircanski, K., Lieberman, M. D., and Craske, M. G. 2012. Feelings into words: Contributions of language to exposure therapy. *Psychological Science, 23*, 1086–1091.

Kotsou, I., Leys, C., and Fossion, P. 2018. Acceptance alone is a better predictor of psychopathology and well-being than emotional competence, emotion regulation and mindfulness. *Journal of Affective Disorders, 226*, 142–145.

Krause, N., Pargament, K. I., Hill, P. C., and Ironson, G. 2016. Humility, stressful life events, and psychological well-being: Findings from the landmark spirituality and health survey. *The Journal of Positive Psychology, 11*, 499–510.

Krüger, T. H., Schulze, J., Bechinie, A., Neumann, I., Jung, S., Sperling, C., Engel, J., et al. 2022. Neuronal effects of glabellar botulinum toxin injections using a valanced inhibition task in borderline personality disorder. *Scientific Reports, 12*, 14197.

Kushlev, K., and Dunn, E. W. 2015. Checking email less frequently reduces stress. *Computers in Human Behavior, 43*, 220–228.

Kushlev, K., and Dunn, E. W. 2019. Smartphones distract parents from cultivating feelings of connection when spending time with their children. *Journal of Social and Personal Relationships, 36,* 1619–1639.

Lambert, J., Barnstable, G., Minter, E., Cooper, J., and McEwan, D. 2022. Taking a one-week break from social media improves well-being, depression, and anxiety: A randomized controlled trial. *Cyberpsychology, Behavior, and Social Networking, 25,* 287–293.

Lanctot, A., and Duxbury, L. 2021. When everything is urgent! Mail use and employee well-being. *Computers in Human Behavior Reports, 4,* 100152.

Larsson, A., Hooper, N., Osborne, L. A., Bennett, P., and McHugh, L. 2016. Using brief cognitive restructuring and cognitive defusion techniques to cope with negative thoughts. *Behavior Modification, 40,* 452–482.

LeMarr, J. D., Golding, L. A., and Crehan, K. D. 1983. Cardiorespiratory responses to inversion. *The Physician and Sportsmedicine, 11,* 51–57.

Leproult, R., Copinschi, G., Buxton, O., and Van Cauter, E. 1997. Sleep loss results in an elevation of cortisol levels the next evening. *Sleep, 20,* 865–870.

Lieberman, M. D. 2019. Affect labeling in the age of social media. *Nature Human Behaviour, 3,* 20–21.

Lieberman, M. D., Eisenberger, N. I., Crockett, M. J., Tom, S., Pfeifer, J. H., and Way, B. M. 2007. Putting feelings into words: Affect labeling disrupts amygdala activity to affective stimuli. *Psychological Science, 18,* 421–428.

Light, K. C., Grewen, K. M., and Amico, J. A. 2005. More frequent partner hugs and higher oxytocin levels are linked to lower blood pressure and heart rate in premenopausal women. *Biological Psychology, 69,* 5–21.

Linehan, M. M. 1993. *Cognitive-behavioral treatment of borderline personality disorder.* New York: Guilford Press.

Linehan, M. M. 1997. Validation and psychotherapy. In A. C. Bohart and L. S. Greenberg (Eds.). *Empathy reconsidered: New directions in psychotherapy.* Washington, DC: American Psychological Association; pp. 353–92.

Linehan, M. M. 2015. *DBT skills training manual,* (2nd ed.). New York: Guilford Press.

Liu, K., Chen, Y., Wu, D., Lin, R., Wang, Z., and Pan, L. 2020. Effects of progressive muscle relaxation on anxiety and sleep quality in patients with COVID-19. *Complementary Therapies in Clinical Practice, 39,* 101132.

Margolis, S., and Lyubomirsky, S. 2020. Experimental manipulation of extraverted and introverted behavior and its effects on well-being. *Journal of Experimental Psychology, 149,* 719–731.

Margolis, S., Stapley, A. L., and Lyubomirsky, S. 2020. The association between extraversion and well-being is limited to one facet. *Journal of Personality, 88,* 478–484.

Mark, G., Iqbal, S., Czerwinski, M., and Johns, P. 2015. Focused, aroused, but so distractable: A temporal perspective on multitasking and communications. *Technologies in the Workplace,* 903–916.

Marlatt, G. A., and Gordon, J. R. 1985. *Relapse prevention.* New York: Guilford Press.

Masi, C. M., Chen, H. Y., Hawkley, L. C., and Cacioppo, J. T. 2011. A meta-analysis of interventions to reduce loneliness. *Personality and Social Psychology Review, 15,* 219–266.

Master, S. L., Eisenberger, N. I., Taylor, S. E., Naliboff, B. D., Shirinyan, D., and Lieberman, M. D. 2009. A picture's worth: Partner photographs reduce experimentally induced pain. *Psychological Science, 20,* 1316–1318.

Masuda, A., Hayes, S. C., Sackett, C. F., and Twohig, M. P. 2004. Cognitive defusion and self-relevant negative thoughts: Examining the impact of a ninety-year-old technique. *Behaviour Research and Therapy, 42,* 477–485.

McRae, K., Jacobs, S. E., Ray, R. D., John, O. P., and Gross, J. J. 2012. Individual differences in reappraisal ability: Links to reappraisal frequency, well-being, and cognitive control. *Journal of Research in Personality, 46,* 2–7.

Mongrain, M., and Trambakoulos, J. 2007. A musical mood induction alleviates dysfunctional attitudes in needy and self-critical individuals. *Journal of Cognitive Psychotherapy, 21,* 295–309.

Montag, C. and Diefenbach, S. 2018. Towards homo digitalis: Important research issues for psychology and the neurosciences at the dawn of the internet of things and the digital society. *Sustainability, 10,* 415.

Nayor, M., Shah, R. V., Miller, P. E., Blodgett, J. B., Tanguay, M., Pico, A. R., Murthy, V. L., Malhotra, R., Houstis, N. E., Deik, A., et al. 2020. Metabolic architecture of acute exercise response in middle-aged adults in the community. *Circulation, 142,* 1905–1924.

Nestor, J. 2020. *Breath: The new science of a lost art.* New York: Riverhead Books.

Nuckowska, M. K., Gruszecki, M., Kot, J., Wolf, J., Guminski, W., Frydrychowski, A. F., Wtorek, J., Narkiewicz, K., and Winklewski, P. J. 2019. Impact of slow breathing on the blood pressure and subarachnoid space width oscillations in humans. *Scientific Reports, 9,* 6232.

Oppezzo, M., and Schwartz, D. L. 2014. Give your ideas some legs: The positive effect of walking on creative thinking. *Journal of Experimental Psychology: Learning, Memory, and Cognition, 40,* 1142–1152.

Panneton, W. M. 2013. The mammalian diving response: An enigmatic reflex to preserve life? *Physiology, 28,* 284–297.

Perlis, M. L., Posner, D., Riemann, D., Bastien, C. H., Teel, J., and Thase, M. 2022. Insomnia. *The Lancet, 400,* 1047–1060.

Poletti, S., Razzini, G., Ferrari, R., Ricchieri, M. P., Spedicato, G. A., Pasqualini, A., Buzzega, C., Artioli, F., Petropulacos, K., Luppi, M., and Bandieri, E. 2019. Mindfulness-based stress reduction in early palliative care for people with metastatic cancer: A mixed-method study. *Complementary Therapies in Medicine, 47,* 102218.

Porcelli, A. J., and Delgado, M. R. 2017. Stress and decision making: Effects on valuation, learning, and risk-taking. *Current Opinion in Behavioral Sciences, 14,* 33–39.

Poulin, M. J., Brown, S. L., Dillard, A. J., and Smith, D. M. 2013. Giving to others and the association between stress and mortality. *American Journal of Public Health, 103,* 1649–1655.

Pumar, M. I., Gray, C. R., Walsh, J. R., Yang, I. A., Rolls, T. A., and Ward, D. L. 2014. Anxiety and depression—Important psychological comorbidities of COPD. *Journal of Thoracic Disease, 6,* 1615–1631.

Querstret, D., Morison, L., Dickinson, S., Cropley, M., and John, M. 2020. Mindfulness-based stress reduction and mindfulness-based cognitive therapy for psychological health and well-being in nonclinical samples: A systematic review and meta-analysis. *International Journal of Stress Management, 27,* 394–411.

Raposa, E. B., Laws, H. B., and Ansell, E. B. 2016. Prosocial behavior mitigates the effects of stress in everyday life. *Clinical Psychological Science, 4*, 691–698.

Reed, J., and Ones, D. S. 2006. The effect of acute aerobic exercise on positive activated affect: A meta-analysis. *Psychology of Sport and Exercise, 7*, 477–514.

Ribeiro, F. S., Santos, F. H., Albuquerque, P. B., and Oliveira-Silva, P. 2019. Emotional induction through music: Measuring cardiac and electrodermal responses of emotional states and their persistence. *Frontiers in Psychology, 10*, 451.

Roemer, L., Orsillo, S. M., and Salters-Pedneault, K. 2008. Efficacy of an acceptance-based behavior therapy for generalized anxiety disorder: Evaluation in a randomized controlled trial. *Journal of Consulting and Clinical Psychology, 76*, 1083–1089.

Ross, L., and Nisbett, R. E. 1991. *The person and the situation: Perspectives of social psychology.* New York: McGraw-Hill Book Company.

Russo, M. A., Santarelli, D. M., and O'Rourke, D. 2017. The physiological effects of slow breathing in the healthy human. *Breathe, 13*, 298–309.

Sacks, O. 2008. *Musicophilia: Tales of music and the brain.* New York: Vintage.

Savulich, G., Hezemans, F. H., van Ghesel Grothe, S., Dafflon, J., Schulten, N., Brühl, A. B., Sahakian, B. J., and Robbins, T. W. 2019. Acute anxiety and autonomic arousal induced by CO_2 inhalation impairs prefrontal executive functions in healthy humans. *Translational Psychiatry, 9*, 296.

Schulte, B. 2015. *Overwhelmed: How to work, love, and play when no one has the time.* New York: Picador.

Seppala, E. M., Hutcherson, C. A., Nguyen, D. T., Doty, J. R., and Gross, J. J. 2014. Loving-kindness mediation: A tool to improve healthcare provider compassion, resilience and patient care. *Journal of Compassionate Health Care, 1*, 5.

Severs, L. J., Vlemincx, E., and Ramirez, J. M. 2022. The psychophysiology of the sigh: I. The sigh from the physiological perspective. *Biological Psychology, 170*, 108313.

Shahar, B., Szsepsenwol, O., Zilcha-Mano, S., Haim, N., Zamir, O., Levi-Yeshuvi, S., and Levit-Binnun, N. 2015. A wait-list randomized controlled trial of loving-kindness meditation programme for self-criticism. *Clinical Psychology and Psychotherapy, 22*, 346–356.

Shapiro, S. L., Astin, J. A., Bishop, S. R., and Cordova, M. 2005. Mindfulness-based stress reduction for health care professionals: Results from a randomized trial. *International Journal of Stress Management, 12*, 164–176.

Sudimac, S., Sale, V., and Kühn, S. 2022. How nature nurtures: Amygdala activity decreases as the result of a one-hour walk in nature. *Molecular Psychiatry.* https://doi.org/10.1038/s41380-022-01720-6

Suppakittpaisarn, P., Wu, CC., Tung, YH., Yeh, YC., Wanitchayapaisit, C., Browning, M. E. H., Chang, CY., and Sullivan, W. C. 2022. Durations of virtual exposure to built and natural landscapes impact self-reported stress recovery: Evidence from three countries. *Landscape and Ecological Engineering.* https://doi.org/10.1007/s11355-022-00523-9

Tangney, J. P. 2000. Humility: Theoretical perspectives, empirical findings and directions for future research. *Journal of Social and Clinical Psychology, 19*, 70–82.

Torre, J. B., and Lieberman, M. D. 2018. Putting feelings into words: Affect labeling as implicit emotion regulation. *Emotion Review, 10*, 116–124.

Toussaint, L., Nguyen, Q. A., Roettger, C., Dixon, K., Offenbächer, M., Kohls, N., Hirsch, J., and Sirois, F. 2021. Effectiveness of progressive muscle relaxation, deep breathing, and guided imagery in promoting psychological and physiological states of relaxation. *Evidence-based Complementary and Alternative Medicine: eCAM, 2021*, 5924040.

Tracy, M. F., Skaar, D. J., Guttormson, J. L., and Savik, K. 2013. Effects of patient-directed music intervention on anxiety and sedative exposure in critically ill patients receiving mechanical ventilatory support: A randomized clinical trial. *JAMA, 309*, 2335–2344.

Uhrig, M. K., Trautmann, N., Baumgärtner, U., Treede, R. D., Henrich, F., Hiller, W., and Marschall, S. 2016. Emotion elicitation: A comparison of pictures and films. *Frontiers in Psychology, 7*, 180.

Vahedi, Z., and Saiphoo, A. 2018. The association between smartphone use, stress, and anxiety: A meta-analytic review. *Stress and Health, 34.*

Vandekerckhove, M., and Wang, Y. L. 2017. Emotion, emotion regulation and sleep: An intimate relationship. *AIMS Neuroscience, 5*, 1–17.

van den Berg, M. M., Maas, J., Muller, R., Braun, A., Kaandorp, W., van Lien, R., van Poppel, M. N., van Mechelen, W., and van den Berg, A. E. 2015. Autonomic nervous system responses to viewing green and built settings: Differentiating between sympathetic and parasympathetic activity. *International Journal of Environmental Research and Public Health, 12,* 15860–15874.

van der Veek, P. P., van Rood, Y. R., and Masclee, A. A. 2007. Clinical trial: Short- and long-term benefit of relaxation training for irritable bowel syndrome. *Alimentary Pharmacology & Therapeutics, 26,* 943–952.

Wacks, Y., and Weinstein, A. M. 2021. Excessive smartphone use is associated with health problems in adolescents and young adults. *Frontiers in Psychiatry, 12,* 669042.

Walsh, L. C., Regan, A., Okabe-Miyamoto, K., and Lyubomirsky, S. 2021. Does putting away your smartphone make you happier? The effects of restricting digital media and social media on well-being. https://psyarxiv.com/c3phw/

Wapner, J. 2020. Vision and breathing may be the secrets to surviving 2020. *Scientific American.* https://www.scientificamerican.com/article/vision-and-breathing-may-be-the-secrets-to-surviving-2020/

Ward, A. F., Duke, K., Gneezy, A., and Bos, M. 2017. Brain drain: The mere presence of one's own smartphone reduces available cognitive capacity. *Journal of Association of Consumer Research, 2,* 140–154.

Wersebe, H., Lieb, R., Meyer, A. H., Hofer, P., and Gloster, A. T. 2018. The link between stress, well-being, and psychological flexibility during an acceptance and commitment therapy self-help intervention. *International Journal of Clinical and Health Psychology, 18,* 60–68.

Williams, M., Teasdale, J., Segal, Z., and Kabat-Zinn, J. 2007. *The mindful way through depression.* New York: Guilford Press.

Wilson, T. D., and Gilbert, D. T. 2003. Affective forecasting. In M. P. Zanna (Ed.), *Advances in experimental social psychology,* Vol. 35, pp. 345–411. Cambridge, Massachusetts: Elsevier Academic Press.

Woine, A., Mikolajczak, M., Gross, J., van Bakel, H., and Roskam, I. 2022. The role of cognitive appraisals in parental burnout: A preliminary analysis during the COVID-19 quarantine. *Current Psychology,* 1–14. Advance online publication. https://doi.org/10.1007/s12144-021-02629-z

Yanagisawa, H., Dan, I., Tsuzuki, D., Kato, M., Okamoto, M., Kyutoku, Y., and Soya, H. 2010. Acute moderate exercise elicits increased dorsolateral prefrontal activation and improves cognitive performance with Stroop test. *NeuroImage, 50,* 1702–1710.

Yang, H., Liu, B., and Fang, J. 2021. Stress and problematic smartphone use severity: Smartphone use frequency and fear of missing out as mediators. *Frontiers in Psychiatry, 12,* 659288.

Yimaz, M., and Huberman, A. D. 2019. Fear: It's all in your line of sight. *Current Biology, 29,* 1232–1234.

Zaccaro, A., Piarulli, A., Laurino, M., Garbella, E., Menicucci, D., Neri, B., and Gemignani, A. 2018. How breath-control can change your life: A systematic review on psycho-physiological correlates of slow breathing. *Frontiers in Human Neuroscience, 12,* 353.

Zeng, X., Chiu, C. P., Wang, R., Oei, T. P., and Leung, F. Y. 2015. The effect of loving-kindness meditation on positive emotions: A meta-analytic review. *Frontiers in Psychology, 6,* 1693.

Zhang, M., Yang, Z., Zhong, J., Zhang, Y., Lin, X., Cai, H., and Kong, Y. 2022. Thalamocortical mechanisms for nostalgia-induced analgesia. *Journal of Neuroscience, 42,* 2963–2972.

Zhenhong, H., Yiqin, L., Lisheng, X., Zhenli, L., Dandan, Z., and Elliott, R. 2018. Critical role of the right VLPFC in emotional regulation of social exclusion: A tDCS study. *Social Cognitive and Affective Neuroscience, 13,* 357–366.

PART THREE

Ans, A. H., Anjum, I., Satija, V., Inayat, A., Ashgar, Z., Akram, I., and Shrestha, B. 2018. Neurohormonal regulation of appetite and its relationship with stress: A mini literature review. *Cureus, 10,* e3032.

Balchin, R., Linde, J. V., Blackhurst, D. M., Rauch, H. L., and Schönbächler, G. 2016. Sweating away depression? The impact of intensive exercise on depression. *Journal of Affective Disorders, 200,* 218–221.

Barber, K. C., Michaelis, M. A. M., and Moscovitch, D. A. 2021. Social anxiety and the generation of positivity during dyadic interaction: Curiosity and authenticity are the keys to success. *Behavior Therapy, 52,* 1418–1432.

Barlow, D. H., Sauer-Zavala, S., Farchione, T. J., Latin, H. M., Ellard, K. K., Bullis, J. R., Bentley, K. H., Boettcher, H. T., and Cassiello-Robbins, C. 2018. *Unified protocol for transdiagnostic treatment of emotional disorders* (2nd ed.). New York: Oxford University Press.

Bartlett, L., Buscot, M. J., Bindoff, A., Chambers, R., and Hassed, C. 2021. Mindfulness is associated with lower stress and higher work engagement in a large sample of MOOC participants. *Frontiers in Psychology, 12,* 724126.

Baumeister, R. F., Bratslavsky, E., Finkenauer, C., and Vohs, K. D. 2001. Bad is stronger than good. *Review of General Psychology, 5,* 323–370.

Baumeister, R. F., and Leary, M. R. 1995. The need to belong: Desire for interpersonal attachments as a fundamental human motivation. *Psychological Bulletin, 117,* 497–529.

Beck, A. T., Rush, A. J., Shaw, B. F., and Emery, G. 1979. *Cognitive therapy of depression.* New York: Guilford Press.

Becker, L., Kaltenegger, H. C., Nowak, D., Rohleder, N., and Weigl, M. 2022. Differences in stress system (re-)activity between single and dual- or multitasking in healthy adults: A systematic review and meta-analysis. *Health Psychology Review, 17,* 78–103.

Berk, L. S., Tan, S. A., Fry, W. F., Napier, B. J., Lee, J. W., Hubbard, R. W., Lewis, J. E., and Eby, W. C. 1989. Neuroendocrine and stress hormone changes during mirthful laughter. *The American Journal of the Medical Sciences, 298,* 390–396.

Bhaskar, S., Hemavathy, D., and Prasad, S. 2016. Prevalence of chronic insomnia in adult patients and its correlation with medical comorbidities. *Journal of Family Medicine and Primary Care, 5,* 780–784.

Blaine, S. K., and Sinha, R. 2017. Alcohol, stress, and glucocorticoids: From risk to dependence and relapse in alcohol use disorders. *Neuropharmacology, 122,* 136–147.

Boggiss, A. L., Consedine, N. S., Brenton-Peters, J. M., Hofman, P. L., and Serlachius, A. S. 2020. A systematic review of gratitude interventions: Effects on physical health and health behaviors. *Journal of Psychosomatic Research, 135,* 110165.

Borkovec, T. D., Wilkinson, L., Folensbee, R., and Lerman, C. 1983. Stimulus control applications to the treatment of worry. *Behaviour Research and Therapy, 21,* 247–251.

Boswell, J. F., Farchione, T. J., Sauer-Zavala, S., Murray, H. W., Fortune, M. R., and Barlow, D. H. 2013. Anxiety sensitivity and interoceptive exposure: A transdiagnostic construct and change strategy. *Behavior Therapy, 44,* 417–431.

Brown, R. P., and Gerbarg, P. L. 2012. *The healing power of the breath.* Boulder, Colorado: Shambhala Publications.

Brunet, H. E., Banks, S. J., Libera, A., Willingham-Jaggers, M., and Almén, R. A. 2021. Training in improvisation techniques helps reduce caregiver burden and depression: Innovative practice. *Dementia, 20,* 364–372.

Cai, L., Liu, Y., and He, L. 2022. Investigating genetic causal relationships between blood pressure and anxiety, depressive symptoms, neuroticism and subjective well-being. *General Psychiatry, 35,* e10087.

Carlucci, L., Saggino, A., and Balsamo, M. 2021. On the efficacy of the Unified Protocol for transdiagnostic treatment of emotional disorders: A systematic review and meta-analysis. *Clinical Psychology Review, 87,* 101999.

Chen, C. Y., and Hong, R. Y. 2010. Intolerance of uncertainty moderates the relation between negative life events and anxiety. *Personality and Individual Differences, 49,* 49–53.

Cherpak C. E. 2019. Mindful eating: A review of how the stress-digestion-mindfulness triad may modulate and improve gastrointestinal and digestive function. *Integrative Medicine, 18,* 48–53.

Craske, M. G., Rowe, M., Lewin, M., and Noriega-Dimitri, R. 1997. Interoceptive exposure versus breathing retraining within cognitive-behavioural therapy for panic disorder with agoraphobia. *The British Journal of Clinical Psychology, 36,* 85–99.

Craske, M. G., Treanor, M., Conway, C. C., Zbozinek, T., and Vervliet, B. 2014. Maximizing exposure therapy: An inhibitory learning approach. *Behaviour Research and Therapy, 58,* 10–23.

Curry, S., Marlatt, G. A., and Gordon, J. R. 1987. Abstinence violation effect: Validation of an attributional construct with smoking cessation. *Journal of Consulting and Clinical Psychology, 55,* 145–149.

Dahne, J., Lejuez, C. W., Diaz, V. A., Player, M. S., Kustanowitz, J., Felton, J. W., and Carpenter, M. J. 2019. Pilot randomized trial of a self-help behavioral activation mobile app for utilization in primary care. *Behavior Therapy, 50,* 817–827.

Daviet, R., Aydogan, G., Jagannathan, K., Spilka, N., Koellinger, P. D., Kranzler, H. R., Nave, G., and Wetherill, R. R. 2022. Associations between alcohol consumption and gray and white matter volumes in the UK Biobank. *Nature Communications, 13,* 1175.

Deacon, B., Kemp, J. J., Dixon, L. J., Sy, J. T., Farrell, N. R., and Zhang, A. R. 2013. Maximizing the efficacy of interoceptive exposure by optimizing inhibitory learning: A randomized controlled trial. *Behaviour Research and Therapy, 51*, 588–596.

Demarinis, S. 2020. Loneliness at epidemic levels in America. *Explore, 16*, 278–279.

De Weck, M., Perriard, B., Annoni, J. M., and Britz, J. 2022. Hearing someone laugh and seeing someone yawn: Modality-specific contagion of laughter and yawning in the absence of others. *Frontiers in Psychology, 13*, 780665.

Dimidjian, S., Barrera, M., Jr., Martell, C., Muñoz, R. F., and Lewinsohn, P. M. 2011. The origins and current status of behavioral activation treatments for depression. *Annual Review of Clinical Psychology, 7*, 1–38.

Ditzen, B., and Heinrichs, M. 2014. Psychobiology of social support: The social dimension of stress buffering. *Restorative Neurology and Neuroscience, 32*, 149–162.

Dugas, M. J., Sexton, K. A., Hebert, E. A., Bouchard, S., Gouin, J. P., and Shafran, R. 2022. Behavioral experiments for intolerance of uncertainty: A randomized clinical trial for adults with generalized anxiety disorder. *Behavior Therapy, 53*, 1147–1160.

Emmons, R. A. and McCullough, M. E. 2003. Counting blessings versus burdens: An experimental investigation of gratitude and subjective well-being in daily life. *Journal of Personality and Social Psychology, 84*, 377–389.

Fekete, E. M., and Deichert, N. T. 2022. A brief gratitude writing intervention decreased stress and negative affect during the COVID-19 pandemic. *Journal of Happiness Studies, 23*, 2427–2448.

Figueiro, M. G., Steverson, B., Heerwagen, J., Kampschroer, K., Hunter, C. M., Gonzales, K., Plitnick, B., and Rea, M. S. 2017. The impact of daytime light exposures on sleep and mood in office workers. *Sleep Health, 3*, 204–215.

Fredrickson, B. L., Mancuso, R. A., Branigan, C., and Tugade, M. M. 2000. The undoing effect of positive emotions. *Motivation and Emotion, 24*, 237–258.

Gass, J. C., Funderburk, J. S., Shepardson, R., Kosiba, J. D., Rodriguez, R., and Maisto, S. A. 2021. The use and impact of self-monitoring on substance use outcomes: A descriptive systematic review. *Substance Abuse, 42*, 512–526.

Gates, P. J., Albertella, L., and Copeland, J. 2014. The effects of cannabinoid administration on sleep: A systematic review of human studies. *Sleep Medicine Reviews, 18*, 477–487.

Gilman, T. L., Shaheen, R., Nylocks, K. M., Halachoff, D., Chapman, J., Flynn, J. J., Matt, L. M., and Coifman, K. G. 2017. A film set for the elicitation of emotion in research: A comprehensive catalog derived from four decades of investigation. *Behavior Research Methods, 49*, 2061–2082.

Gleichgerrcht, E., and Decety, J. 2013. Empathy in clinical practice: How individual dispositions, gender, and experience moderate empathic concern, burnout, and emotional distress in physicians. *PLoS ONE, 8*, e61526.

Gu, J., Strauss, C., Bond, R., and Cavanagh, K. 2015. How do mindfulness-based cognitive therapy and mindfulness-based stress reduction improve mental health and wellbeing? A systematic review and meta-analysis of mediation studies. *Clinical Psychology Review, 37*, 1–12.

Gu, Y., Ocampo, J. M., Algoe, S. B., and Oveis, C. 2022. Gratitude expressions improve teammates' cardiovascular stress responses. *Journal of Experimental Psychology, 151*, 3281–3291.

Guo, L. 2023. The delayed, durable effect of expressive writing on depression, anxiety and stress: A meta-analytic review of studies with long-term follow-ups. *The British Journal of Clinical Psychology, 62*, 272–297.

Hari, J. 2023. *Stolen focus: Why you can't pay attention—and how to think deeply again.* New York: Crown.

Hewig, J., Hagemann, D., Seifert, J., Gollwitzer, M., Naumann, E., and Bartussek, D. 2005. A revised film set for the induction of basic emotions. *Cognition and Emotion, 19*, 1095–1109.

Hilbert, A., and Tuschen-Caffier, B. 2007. Maintenance of binge eating through negative mood: A naturalistic comparison of binge eating disorder and bulimia nervosa. *The International Journal of Eating Disorders, 40*, 521–530.

Hill, D., Conner, M., Clancy, F., Moss, R., Wilding, S., Bristow, M., and O'Connor, D. B. 2022. Stress and eating behaviours in healthy adults: A systematic review and meta-analysis. *Health Psychology Review, 16*, 280–304.

Hoge, E. A., Bui, E., Mete, M., Dutton, M. A., Baker, A. W., and Simon, N. M. 2022. Mindfulness-based stress reduction vs escitalopram for the treatment of adults with anxiety disorders: A randomized clinical trial. *JAMA Psychiatry.* doi:10.1001/jamapsychiatry.2022.3679

Huberman, A. 2021. Toolkit for sleep. *Huberman Lab*. https://hubermanlab.com/toolkit-for-sleep/

Kahneman, D., and Tversky, A. 1979. Prospect theory: An analysis of decision making under risk. *Econometrica, 47*, 263–291.

Kanter, J. W., Manos, R. C., Bowe, W. M., Baruch, D. E., Busch, A. M., and Rusch, L. C. 2010. What is behavioral activation? A review of the empirical literature. *Clinical Psychology Review, 30*, 608–620.

Kocovski, N. L., Fleming, J. E., Hawley, L. L., Huta, V., and Antony, M. M. 2013. Mindfulness and acceptance-based group therapy versus traditional cognitive behavioral group therapy for social anxiety disorder: A randomized controlled trial. *Behaviour Research and Therapy, 51*, 889–898.

Kruger, J., and Evans, M. If you don't want to be late, enumerate: Unpacking reduces the planning fallacy. *Journal of Experimental Social Psychology, 40*, 586–598.

Krueger, K. R., Murphy, J. W., and Bink. A. B. 2019. Thera-prov: A pilot study of improv used to treat anxiety and depression. *Journal of Mental Health, 28*, 621–626.

Kruse, E., Chancellor, J., Ruberton, P. M., and Lyubomirsky, S. 2014. An upward spiral between gratitude and humility. *Social Psychological and Personality Science, 5*, 805–814.

Kushlev, K., Heintzelman, S. J., Oishi, S., and Diener, E. 2018. The declining marginal utility of social time for subjective well-being. *Journal of Research in Personality, 74*, 124–140.

Layous, K., Chancellor, J., and Lyubomirsky, S. 2014. Positive activities as protective factors against mental health conditions. *Journal of Abnormal Psychology, 123*, 3–12.

Lee, D. H., Rezende, L. F. M., Joh, H. K., Keum, N., Ferrari, G., Rey-Lopez, J. P., Rimm, E. B., Tabung, F. K., and Giovannucci, E. L. 2022. Long-term leisure-time physical activity intensity and all-cause and cause-specific mortality: A prospective cohort of US adults. *Circulation, 146*, 523–534.

Lee, Y. C., Lu, C. T., Cheng, W. N., and Li, H. Y. 2022. The impact of mouth-taping in mouth-breathers with mild obstructive sleep apnea: A preliminary study. *Healthcare, 10*, 1755.

Linehan, M. M. 2015. *DBT skills training manual* (2nd ed.). New York: Guilford Press.

Lundberg, J. O., Settergren, G., Gelinder, S., Lundberg, J. M., Alving, K., and Weitzberg, E. 1996. Inhalation of nasally derived nitric oxide modulates pulmonary function in humans. *Acta Physiologica Scandinavica, 158,* 343–347.

Lyubomirsky, S., Dickerhoof, R., Boehm, J. K., and Sheldon, K. M. 2011. Becoming happier takes both a will and a proper way: An experimental longitudinal intervention to boost well-being. *Emotion, 11,* 391–402.

Lyubomirsky, S., and Layous, K. 2013. How do simple positive activities increase well-being? *Current Directions in Psychological Science, 22,* 57–62.

Madore, K. P., and Wagner, A. D. 2019. Multicosts of multitasking. *Cerebrum, 2019,* cer-04-19.

Magnon, V., Dutheil, F., and Vallet, G. T. 2021. Benefits from one session of deep and slow breathing on vagal tone and anxiety in young and older adults. *Scientific Reports, 11,* 19267.

Mark, G., Gudith, D., and Klocke, U. 2008. The cost of interrupted work: More speed and stress. https://www.ics.uci.edu/~gmark/chi08-mark.pdf.

Masi, C. M., Chen, H. Y., Hawkley, L. C., and Cacioppo, J. T. 2011. A meta-analysis of interventions to reduce loneliness. *Personality and Social Psychology Review, 15,* 219–266.

McRaven, W. H. 2014. University of Texas at Austin 2014 commencement speech. [Video]. YouTube. https://www.youtube.com/watch?v=pxBQLFLei70.

McRaven, W. H. 2017. *Make your bed: Little things that can change your life . . . and maybe the world.* New York: Grand Central Publishing.

Mikkelsen, K., Stojanovska, L., Polenakovic, M., Bosevski, M., and Apostolopoulos, V. 2017. Exercise and mental health. *Maturitas, 106,* 48–56.

Monfort, S. S., Stroup, H. E., and Waugh, C. E. 2015. The impact of anticipating positive events on responses to stress. *Journal of Experimental Social Psychology, 58,* 11–22.

Myllymäki, T., Kujala, U. M., and Lindholm, H. 2018. Acute effect of alcohol intake on cardiovascular autonomic regulation during the first hours of sleep in a large real-world sample of Finnish employees: Observational study. *JMIR Mental Health, 5,* e23.

National Sleep Foundation. 2012. *Bedroom poll.* https://www.sleepfoundation.org/wp-content/uploads/2018/10/NSF_Bedroom_Poll_Report_1.pdf.

Natraj, N., and Ganguly, K. 2018. Shaping reality through mental rehearsal. *Neuron, 97*, 998–1000.

Nestor, J. 2020. *Breath: The new science of a lost art.* New York: Riverhead Books.

Newman, D. B., Gordon, A. M., and Mendes, W. B. 2021. Comparing daily physiological and psychological benefits of gratitude and optimism using a digital platform. *Emotion, 21*, 1357–1365.

Nuckowska, M. K., Gruszecki, M., Kot, J., Wolf, J., Guminski, W., Frydrychowski, A. F., Wtorek, J., Narkiewicz, K., and Winklewski, P. J. 2019. Impact of slow breathing on the blood pressure and subarachnoid space width oscillations in humans. *Scientific Reports, 9*, 6232.

Ostafin, B. D., and Proulx, T. 2020. Meaning in life and resilience to stressors. *Anxiety, Stress, and Coping, 33*, 603–622.

Papa, A., Sewell, M. T., Garrison-Diehn, C., and Rummel, C. 2013. A randomized open trial assessing the feasibility of behavioral activation for pathological grief responding. *Behavior Therapy, 44*, 639–650.

Pennebaker, J. W. 2018. Expressive writing in psychological science. *Perspectives on Psychological Science, 13*, 226–229.

Pennebaker, J. W., and Smyth, J. M. 2016. *Opening up by writing it down: How expressive writing improves health and eases emotional pain* (3rd ed.). New York: Guilford Press.

Ramirez, G., and Beilock, S. L. 2011. Writing about testing worries boosts exam performance in the classroom. *Science, 331*, 211–213.

Ritterband, L. M., Thorndike, F. P., Ingersoll, K. S., Lord, H. R., Gonder-Frederick, L., Frederick, C., Quigg, M. S., Cohn, W. F., and Morin, C. M. 2017. Effect of a web-based cognitive behavior therapy for insomnia intervention with 1-year follow-up: A randomized clinical trial. *JAMA Psychiatry, 74*, 68–75.

Rizvi, S. L. 2019. *Chain analysis in dialectical behavioral therapy.* New York: Guilford Press.

Russo-Netzer, P., and Cohen, G. L. 2022. If you're uncomfortable, go outside your comfort zone: A novel behavioral stretch intervention supports the well-being of unhappy people. *The Journal of Positive Psychology*, https://doi.org/10.1080/17439760.2022.2036794.

Safer, D. J., Telch, C. F., and Check, E. Y. 2009. *Dialectical behavior therapy for binge eating and bulimia.* New York: Guilford Press.

Sakurada, K., Konta, T., Watanabe, M., Ishizawa, K., Ueno, Y., Yamashita, H., and Kayama, T. 2020. Associations of frequency of laughter with risk of all-cause mortality and cardiovascular disease incidence in a general population: Findings from the Yamagata study. *Journal of Epidemiology, 30,* 188–193.

Salmon, P. 2001. Effects of physical exercise on anxiety, depression, and sensitivity to stress: A unifying theory. *Clinical Psychology Review, 21,* 33–61.

Sandstrom, G. M., Boothby, E. J., and Cooney, G. 2022. Talking to strangers: A week-long intervention reduces psychological barriers to social connection. *Journal of Experimental Social Psychology, 102,* 104356.

Sandstrom, G. M., and Dunn, E. W. 2014. Is efficiency overrated? Minimal social interactions lead to belonging and positive affect. *Social Psychological and Personality Science, 5,* 436–441.

Sandstrom, G. M., and Dunn, E. W. 2014. Social interactions and well-being: The surprising power of weak ties. *Personality & Social Psychology Bulletin, 40,* 910–922.

Schickedanz, A., Perales, L., Holguin, M., Rhone-Collins, M., Robinson, H., Tehrani, N., Smith, L., Chung, P. J., and Szilagyi, P. G. 2023. Clinic-based financial coaching and missed pediatric preventive care: A randomized trial. *Pediatrics,* 151, e2021054970.

Schleider, J. L., Mullarkey, M. C., Fox, K. R., Dobias, M. L., Shroff, A., Hart, E. A., and Roulston, C. A. 2022. A randomized trial of online single-session interventions for adolescent depression during COVID-19. *Nature Human Behavior, 6,* 258–268.

Schoenfeld, T. J., Rada, P., Pieruzzini, P. R., Hsueh, B., and Gould, E. 2013. Physical exercise prevents stress-induced activation of granule neurons and enhances local inhibitory mechanisms in the dentate gyrus. *The Journal of Neuroscience, 33,* 7770–7777.

Segal, Z. 2016. The three-minute breathing practice. *Mindful.* https://www.mindful.org/the-three-minute-breathing-space-practice/.

Seligman, M. P. 2006. *Learned optimism: How to change your mind and your life.* New York: Vintage.

Singh, B., Olds, T., Curtis, R., Dumuid, D., Virgara, R., Watson, A., Szeto, K., O'Connor, E., Ferguson, T., Eglitis, E., Miatke, A., Simpson, C. E., and Maher, C. 2023. Effectiveness of physical activity interventions for improving depression, anxiety and distress: an overview of systematic reviews. *British Journal of Sports Medicine*, bjsports-2022-106195. https://doi.org/10.1136/bjsports-2022-106195

Sloan, D. M., Marx, B. P., Resick, P. A., Young-McCaughan, S., Dondanville, K. A., Straud, C. L., Mintz, J., Litz, B. T., and Peterson, A. L. 2022. Effect of written exposure therapy vs cognitive processing therapy on increasing treatment efficiency among military service members with posttraumatic stress disorder: A randomized noninferiority trial. *JAMA Network Open, 5*, e2140911.

Smyth, J., Johnson, J., Auer, B., Lehman, E., Talamo, G., and Sciamanna, C. 2018. Online positive affect journaling in the improvement of mental distress and well-being in general medical patients with elevated anxiety symptoms: Evidence from a preliminary randomized controlled trial. *JMIR Mental Health, 5*, e11290.

Sproesser, G., Schupp, H. T., and Renner, B. 2014. The bright side of stress-induced eating: Eating more when stressed but less when pleased. *Psychological Science, 25*, 58–65.

Stietz, J., Jauk, E., Krach, S., and Kanske, P. 2019. Dissociating empathy from perspective-taking: Evidence from intra- and inter-individual differences research. *Frontiers in Psychiatry, 10*, 126.

Stothard, E. R., McHill, A. W., Depner, C. M., Birks, B. R., Moehlman, T. M., Ritchie, H. K., Guzzetti, J. R., Chinoy, E. D., LeBourgeois, M. K., Axelsson, J., and Wright, K. P., Jr. 2017. Circadian entrainment to the natural light-dark cycle across seasons and the weekend. *Current Biology, 27*, 508–513.

Sun, J., Harris, K., and Vazire, S. 2020. Is well-being associated with the quantity and quality of social interactions? *Journal of Personality and Social Psychology, 119*, 1478–1496.

Tait, R. J., Paz Castro, R., Kirkman, J. J. L., Moore, J. C., and Schaub, M. P. 2019. A digital intervention addressing alcohol use problems (the "Daybreak" program): Quasi-experimental randomized controlled trial. *Journal of Medical Internet Research, 21*, e14967.

Taylor, S. E., Klein, L. C., Lewis, B. P., Gruenewald, T. L., Gurung, R. A., and Updegraff, J. A. 2000. Biobehavioral responses to stress in females: Tend-and-befriend, not fight-or-flight. *Psychological Review, 107*, 411–429.

Vincent, N., and Lionberg, C. 2001. Treatment preference and patient satisfaction in chronic insomnia. *Sleep, 24*, 411–417.

Vyas, S., Even-Chen, N., Stavisky, S. D., Ryu, S. I., Nuyujukian, P., and Shenoy, K. V. 2018. Neural population dynamics underlying motor learning transfer. *Neuron, 97,* 1177–1186.e3.

Willcox, B. J., Willcox, D. C., and Suzuki, M. 2017. Demographic, phenotypic, and genetic characteristics of centenarians in Okinawa and Japan: Part 1— Centenarians in Okinawa. *Mechanisms of Ageing and Development, 165,* 75–79.

Williams, M., Teasdale, J., Segal, Z., and Kabat-Zinn, J. 2007. *The mindful way through depression.* New York: Guilford Press.

Wood, A. M., Maltby, J., Gillett, R., Linley, P. A., and Joseph, S. 2008. The role of gratitude in the development of social support, stress, and depression: Two longitudinal studies. *Journal of Research in Personality, 42,* 854-871.

Wright, K. P., Jr., McHill, A. W., Birks, B. R., Griffin, B. R., Rusterholz, T., and Chinoy, E. D. 2013. Entrainment of the human circadian clock to the natural light-dark cycle. *Current Biology, 23,* 1554–1558.

Wu, J., Balliet, D., Kou, Y., and Van Lange, P. A. M. 2019. Gossip in the dictator and ultimatum games: Its immediate and downstream consequences for cooperation. *Frontiers in Psychology, 10,* 651.

Yemiscigil, A., and Vlaev, I. 2021. The bidirectional relationship between sense of purpose in life and physical activity: A longitudinal study. *Journal of Behavioral Medicine, 44,* 715–725.

Zaccaro, A., Piarulli, A., Laurino, M., Garbella, E., Menicucci, D., Neri, B., and Gemignani, A. 2018. How breath-control can change your life: A systematic review on psycho-physiological correlates of slow breathing. *Frontiers in Human Neuroscience, 12,* 353.

Zander-Schellenberg, T., Collins, I. M., Miché, M., Guttmann, C., Lieb, R., and Wahl, K. 2020. Does laughing have a stress-buffering effect in daily life? An intensive longitudinal study. *PLoS ONE, 15,* e0235851.

A FINAL NOTE

Motto, J. A., and Bostrom, A. G. 2001. A randomized controlled trial of postcrisis suicide prevention. *Psychiatric Services, 52,* 828–833.

Acknowledgments

I can't thank the following people enough for being the least stressful and most joyful team to work with on shaping an idea into a beautiful book: Rachael Mt. Pleasant, I'm grateful beyond words for your faith in this project and your insightful edits, attention to detail, and kindness; Lia Ronnen, Sarah Smith, Barbara Peragine, Kim Daly, Erica Jimenez, Sofia Khu, Jacquelynne Hudson, Rebecca Carlisle, Moira Kerrigan, Cindy Lee, and Ilana Gold, you have each gone above and beyond—it's been a dream to publish with Workman. Lindsay Edgecombe, I am amazed by your poise and strength and feel lucky to call you my agent. Paula Derrow, you have taught me so much about good writing and generosity.

This book began when Roberta Zeff published my article on five-minute stress resets in the *New York Times*, and I'm so thankful to her and to the tireless editors, especially Tim Herrera and Adam Kirsch, I've worked with over the years. I'm also grateful to Rozalina Burkova for the beautiful accompanying illustrations.

One of the greatest perks of writing this book has been delighting in the wisdom and generosity of the dozens of experts, mentors, and fascinating people who agreed to talk to me. An extra-big thank you to: Cory Newman, Jeremy Jamieson, Sharon Salzberg, Ed Watkins, Jessica Schleider, Richard Brown, Patricia Gerbarg, Tola T'Sarumi, Arthur Robin Williams, Robert Whitaker, Joshua Smythe, James Pennebaker, William Gerin, George Slavich, Jack Feldman, BJ Miller, Jonathan Fader, Peter Shore, Neal Brennan, Wendy Berry Mendes, Hawthorne Smith, Michael Perlis, Ramit Sethi, John Moynihan, Keeley Abram, Jennifer Aaker, Naomi Bagdonas, and Celeste Headlee.

I'm so grateful to the many colleagues and people who inspire me and who have cheered me on over the years, especially Adam Grant, Kirsten Thompson, Sarah Miller Lipton, Matt Kagan, Lois Berman, Tracy Kisner, Dan Goodman, Emanuel Maidenberg, Sari Eitches, Dennis Greenberger, Annalise Caron, Simon Rego, Juli Fraga, Eleanor Goldberg, Amanda Setton,

David Biello, Jonathan Cohen, Mayim Bialik, Alex Cooper, and Meghan Keene. An extra-special thanks to Nikki Cooper Baker, Kate Ballen, and Sonia Taitz for reading so many drafts and generously providing the most useful feedback. It means so much to know you are always there. And to Daniella Kahane and Jenna Strongwater for your impeccable taste and sharing your design input while offering so much sympathetic joy.

I am endlessly grateful for the opportunity to work with my clients. I can't believe how fortunate I am to know you and to witness your courage and growth. I'm also thankful for the pioneers in the field of psychology, especially Marsha Linehan, Steve Hayes, Aaron Beck, Zindel Segal, and Dave Barlow, whose ideas and research I've referenced. They've given me an invaluable road map and I am continuously appreciative of their dedication to alleviating suffering.

My late grandparents Dr. Emil and Sylvia Seletz made me realize the power of being present, persevering (especially in creative endeavors), and making people feel cherished and inspired me to pursue a career in clinical psychology, and Simon and Gita Taitz, Holocaust survivors, taught me about resilience. Thank you to my parents, Emanuel Taitz and Dr. Josepha Seletz, who go above and beyond; to my sisters, Michelle and Rebecca, who are also the most fun aunts; and to my in-laws, Karen and Bill, for being such devoted grandparents. Jimmy, Sonia and Paul, and Moshe, I'm so happy you're family. And to Ana and Marley, who feel like family.

Sylvie, Eli, and Asher, I can't put into words how blessed I feel to be your mother—you each have a huge heart and strive to do right and I am so grateful for the opportunity to guide you. And Adam, from instantly laughing and saying yes when I asked about sharing your horrible bad day story in this book to organizing countless fun Sundays so I could write, I'm so lucky to have you as a partner because my dreams are your dreams—and vice versa.

To all of my friends and extended personal and professional communities, you know who you are, and I'm so touched—social support is all it's cracked up to be.

And thank *you*—imagining you reading this motivated me to write it, and I'm moved by your willingness.

About the Author

Jennifer L. Taitz is a clinical psychologist and an assistant clinical professor in psychiatry at the University of California, Los Angeles. Dr. Taitz completed her fellowship in psychology at Yale University School of Medicine and achieved board certifications in both cognitive behavioral therapy and dialectical behavior therapy. Passionate about spreading hope to a wider audience, she enjoys writing for publications such as the *New York Times*, the *Wall Street Journal*, and *Harvard Business Review* and sharing her work on leading podcasts ranging from NPR's *Life Kit* to Spotify's *Call Her Daddy*. In addition to treating clients in her private therapy practice, LA CBT DBT, she is the author of *How to Be Single and Happy: Science-Based Strategies for Keeping Your Sanity While Looking for a Soul Mate* and *End Emotional Eating: Using Dialectical Behavior Therapy Skills to Cope with Difficult Emotions and Develop a Healthy Relationship to Food*. Both books earned the Association of Behavioral and Cognitive Therapy Self-Help Book Seal of Merit for allegiance to research and readability.

Dr. Taitz is donating a percentage of her profits from this book to the Arc of the United States, an organization that promotes the human rights and inclusion of individuals with intellectual and developmental disabilities; Breath-Body-Mind Foundation, which offers disaster survivors evidence-based techniques to enhance their resilience and well-being; and Second Nurture, a charity that educates and supports families who want to foster or adopt.